The
TALENT
MASTERS

The
TALENT
MASTERS

Why Smart Leaders Put People
Before Numbers

BILL CONATY AND RAM CHARAN

CROWN
BUSINESS
NEW YORK

Published in the United States by Crown Business, an imprint of the
Crown Publishing Group, a division of Random House, Inc., New York.
www.crownpublishing.com

CROWN BUSINESS is a trademark and CROWN and the Rising Sun
colophon are registered trademarks of Random House, Inc.

Crown Business books are available at special discounts for bulk
purchases for sales promotions or corporate use. Special editions,
including personalized covers, excerpts of existing books, or books with
corporate logos, can be created in large quantities for special needs. For
more information, contact Premium Sales at (212) 572-2232 or e-mail
specialmarkets@randomhouse.com.

Library of Congress Cataloging-in-Publication Data is available upon request.

ISBN 978-0-307-46026-4

Printed in the United States of America

Design by Lauren Dong

10 9 8 7 6 5 4 3 2 1

First Edition

To the many great business and human resource leaders who have inspired me over the years and to my family for supporting my efforts to make a difference in the HR world

—BILL CONATY

To the hearts and souls of the joint family of twelve siblings and cousins living under one roof for fifty years whose personal sacrifices made my formal education possible

—RAM CHARAN

Contents

The
TALENT
MASTERS

TALENT Is the EDGE
No Talent, No Numbers

If businesses managed their money as carelessly as they manage their people, most would be bankrupt.

The great majority of companies that control their finances masterfully don't have any comparable processes for developing their leaders or even pinpointing which ones to develop. No matter how much effort they put into recruiting, training, and assessing leaders, their talent management remains hit-or-miss: governed by superficial criteria and outdated concepts, dependent as much on luck as on skill. These are the companies that wake up some morning suddenly realizing they need a new CEO but don't know where to start looking. More pervasively, by repeatedly putting people into the wrong jobs, they waste both human and financial capital when those people don't perform.

How did this come to be? After all, it's clear enough that people make the decisions and take the actions that produce the numbers. Talent is the leading indicator of whether a business is headed up or down. Everyone agrees that it's a company's most important resource. But a spreadsheet full of numbers is a lot easier to parse than the characteristics unique to a human being. You can control what you're doing; the numbers are unambiguous, the outputs are clear. People, not so much. Better to leave that to the HR staff or search firms, particularly since the pressure to make your numbers quarter after quarter is so great that there's no time to waste on the soft stuff. And of course the law requires financial reports.

You've no doubt noticed, however, that making money has gotten harder. It will remain so for the imaginable future. In the fast-changing global marketplace, the half-life of core competencies grows ever shorter. All of the familiar competitive advantages such as market share, brand, scale of a business, cost structure, technological know-how, and patents are constantly at risk.

Talent will be the big differentiator between companies that succeed and those that don't. Those that win will be led by people who can adapt their organizations to change, make the right strategic bets, take calculated risks, conceive and execute new value-creating opportunities, and build and rebuild competitive advantage.

Only one competency lasts. It is the ability to create a steady, self-renewing stream of leaders. Money is just a commodity. Talent supplies the edge. We can't put it any better than Ron Nersesian, the head of Agilent Technologies' Electronic Measurement Group: "Developing people's talent is the whole of the company at the end of the day. Our products all are time-perishable. The only thing that stays is the institutional learning and the development of the skills and the capabilities that we have in our people."

Managing people with precision is without question harder than managing numbers, but it is doable and gets easier once you know how. Companies such as GE, P&G, Hindustan Unilever, and some others analyze talent, understand it, shape it, and build it through a combination of disciplined routines and processes, and something even rarer and harder to observe from outside: a collective expertise, honed through years of continuous improvement in recognizing and developing talent.

These companies have disproved the myth that the judgment of human potential is a "soft" art. Their rigorous, iterative, and repetitive processes convert subjective judgment about a person's talent into an objective set of observations that are specific, verifiable, and ultimately just as concrete as the analysis of a financial statement.

They have embedded in their culture the habits of observing talent, making judgments about it, and figuring out how to unleash it. They draw from their large toolboxes and creative imaginations to accelerate each leader's growth. Their executives are expected to make developing, deploying, and refreshing leadership talent an everyday, top-of-the-mind part of their jobs, and they are held accountable for how well they do it.

These companies are building for the long term. We call them talent masters, and this book will show you how they do it.

SEARCHING FOR THE SPECIFICS

One reason hardheaded managers disdain the "soft stuff" is that it so often reflects soft thinking. Take some of the criteria human resources staffs commonly use to evaluate leadership competencies. They'll rank people on a scale according to labels like these: "strategic," "innovative," "master communicator," "very bright," "analytic," "intuitive," and so on. These cryptic descriptions are so broad that they are worthless in the real world of managing. They cannot even predict whether a person is a good or poor fit for a given job, much less capture the unique abilities of an outstanding leader.

An exercise in a course at Wharton's advanced management program exposes the futility of buzzword descriptors. The instructor at a recent session asked the participants to explain Steve Jobs's distinguishing talent. Put aside his controversial personality and behaviors for the moment, the instructor advised. What we want to know is why he has beaten all expectations in his second act at Apple. (Including his own; when Apple's market value overtook Microsoft's in June

2010, Jobs called the development "surreal.") In the dozen years since he reclaimed the failing company, he has turned it into a hard-driving, cash-generating machine. He doesn't just develop new products; he changes games. The iPod, iPhone, and iPad, along with iTunes, have created massive disruptions, forcing players in the music and telecom industries—among others—to change their business models.

There's enough information available about the way Jobs thinks, behaves, and makes decisions that anyone who cared to could assess his real talent in several dimensions and describe it in clear language with specificity and nuance. Most people don't even try.

When the instructor at Wharton asks participants the question about what Jobs's talent is, hands shoot up all over the room. He's creative, innovative, entrepreneurial; he's a master of communication; he breaks the paradigm, creates new businesses; he changes the game of other people. After a couple of minutes the instructor calls a halt. "You can't do it in buzzwords," he says. "To really define a person's talent, you need to express your full thought about a human being in whole sentences with nuances that are specific to that person. And you have to get the information by closely observing the person's actions, decisions, and patterns of behavior." He shows the way by asking some probing questions. "How is he creative?" Somebody replies, "He figures out what will be a great product." Okay, but how does he do that? "He interacts with consumers." Fine, but how does he interact with consumers? Somebody has read that he hangs out with young people. Another observes that he is always looking for upcoming technologies ahead of others. Still no cigar.

The instructor next gives the executives information they can use to drill down and get to the real nature of Steve Jobs's talent. For starters, they hear a tale from one Apple director about the special board meeting held after Jobs accepted the post. Jobs walked up to the wall of the conference room where Apple's roughly two dozen current products were on display and began taking them down, one at a time. When he was done, only four were left. Those were the ones, he said, that would give Apple new life by differentiating it in the marketplace.

The story provided two observable and verifiable facts about Jobs: he understands what appeals to customers, and he acts decisively. Now the instructor asks people to explain what the creation of the iPod reveals about his talent. The first replies from the group point to his grasp of technology. But the technology already existed, someone else notes—other people were making MP3 players. The discussion that follows leads to a more meaningful conclusion: the success of the iPod was the result of a great insight coupled with brilliant execution. At the time, Napster had created an uproar in the market for recorded music with its file-sharing service that allowed users to swap downloaded MP3 files with each other. Napster's game was ultimately found illegal (it was essentially based on theft), but Jobs saw that the technology could create a legal market by ensuring the music industry a stream of revenues. And the market would be huge—a new social phenomenon, in fact—because it would liberate music lovers by enabling them to make their own buying choices legally and affordably, at any time, in any quantity. Then he created a product that was so easy to use and stylish that he could sell it at a high price, with fat margins. And we all know the rest of the story. By far the bestselling MP3 player ever, the iPod lifted the Apple brand to unprecedented heights, giving Mac sales a boost and reestablishing the company's reputation as a leader in innovation.

Drilling further, the instructor brings out another important observable fact. Jobs spends almost all his time internally with roughly a hundred experts in software, hardware, design, and the technologies of metal, plastic, and glass. Every Monday morning he brings them together to review products and the challenges of designing and executing them. It's one of his social processes for connecting multiple disciplines to create compelling products, and he's been doing it rigorously for a dozen years. Four hours a week, fifty weeks a year, for twelve years equals 2,400 hours spent building mental and relationship capital by connecting the newest ideas of diverse brilliant and passionate minds. It's the kind of approach that turns an athletic team into an unsurpassed champion. Jobs is one of the few CEOs with such a disciplined practice of connecting the dots.

Now the discussion gets rolling in earnest as the class begins piecing together the specific traits that define his genius. Somebody says, "So that's the real process of connecting with the customers, through his own mind and expertise." Somebody else raises her hand and says, "It's interesting that more than once he was able to identify an opportunity others didn't see." Another person: "It's more than that—he creates opportunities, like the iPhone."

Aha, the iPhone. What did he really do that has made it such a phenomenon? "He broke the paradigm." What does that mean? "He was able to figure out a new business model." Now eyes are lighting up. Until that point, the margins and brands of handset makers were controlled by the carriers. It not only won Apple the largest share of the smart-phone market but also generated new revenue streams enjoyed by no other phone maker. Jobs produced the most functional and elegant handset ever. Always tremendously protective of his brand and margins, he gave the iPhone to one carrier exclusively, AT&T. In exchange, Apple got the price it wanted and—for the first time in telecom history—a share of the carrier's revenue from the usage of a phone (supported by the higher rates users paid for their service). This was groundbreaking. Finally, it made money on the sale of its countless applications. Most of the new revenue streams flow straight to the bottom line, producing cash every day and making the iPhone Apple's biggest moneymaker. Jobs's verifiable action shows not only his business acumen but also the audacity and courage he exercised to reverse the power balance between a mighty carrier and a lowly handset supplier.

CALIBRATING STEVE JOBS

What does deconstructing Jobs have to do with developing talent? Just this: the Wharton exercise mirrors on a small scale what talent masters do, which is to develop precision of observation, thought, and expression. Working with the instructor, the class wrapped up its exercise with this concise summary:

Steve Jobs's natural talent is to imagine not only what consumers want now but also what they will want in the future—and pay a premium price for. He searches for discontinuities in the external landscape. He figures out trajectories of new opportunities. Then he conceives and executes not only differentiated products that yield high margin and high brand recognition, but also business models that will exploit them most profitably.

He views a product as an experience, not just an object. He can visualize what it will look and feel like, and can then execute it to near perfection. He makes advanced technology friendly to consumers based on his uncommon talent for connecting it to user experience. He has an innate feel for design, convenience, simplicity, and elegance in the product. He connects the best ideas from widely diverse disciplines to create the consumer experience he's striving for. He figures out precisely what problems need to be solved, however impossible they may seem, and searches for the best people to solve them, regardless of their status.

He is a master of communications. He crafts simple messages that connect with audiences, leveraging his record of innovation to create buzz and build demand for a new product even before it is launched. He relates with consumers, employees, and partners, and turns them into rabid fans. He builds their trust in him, in Apple, and in the Apple brand.

Bear in mind that these individual items combine to form a blend unique to that individual. It's how the traits blend together that matters.

Talent masters do not resort to vague clichés or rely on batteries of mechanistic tests to assess talent. Instead they study the behavior, actions, and decisions of individuals, and link these to actual business performance. Their observations are rigorous, specific, and nuanced. Over time, as other leaders discuss them openly and candidly, the observations become verified as facts. They dig to understand an individual's unique combination of traits. The purpose is to know what the person is, describe his characteristics in complete thoughts using full sentences, and learn how the key items combine into a unified whole.

In a word, they work to become *intimate* with their talent—that is, to know the essence of each individual. Intimacy is what makes the soft skill of judging people as hard as the skill of interpreting numbers. In fact, it's similar to the relationship top financial people have with their subject matter. Their total command of numbers, both their own and those of competitors, comes from a knowledge so intimate that it becomes intuitive: they live with the numbers.

Masters of talent build a similar depth of knowledge about people, a database in their minds. They make detailed, specific, and accurate observations about them and compare them with other people they've observed. Every encounter invokes an observation. Accumulation of these observations, done consciously, produces a complete picture of the whole person. This deeper, more accurate knowledge is the key to high-quality decisions about leaders.

PUTTING SUE IN THE RIGHT JOB

Here's an example of how important deep knowledge of an individual is to both the person and the organization. It's the true story of a disguised up-and-coming star in one global company.

Sue's past performance and experience suggested that she

was full of promise when she joined Lindell Pharmaceuticals in 2006. Her business career started at 3M, where she sold technical products to the pharmaceutical industry for three years. She then went off to Wharton to get her MBA, graduating in the top third of her class. After that she joined McKinsey, and over the course of two years successfully consulted mainly in marketing and sales with pharmaceutical makers, a hospital chain, and a health insurance company.

After hiring Sue, Lindell made her sales manager of its Pennsylvania and New Jersey territory, overseeing some one hundred salespeople and ten supervisors whose customers include health insurance companies, hospitals, and pharmacy chains. She more than lived up to her promise. After two years she was outperforming all other territory managers in the region and setting new records for revenues and market share.

Among other things, Sue installed a software-based program that raised the productivity of her people. Based on records of what drugs doctors prescribed most, it cut the administrative work of the sales force and let them spend more time in the offices of their potential best customers. As other regions started to emulate her, the tool rapidly became a new practice for the company.

People were watching. Lindell's CEO is serious about creating a pipeline of future leaders. Top management identifies high-potential leaders early, and gives them experiences that will develop them to their fullest potential. Sue's boss Laura, the regional president, met quarterly with Jorge, Lindell's executive vice president for sales; Bill, the CEO for North America; and Sam, the head of human relations for North America, to review leaders who were ready for promotion or experience elsewhere. The routine included not only discussions of the people but also informal visits with groups of them in their own environments, typically over breakfast. At their spring 2008 meeting, Laura, Bill, and Jorge put Sue on their list of fast-track candidates to be watched especially closely.

That was also the year the world changed. Health care reform became a contentious topic, with critics arguing that "big pharma" was wasting too much money on advertising and pushing products onto doctors. Prices came under pressure as the decision-making power shifted from the companies to insurers, hospital chains, and pharmacy benefits managers. Partly as a result, pharmaceutical salespeople were obliged to start practicing what is generally known as value selling. Instead of simply pushing product, they had to demonstrate how their company or product could create more benefits for all stakeholders, including the patients themselves.

Sue quickly grasped the new reality. She figured out the procedures and metrics required for the new selling approach: analyzing what customers were buying, cross-referencing usage patterns with patient data to gain insights into efficacy, giving customers ideas about how to bring total costs down while improving patient care, and training their people in using the techniques. Importantly, she designed a proprietary system for tracking patients' adherence to their prescriptions. Patients who don't take medications as prescribed are a major and widespread problem for health care providers, since they often end up sicker and requiring more care than they did before. She put her sales force through intensive training exercises, tested them, and sent them out into the field. She also replaced a part of her sales force with people who understood business as well as selling—she had learned that the knowledge could be a valuable selling tool.

Her territory's sales soared. When Laura, Jorge, Bill, and Sam met at the end of the year, they agreed that it was time to take a very close look at this rising star. The four were scheduled to attend a conference at Sue's offices in Philadelphia, and they arranged to take her out for a dinner where they questioned her at length and in depth about how she was achieving her extraordinary results. Learning that Sue would be calling on one of the company's five largest customers the next day in Cleveland, Laura invited herself along to observe. After the meeting's successful conclusion, Sue returned to Philadelphia and Laura settled down on the plane to New York to review and write up what she'd seen. These were her key points:

- "Sue met with the customer's chief buyer, executive vice president, CFO, and chief medical officer, and they were all deeply impressed with her two-hour presentation. They could see that she understood the guts of their business from their viewpoint rather well, including the challenges they faced in the new environment. She showed a mastery of their financial details that few salespeople have, even to understanding key items of their balance sheet."
- "She established a rapport with them and quickly built relationships. She excelled in the give-and-take of two-way dialogue. I could see the customers nod appreciably as she answered their questions. She was to the point. They were superattentive when she showed them how to monitor patients' use of their prescriptions, and blown away by the financial analysis she had done showing what our company could do to help them improve their performance."

Laura called Jorge, the EVP of sales, the next day to relay her observations. "What other talents has she shown?" he asked. Laura replied that Sue had proved to be a good judge of people, as evidenced by the choices she made when she replaced a third of her sales force. She continually upgrades her organization, Laura added, and had brought in major new ideas. She was ahead of the curve and a successful change agent. They agreed that she had reshaped her job, was now outgrowing it, and was definitely on a fast track for promotion. Jorge said he would put her on the list of high-potential people to discuss at an upcoming full-day meeting with Sam, the head of HR—always a participant in such meetings—and Bill, the North America CEO.

The traditional next step at Lindell would be to make Sue regional sales president in the coming twelve months. If she succeeded, she would most likely move up over time to become executive vice president for sales for North America. Everyone agreed that she should be promoted sooner, but that's where the easy agreement ended. Jorge, convinced that she could do great things for Lindell's sales organization, wanted to follow the standard route. Sam demurred, saying, "We need to think bigger for her." Her judgment and major decisions had been uniformly good, he pointed out. "She clearly understands business. She has an affinity for people, builds relationships, and brings in new ideas. I think we should put her onto the general management P&L [profit and loss] track by making her a brand manager." Laura agreed with Jorge, and talked for a couple of minutes about Sue's value to the sales organization and questioning whether someone so young could handle a P&L responsibility.

Then Bill spoke up. "Tell me more about why this would be a good idea, Sam," he said. The HR director reiterated her achievements and turned to her career needs and aspirations. "Sue has the capacity to go far in this company," he said. "I can see her being one of the top ten or fifteen officers someday. And one problem with the sales job is that it would deny her some important opportunities. As a brand manager, she'd not only be getting the P&L experience but also broadening the scope of her people relationships. She'd be interacting with headquarters, and also with other brand managers from around the world. This would make a huge difference in her personal growth.

"And there's another issue. You're aware that few regional presidents have gone over to brand management. Here's why. The transition gets tougher the more time you spend in your discipline. The person who crosses over earlier is more flexible and adaptable. Compensation can also be a problem, because it's a downward move—the sales president will have been making more than she would as a brand manager."

The others were starting to see his point. After a few minutes of debate, Bill said, "Let's sum up the reasons why she's ready for a management job. She delivers results and brings in big ideas; upgrades her people and makes good choices in selecting new ones; adjusts quickly to changes in the environment and acts decisively and with impressive speed; understands the customers' total business, which shows that she has business acumen; is able to build relationships at high levels externally and at all levels internally.

"We haven't seen talents like this in a territory sales manager for a long time," he concluded.

"What if she doesn't work out?" asked Jorge.

"We'd bring her back into sales as the regional president," said Sam. "It would no doubt be a blow, but I don't think it would cripple her. She's shown that she can learn from experience. She would return to sales having learned a lot, broadened her experience, and become better prepared for that job."

Persuaded by now that the move made sense, Laura added a final thought: "If we don't give her this shot, will we risk losing her to a competitor?" No one felt the need to reply.

Bill looked around. "So we're agreed?" he asked. Everyone nodded in assent. "Laura, give her a call soon. Tell her she's been doing a great job, should keep doing it, and expect that she'll be getting a new one within ninety days."

Laura grinned. "I bet she's going to be surprised," she said. "I know she wanted to get into general management, but I am sure she didn't imagine it would come this soon— or even at all in this company."

By now you may be thinking that this is a fairy tale. You can't recall any instance of people in your organization taking such a thoughtful, painstaking approach to placing a leader in a job. Just the candor and ease that mark their conversations are alien to your culture. It's unimaginable that people would cooperate like that. But as we will see repeatedly in this book, it's how people work in a talent master organization.

We extract several important lessons from the Steve Jobs and "Sue" stories:

- Talent masters understand the subtleties that differentiate people. Two individuals may share the same set of characteristics, but those characteristics will combine differently in them in ways that differentiate their leadership capabilities. (Case in point: Steve Jobs.) Talent masters assess and express what each person is in reality, not against some predetermined checklist. They obtain insights through observing the person's actions, decisions, and behaviors. They look for the specifics of how various traits combine. And they express all these in complete thoughts that are verifiable, not cryptic single words such as "strategic."

- Sue was one of many territory sales managers at Lindell, but her combination of traits stood out. She had business acumen, cognitive bandwidth, and personality traits such as being able to build relationships and adapt to rapid change. Together these enabled her to make high-leverage decisions that delivered numbers above and beyond those of her colleagues in similar positions.

- Lindell's leaders could see the totality of Sue's skills and traits only because they had engaged in many candid conversations with and about her and observed her interacting with customers. Talent masters spot, find, and develop people like Sue through predictable, consistent, repetitive processes that develop candor and trust through the give-and-take of vigorous dialogue.

This system, based on intimate knowledge through the observations of actions, decisions, and behaviors, grows raw talent to its full potential.

- The plan they settled on was centered on increasing not just her *capacity*—her ability to get more of the same work done. More important, it would raise her *capability,* which means achieving more through doing a higher level of work. Increasing capability leads to the kind of growth that expands cognitive bandwidth and produces higher levels of leadership. Becoming a brand manager would grow her capability by an order of magnitude.

- Nobody knew for sure if Sue was fully ready for the job. But talent masters often place such bets on high-potential leaders for three good reasons. First, people facing a stretch situation aren't likely to be overconfident and are eager to learn from others. Second, it helps to retain talented people who are itching to advance and may look to greener pastures if they don't get the chance. Third, successful stretches will attract better candidates in the future because ambitious and capable people will know that they won't have to wait for slots to open.

- Getting to the core of a person's values, behaviors, beliefs, and talents may seem like a lot of work, but masters understand that the return on time is huge. It's like analyzing a business problem or opportunity: we drill down to find the causes, understand the context, and assess options. Similarly, when we get to know a person, we are able to develop insights and options to speed his or her growth and development. This is especially important for companies that rely on specialized knowledge and need to quickly develop the leadership potential of their experts. Decisions like the one for Sue build organizational capacity.

- Insight into an individual's talents and foresight into

where the leader could go turn traditional succesion planning on its head. Rather than finding people to fill positions, it puts the emphasis on opening paths for leaders to grow their talents and become ever more capable. The ultimate payoff is seamless successions to the CEO job and other high-leverage positions. Rarely if ever do talent masters need to turn outside for a chief executive.

INSTITUTIONALIZING GOOD JUDGMENTS

Just about any organization will have some great natural judges, but none have enough to build a program around. Those making the judgments have to know the talent well— or better yet, intimately. They have to know all about the job the person is being considered for. They have to know how the person stacks up against other candidates for the job, which means they have to know all about those people, too.

The first thing to understand about talent masters is that they can identify a person's talent more precisely than most people because they excel at observing and listening. They use these abilities to see the whole person—her skills and experience, of course, but also such things as her judgment, personality, and ability to build relationships, not just characteristics defined by buzzwords. They understand the nature of an individual's shortcomings—the difference between a fatal flaw that will keep him from advancing and a development need that can be fixed.

Talent masters have developed their abilities through constant and intense practice. They accumulate observations and connect them into verifiable inferences about people. They can compare different people with the same exactitude as they compare different sets of numbers. Paradoxically, comparing people is both harder and easier than comparing numbers.

It's harder because it takes a lot of practice to overcome the biases and psychic filters that so often cloud good judgment; but it's easier because in the end there are fewer data points and variables to take into account.

Talent masters institutionalize this expertise in their companies. It's practiced, imitated, tracked, and learned by all leaders until it becomes second nature, part of the established processes and daily routines. And they use it to create their own supply of good judges. They calibrate individuals through myriad dialogues, using information collected through many observations of decisions, actions, and behaviors and refined in group discussions. The dialogue is informal and fact driven. The discipline of pooling leaders' judgments about other leaders is comprehensive, continuous, and part of the culture. It integrates the development of people with the running of the business, and connects their leadership strengths and weaknesses with the business results. The judgments continue to improve with practice and experience.

Masters do this most visibly in formal reviews and processes, often adapted from the ones GE pioneered (which we will show you in the next chapter). But equally important are processes that you can't see. These are what we call social processes.

Any time two or more people work together there's a social process in which they exchange information and ideas, exercise power, and express their values through what they say and do. Unlike business processes, where the participants' roles and goals are specified, social processes usually operate in the background. The prescribed outcome of a budget meeting, for example, is efficient allocation of resources. But the actual outcome is often the result of a social process in which the players exercise personal influence and power to jockey for those resources. Participants, as well as the leader in charge of the process, may or may not be aware of how their behaviors and dialogue shape the results.

No less than business processes, social processes can be

managed and led to improve the outcome. Through the content of the dialogue and the attitudes and values that are conveyed verbally and nonverbally, talent masters use them to identify great leaders and help them grow. No company can achieve talent mastery without embedding talent in the organization's social processes.

PRINCIPLES OF THE TALENT MASTERS

Our collaboration on this book began with the desire to crystallize into principles the many things we've learned working with people and companies we have identified as talent masters. These principles comprise the framework within which talent masters operate, and they provide the way for you to diagnose your company's talent development capability.

1. An enlightened leadership team, starting with the CEO. Ordinary CEOs plan for their companies' futures in terms of financial and strategic ambitions. The enlightened CEO recognizes that his top priority for the future is building and deploying the talent that will get it there. He is deeply committed to creating a culture of talent mastery, and personally involved in executing it. As a role model, he is crucial to getting everyone on board and shaping the social systems that will make or break the formal processes of leadership development. We find that such leaders invest at least a quarter of their time in spotting and developing other leaders; at GE and P&G, it's closer to 40 percent.

2. Meritocracy through differentiation. This is the mother's milk of helping talent reach its potential. Memorize this slogan: Differentiation breeds meritocracy; sameness (the failure to differentiate people) breeds mediocrity. The latter happens all too often in companies that automatically equate high performance with achieving or exceeding agreed-upon financial goals. Without exception, talent masters dig into the many causes underlying performance so that they can recognize and reward leaders according to their talents, behaviors, and values.

3. **Working values.** All companies have values, stated or unstated. Some are meaningful, many are boilerplate. What we call working values have a real impact on how well results are delivered, because they govern how people work and behave. They're the values people live by, because they are absolutely expected of both leaders and employees. For example, one value we see among talent masters is the obligation of leaders to develop other leaders. Values aren't always labeled as such. Hindustan Unilever distinguishes the what and the how of leadership, the "what" referring to getting things done and the "how" to the values component, "acting in a way others will admire and want to follow." At Procter and Gamble, says CEO Bob MacDonald, "We talk a lot about character, which I define as putting the needs of the organization above your own needs." By whatever name, masters repeat and repeat and repeat their values, and reinforce them by linking recognition and rewards with them.

4. **A culture of trust and candor.** A company can develop its people only if it has accurate information about their strengths and development needs, and it can only get that information if people can talk candidly—that is, honestly and openly. Candor gets the truth out. It enables keener observations, greater insight, and better descriptions. It's easy to cite a leader's strengths but edgier to pinpoint their development needs and expect them to accept and address them. As we will see throughout this book, creating a culture of candor is the hardest part of becoming a talent master. People can talk candidly only if they trust the system to respect honesty and confidentiality. Talent masters work strenuously to ensure trust by insisting on candor in all of the company's dialogues, whether one-on-one, in group settings, or in appraisals.

5. **Rigorous talent assessment.** Talent masters have the same goal and results orientation in their people processes as

they do in their financial systems. They set explicit time-based people development goals and discuss the why and how of these goals. They review people as thoroughly and regularly as they review operations, business performance, strategy, and budgets. Crucially, they integrate the people reviews with each of the others, gathering and updating the information as the person progresses. Like the financial systems, the people systems have rhythm and rigor, and evolve over time as new needs arise.

6. A business partnership with human resources. Talent masters use human resource leaders as active and effective business partners, raising them to the same, if not higher, level as the chief financial officer. The HR function will only be as strong as the CEO wants it to be, and if the CEO doesn't have high expectations for it, HR will remain second tier. Just as the CFO is the trustee of the financial system, the chief human resources officer is the trustee of the people system.

7. Continuous learning and improvement. Talent masters recognize that a fast-changing business environment requires constant change and updating of both their leaders' skills and their own leadership criteria. They give leaders training on specific topics, and they adjust their talent development plans according to the external changes they see as likely in the years to come.

WHO ARE THE TALENT MASTERS?

The companies that form the core of our research are at various stages of evolution. Some have been world leaders for decades; others are works in progress. Whether old hands or newcomers, they follow the principles we've laid out consistently and intensively—with almost religious fervor. Our purpose is not that you copy the masters as they are. Rather, it's to give you the opportunity to pick and choose tried and proven ideas.

All companies have formal processes for managing talent, some of them good and some not so good. The masters have superlative ones. But these are the easy things to see, and they're not the most important. The thing you can't see from outside—the black box where the real secret of mastery resides—is in the social systems of their companies. We will make them visible to you.

Our work is not the product of statistical research, which is fine for showing correlations but little help in determining cause and effect. Ours is observational research, drawn directly from the experiences of the players and quite often in their own voices. We chose our companies because we know them well—in many cases we've worked in or with them for decades—and we understand their social systems. We have been able to go inside their black boxes to observe what they do and how they do it. Now we will take you with us to see the masters in action: not only the tools and techniques they use but also the questions they ask, the conversations they hold, and the living dynamics of their decision making.

The book is divided into four parts. The first is an in-depth exploration of General Electric's much-admired talent management system. It's necessarily a long section, because there are so many aspects to explain. We'll take you inside so you can see how and why it works.

We begin with GE for two reasons. First, we know it intimately from our long experience with its unique system of talent development: Ram Charan's forty consecutive years of working with, observing, and teaching GE leaders at all levels and Bill Conaty's like number of years living within and helping to adapt the system to the evolving external landscape. Second, GE is the go-to company for students of talent management—widely admired and copied, and a pioneering practitioner of the principles we've enumerated. It's also a celebrated producer of leaders for other companies. Among its satisfied customers are the world's foremost executive recruiters. "GE has been and continues to be the best source of talent for a wide range of industries and functions due to its unique programs for developing leaders," says Tom Neff, chairman of Spencer Stuart U.S. Gerry Roche, senior chairman of Heidrick & Struggles, adds, "GE devotes more time, attention, and money to the long-term objective of people development than any company I know. It is still the gold standard for smart companies that want to find the next great CEO."

There are many ways up every mountain, and the four companies in part II illustrate the wide range of approaches to talent mastery. Be prepared for surprises when you reach chapter 5, on Hindustan Unilever (HUL). One of the leading producers of CEO and marketing leadership in Asia, it has developed a unique system of talent development, one in which top executives can be seen recruiting on campuses and spending evenings in small Indian towns with management trainees. We know of no company whose top management makes deeper personal commitments to developing leaders.

When it comes to developing global leaders, Procter & Gamble (chapter 6) has few if any equals. The company has found that there's no substitute for experience—in particular, the experience a leader gains through stretch assignments in different countries and cultures. It has also been ahead of the pack in building databases for talent management, and is now adding social media to the tools for increasing collaboration and global insight throughout the company.

Agilent Technologies CEO Bill Sullivan (chapter 7) faced a problem common among companies in expertise-based industries such as high-tech, biotechnology, and pharmaceuticals: the need for leaders with both business skills and technical expertise. Such people are rare, so Sullivan decided he would build his own "best-in-class" management bench. In discovering a way to home-grow leaders with both qualities, Sullivan has produced a model for others in the same boat.

How deeply do you know yourself? It's not a frivolous question. As the burgeoning field of behavioral economics shows us, unconscious behaviors have big implications for business leaders. Novartis (chapter 8) is in the vanguard here. Its talent management includes numerous tools and programs to help leaders learn about what goes on down under. The approach is unique—even startling—but any company or leader will benefit from understanding how surfacing the leader within adds real depth to talent development.

Part III (chapters 9, 10, and 11) focuses on talent masters who've joined the game only recently. Companies like GE, P&G, and HUL had decades to hone their systems and processes, but few in today's high-speed world have the luxury of time. We'll show how Goodyear, not too long ago the epitome of a tired rust belt company, has rapidly reinvented itself. Its new strategy was to get out of a commodity business and market differentiated products to consumers around the world. But CEO Bob Keegan understood that a radically different strategy would require new people. He began by replacing most of the leadership team with carefully chosen outsiders and developing the social processes and systems to build an entirely new leadership culture.

UniCredit CEO Alessandro Profumo also had a bold strategy that required a new leadership team, but unlike Keegan, he couldn't bring in a raft of outsiders. In turning his Italian bank into a pan-European financial institution, he would have to work with existing leaders in diverse countries and cultures, unifying them in a new mind-set—and doing the job quickly. He accomplished this by enlisting an experienced HR executive as a business partner who could understand the realities and culture of his new company and create the necessary systems and social processes.

Clayton Dubilier & Rice (CDR) and TPG, two of the top private equity firms, might seem to be outliers on the subject of talent mastery. Aren't outfits like this the "barbarians at the gates," the strippers and flippers who buy businesses, cut them to the bone, and then sell for big profits? Whatever may have been true in the past, private equity is emerging as an increasingly important sector in the world economy. None has been more aggressive in marrying its mastery of finance with mastery of talent than CDR. It has brought in retired business leaders, most notably Jack Welch of GE, A. G. Lafley of P&G, Ed Liddy of Allstate, Paul Pressler of Gap, and Vindi Banga of HUL, to help it win a redefined competitive game and strengthen the talent management systems of the companies in its portfolio. Other PE giants, such as KKR and Cerberus, are concentrating on developing stronger HR teams to build their own talent.

Korea-based LGE became a global player with its low-cost, high-quality consumer electronics goods. CEO Yong Nam wanted to take it to the next level, establishing its brand as a leader in innovation with strong ties to local markets. Doing that would require replacing its homogeneous Korean leadership bench with executives who could relate to the local markets. His challenge was how to do this without undermining the things that worked. His unique solution could be another model for others facing similar challenges.

We've got practical how-to advice for you in part IV. It's a talent mastery tool kit filled with specifics about what to know and what to do—information you can put to work on Monday morning. Among the topics are guidelines for talent reviews, continuous learning programs that produce business results, using HR as a business partner, and ensuring smooth successions. There's also a checklist for assessing your own company's talent management capabilities.

Talent mastery doesn't guarantee unbroken success. As this book went to press, Yong Nam of LGE had stepped aside because of the company's poor showing in the smart phone market, and Alessandro Profumo of UniCredit was reportedly engaged in a power struggle with his board. Neither issue related to their masterful work on talent management. Even the best leaders are susceptible to misjudging business issues, especially in situations involving considerable risk. In fact, every one of our companies has run into rough spots at one time or another, and there's no guarantee that they won't again. And think of two talent masters—say, P&G and HUL—duking it out in the same markets. At any given time, one will be on top and the other running behind.

A good ball club is good because of the talent of its coach and players, nothing else. Talent masters, with their depth of strong leaders, catch mistakes, make changes, and come back stronger than others who stumble. What we have observed, and can assert with confidence, is that talent is the single most important key to longevity. The better a company's leaders, the sooner it will get back on track.

Part I

WHAT
A MASTER DOES
Inside GE's Talent
Management System

Any research into the art and science of the talent masters necessarily starts with General Electric. Always an innovator in the field, GE became a hotbed of revolution under the legendary Jack Welch, CEO from 1981 to 2001. He made every one of the principles laid out in the first chapter a part of his company's talent management system, and they continue to guide the company as it evolves. As we noted in the first chapter, GE's leadership development is probably more widely benchmarked and emulated than that of any other company.

But benchmarking or emulating isn't necessarily the same as knowing. Executives who come to study GE listen attentively to the presentations it gives, but few come away truly understanding its guts. They can identify with the elements they recognize—the values, the processes that make up the operating system that GE calls the playbook—and say, "Yes, we have something very similar." What they don't often grasp are the subtler factors that make the system work, which are instinctive and take place routinely in GE culture: the straightforward and candid discussions through which leaders get to the heart of issues, the linkage of business processes with talent processes, the social systems that integrate the seemingly discrete meetings into a constant process—in short, the elements that characterize being a talent master.

Most companies partition their management systems into discrete areas: "Today we talk about people, tomorrow we talk about strategy, next week we talk about operations and budgets." At GE, all are part of a continuous loop. For example, both strategic plan meetings and operation reviews include a thorough review of the people needed to execute the plan. People sessions start with a business overview, since business results come directly from the people involved. Business reviews always start with an assessment of the leadership team. Every encounter is both a coaching opportunity and a chance to register an observation that over time adds to the "intimacy" data bank.

The system works only because it is rigorous and constantly challenges people to prove themselves. Leaders are rewarded as much on how well they lead people as they are on the numbers they deliver. In addition to looking at their top- and bottom-line results, business leaders consistently focus on answering questions such as:

- Who are the promising leaders?
- Where do they fit? How can they do better?

- What can we do to help them realize their potential faster?
- How well are we doing as a company in developing the leaders we need?

Dialogues are candid, unreservedly so. Between the meetings devoted to business results and people development, GE's social processes continue the dialogues both formally and informally, day by day, week by week. The leaders come to know their people intimately, and vice versa, through not only the scheduled meetings and reviews but also daily interactions and networking in social settings. At the top, especially, there are no strangers. The CEO and senior vice president of HR know the top six hundred people in the company intimately—their families, their hobbies, their likes and dislikes, their skills, strengths, psychological tendencies, and development needs. These six hundred executives have become almost a family.

The people who benchmark can't hope to see all these things, because they can't see them in action, which is the only way to fully understand them. But you can. The three chapters in this section bring you inside GE for a tour unlike any you've ever had. Your journey will take you alternately through clear and comprehensive explanations of the system, and intimate personal stories that show how it plays out in real life.

Chapter 2 shows how GE executives swiftly and surely managed a surprise high-level resignation, an event that often as not causes chaos elsewhere in the corporate world.

Chapter 3 is the complete road map and instruction manual for the GE system, explaining all its extraordinary details and showing how the parts function as a whole. Chapter 4 brings you back down to human scale with the remarkable stories of two individuals whose experiences illustrate the care that GE takes in developing its leaders' careers.

Chapter 2

The SAME-DAY SUCCESSION
What GE Did When Larry Johnston Quit

When Bill Conaty got a call from Larry Johnston late one Friday afternoon in 2000, nothing seemed out of the ordinary at first. Johnston, CEO of GE's $6 billion appliance business in Louisville, Kentucky, said he might be at GE headquarters in Fairfield, Connecticut, on Monday and might stop in to see him.

"Great," replied Conaty. "Or we can talk now if you want."

Johnston said, "No, I don't need anything now, but maybe on Monday."

Knowing Johnston well, Conaty thought that sounded a little strange, and after thinking about it he tried calling him back in Louisville. He couldn't reach him; he tried again several times over the weekend, but no luck. Johnston was a guy who would always return his calls quickly, so it was definitely troubling.

Johnston finally called early Monday morning to say that he was in the corporate guesthouse and wanted to come over. Now Conaty knew for sure that something was wrong, but he never could have imagined what came next.

Within an hour Johnston was in his office, very subdued. After asking Conaty to shut the door, he said, "Look, I'm leaving."

Conaty said, "Larry, you can't leave! Why would you?"

Johnston explained that he'd taken an offer from the Albertson's grocery store chain to be their CEO, adding, "It's the opportunity of a lifetime, a phenomenal financial package, and it's not with a GE competitor." He first told Conaty that he didn't return his calls over the weekend at the request of his new employer, but it was more revealing when he added, "And I didn't want to be talked out of it."

"I tried to pull him back off the cliff," recalls Conaty, "but as I exhausted all my moves it became clear to me that Larry had already jumped." Numbly he walked Johnston down the hall to the office of Jeff Immelt, who had recently been named Jack Welch's successor as CEO, and the three men sat down uncomfortably. Johnston had worked closely with and for Immelt over the years at the Appliances business, and later at Medical Systems, so they knew each other well. "Larry was a very good salesman, but Jeff was a great salesman," says Conaty, "and my feeling was, 'Maybe Jeff can talk him out of this.' I went back to my office and waited for either the black or white smoke to emerge from Immelt's office."

Most companies come unhinged in the face of such an unexpected departure, as HP did recently when Mark Hurd abruptly resigned. There's a mad scramble to get a search firm and screen candidates. In the meantime an interim leader gets shoved into the job, and now the ship has only half a rudder. As weeks go by—maybe even months—uncertainty and rumors sap morale and efficiency. Some internal contenders for the job are apt to get caught up in jockeying for position. One may play it safe to avoid making mistakes. Somebody may make a bold but rash move in hopes of scoring a coup. Competitors will see the leadership vacuum as an opportunity to make gains or pirate talent made uneasy by the uncertainty. By the time the company finally finds the right successor, it will have its hands full getting things back on course, and the organization may have suffered long-term damage.

This does not happen at GE and other talent masters. McDonald's Corporation, for instance, named a new CEO successor within hours of losing their incumbent CEO to a fatal heart attack in the middle of the night. At GE, many people remember that the company had three strong, well-vetted internal candidates to succeed Welch. But unlike most companies, it has the same set of options at all organizational levels. They know enough about each leader to quickly install the person best suited for the job and its upcoming challenges while minimizing organizational disruption.

Many companies feel good because they have succession plans, with a candidate earmarked for each box on the chart. They shouldn't. A predetermined choice freezes the job's frame of reference at the time of the choosing. In a fast-changing business world, the person who is right for a job today may be wrong in a year or even six months. Multiple candidates offer a better shot at getting someone who's equipped to deal with the new conditions.

Fewer than 5 percent of GE's top six hundred leaders leave voluntarily, because they get a satisfying variety of experiences in a meritocratic culture. But other companies are always looking for GE talent, and the offer of a top position can be hard to resist. When a valued leader does leave the fold—even one who may seem indispensable at the moment—the people in charge know what to do. They understand the business, know the candidates' strengths and development needs, and are well prepared to fill the slot with the right match quickly—even in a matter of hours. The goal is clear: no pause, no time for people to commiserate, no laxity in decision making, and no opportunity for the competition to poach talent.

When Larry Johnston resigned, GE set itself a new record for speed, naming his successor and three others down the line in half a day and announcing the changes before the day was over. That performance has been the model to shoot for ever since. GE does not allow a top leadership vacuum to exist, even for a day.

. . .

As he waited, Conaty couldn't stop thinking about Johnston. Few critical departures had caught him off guard in his forty-year career, and as he thought back to the Friday call, he faulted himself for not having been on top of the situation. He sensed that Johnston had been right at the cusp of saying more. Maybe things would have turned out differently if he had kept Larry going, he thought.

The whole thing was especially painful because Johnston had been doing a very good job running Appliances—and Conaty had taken a bit of a chance in helping him to get his first P&L job two years before. Johnston had been head of sales at Appliances when its CEO retired, and had hoped for a shot at the job. "Back then Jack Welch and I recognized Larry as a world-class sales and marketing guy, but had a tougher time visualizing him running a big GE business," says Conaty. The job as CEO of Appliances went to Dave Cote, who ran the GE Silicones business at the time. (Cote is now chairman and CEO of Honeywell International.)

Conaty continues: "About six months after Cote took over in Appliances we decided at a Session C review that we would give Larry the opportunity to go fix our European medical business, which was in rough shape." Session C is the yearly meeting where senior leaders reviewed the company's leadership. "Larry had always indicated that he wanted to run a P&L business, and this was his reward for staying on and helping Cote out in Appliances instead of whining and undermining him.

"I remember Larry's reaction when I called to test his interest in the medical job. I reached him at a big sales conference and he was returning my call from a bank of pay phones in the conference center. I said, 'I have some interesting news. We finally have a business for you.' Larry said, 'You're kidding!' I said, 'No, but it's totally screwed up.' He says, 'I love it!' I said, 'It isn't pretty and a couple of guys already tripped on it. But it's in Paris.' Larry was ecstatic: 'Fantastic! When do I start?' "

Johnston jumped into the job with both feet and fixed a problem business whose solution had eluded others. He not only proved himself a solid business leader but also won people over with his charm. When Cote resigned to become CEO of TRW, Welch and Conaty were happy to offer Johnston the top spot at Appliances.

And now here he was saying sayonara. "I kept hoping that Jeff Immelt would work his salesman's magic," says Conaty. "But when he called me back in, there they sat, looking dejected. They're both big guys, Immelt six foot four, Johnston a couple of inches taller, but both seemed at least a foot shorter. They were slumped down, elbows on knees. 'He's gone,' Jeff said, looking up at me bleakly. 'I can't talk him out of it.' "

Conaty gave it a halfhearted last shot with a bit of humor. " 'C'mon, Larry, cut the crap,' I said. 'You've lived in Paris and now you're going to Boise, Idaho, the location of Albertson's headquarters?' Larry sort of chuckled and said, 'Well, everything isn't perfect, but I've got to do this for me and my family.' Jeff smiled faintly, looking beaten." Both Conaty and Immelt sat there for a few minutes just basically shaking their heads in disbelief.

At the time Jeff Immelt was transitioning to the job of chairman and CEO of GE, Jack Welch was still around, and Conaty and Immelt told Larry, "You just stay here in Jeff's office, Larry, make whatever business calls you gotta make—but we don't want word to get out that you're leaving before we talk to Jack and determine our game plan."

AN IMPROMPTU SESSION C

Conaty and Immelt walked over to Welch's office feeling like failures; it would be a big surprise for Welch too. Conaty recalls, "Jack's response—expletive deleted—was, 'Okay, who are we putting in the job? How are we going to protect the company?' Then he added, 'I want us to name his successor today.'" Conaty suggested that maybe they should take another day to work it out. "'Bullshit,' Jack replied. 'Let's announce today.'" So they immediately put an action plan together, first calling Larry into Welch's office. The first thing Welch said was, "You big axxxxxxx!" But he didn't spend any time trying to talk him out of it. Welch had already turned the page.

The group discussed the top four candidates they had previously designated as potential successors. Johnston took part in the discussion, though uncomfortably; he wanted to get out of that office and return to Louisville. But they couldn't let him go alone and announce his departure. "That would put everybody there in a panic," says Conaty, "because Larry was kind of a local hero: a big man in stature and presence, big in the community as well as the business." Welch told Johnston, "You just hang around in an office, Larry, while we finalize our plan. By the way, Jeff and Bill will be accompanying you on your return trip to Louisville to announce your departure and your successor."

How did Welch have four potential candidates at his fingertips? The answer demonstrates the strength and power of the GE system of talent mastery, one centered on the Session C system. While Session C and its follow-up cycle stretches through the year, the dynamism of the process comes from the informal day-to-day discussions between the CEO and the senior vice president of human resources as they constantly assess the company's top leaders. These frequent dialogues expand their mental databases with current information gleaned from many other people as well. They do not have to grope around in the dark to figure out who is suitable for a specific job.

Welch, Immelt, and Conaty started with a quick review of the Appliances business itself. It built low-margin products in a highly competitive industry where every dollar earned was a struggle. Though it was only a small part of GE's portfolio, its huge brand recognition made it disproportionately important to the company. GE needed to protect that brand by keeping it in the hands of strong leadership. (Also, it was important to dampen recurring outside speculation that GE would get rid of the business, though there were no plans to do so at the time.) What mattered most was keeping it from disrupting the bigger picture of GE by turning off customers such as Home Depot, Lowe's, and Best Buy and losing business to major competitors such as Whirlpool.

GE grooms people with leadership potential by giving them increasingly challenging jobs in different businesses. Of the four backup candidates, only one was in Appliances: Jim Campbell, the vice president of sales and marketing. The other three were proving themselves as P&L leaders elsewhere, and in most cases one would have gotten the job. But this was not a normal situation. The issue for GE's talent masters is always to pick someone who best meets the challenges of the current environment—in this case protecting the brand and customer relationships. It wasn't that the business environment had radically changed: the real issue was continuity. Johnston was a good business manager, but more important, his great talents for selling and building customer relations were instrumental in the division's success. He was a master in dealing with customer problems and complaints at the highest level. The business needed more of the same.

Campbell had much of Johnston's magic, which made him a prime contender. But the decision makers had myriad risks to consider. Lacking major P&L experience, could he handle being CEO of an entire business? If he failed and had to be replaced, it would be the third turnover of leadership in the business in four years, a sign of instability that could damage the brand and morale inside the organization. Second, what would be the repercussions? Would choosing an insider unsettle leaders elsewhere in GE who were already managing smaller P&Ls successfully and waiting to move up to bigger jobs like running the Appliances unit?

This is why being a talent master is a total leadership job, rather than the sole province of human resources. HR can facilitate, assist, and gather information, such as doing a 360-degree assessment, and pose challenging questions. But filling a key job requires intimate knowledge about how the particulars of the business affect leadership criteria at any given time. Senior leaders cannot delegate such judgments.

The overriding need to protect customer relationships seemed to outweigh the risks. Also, it would be good to show the Appliances team that one of their own was valued highly enough to be the next CEO. Those became the non-negotiable criteria. Astutely, Jack Welch was thinking along these lines as well: *Let's use this as an opportunity to go on the offensive and act quickly to promote a number of internal Appliances leaders.* What a terrific way it would be to energize rising stars within the business and defuse the feelings over Larry's departure.

Still, they had to be confident that Jim could handle this huge general management challenge. Could he be as good as Larry? For that matter, might he even be better? Jim was well known by the top people in the company. The three men had before them a ton of data gleaned in Session C and operating reviews, including observations about his skills, personality, traits, judgment, relationships, and continuous learning. But they also needed a better feel for how his organization would support him in the CEO role. They had to get a quick, informal answer from reliable sources who would be honest and candid.

Here's where a trusting relationship between the corporate HR function and the business leaders, built over many years—one that reassures sources that their confidences will never be violated—pays off. As you'll also see in other stories, HR needs to be the trustee of the company's social system to make these discussions worthwhile and productive.

Conaty quickly began getting judgments about Jim Campbell from key leaders at Louisville. In private conversations, he accomplished three more things: he would get a handle on the likely chemistry among the top people and Campbell in his new job; he would be able to explain the merits of selecting him; and he would get a feel for any concerns about gaps in skills—whether, for example, Campbell's lack of manufacturing experience would hamper him.

The reviews were boffo: "Jimmy? He's great!" and "I can't think of anyone who deserves it more." Conaty could tell by the tone of voice and choice of words that the people in Louisville were true to GE culture in their candor. Dick Segalini, the vice president of production operations, gave the most reassuring endorsement of all: "I love Jim Campbell. He won't have to worry about the operating side. I'll make sure he succeeds." Appliances had a strong and experienced CFO in Steve Sedita, so the finance side was covered. And Larry Johnston himself was enthusiastic about the choice since he knew that Campbell would follow through on the customer initiatives that he had started.

Their concerns alleviated, the corporate team wrestled with the domino effect set off by Campbell's promotion. They knew the leaders several levels down in Appliances—their skills, personalities, and raw talents. Who would fill Campbell's job? They quickly decided it would be Lynn Pendergrass, who reported to Campbell as general manager of Refrigeration. And who would fill her job? Len Kosar, a sales manager. That meant three people in Louisville were getting big, unexpected promotions inside the business, with more to follow in filling their jobs.

"The most shocked guy in Louisville was Jim Campbell," says Conaty, "since he was minding his own business, focused on his aspiration of being one of the best sales leaders in the company. His personal assessment in the annual resume he submitted to GE headquarters was that he was continuing to grow and develop in his current assignment, and he gave no sign of wanting to be CEO of the entire Appliances business. Since 'running for office' can be deemed as the kiss of death in GE, Campbell was trusting the GE system to take care of his career."

A SHOCK BECOMES A TRIUMPH

By 1:00 p.m. Immelt, Johnston, and Conaty were on a plane to Kentucky. The conversation during the flight was cordial, because they had resolved where they were going with the organization changes in Appliances. Jeff Immelt, skilled at drawing people out with incisive questions, asked Larry things such as "What would you be worried about if you were continuing to run the Appliances business right now?" Larry, clearly eager to help, enumerated the challenges and issues he was dealing with in a tough industry.

Alerted early in the afternoon that Larry wanted to meet with him, Campbell walked into Larry's office later that day expecting the usual weekly exhortation to get more sales. But there sat Conaty and Immelt along with Johnston.

"Larry's leaving and you're the new CEO," Immelt told him.

Campbell was gobsmacked. "Are you shitting me?" he said. "The whole thing?"

Shortly thereafter Immelt, Conaty, and Johnston met with the Appliances senior staff and made the announcement. Bill Conaty describes the scene: "Jeff and I made it as upbeat as possible. 'Larry is leaving,' Jeff said, adding with a grin, 'And he's a jerk for doing it!' That got a laugh. 'Jim Campbell is replacing him.' Applause all around. 'Jim is being replaced by Lynn.' More applause. 'Lynn is being replaced by Len.' Even more applause and smiles: *Wow, three people got elevated, and they're all from inside!* It was seen as a major win for Louisville. The media played it up as good news, with the three locals moving up, and most of the customer base said they picked the right guy in Campbell. Bottom line: *Too bad about Larry, we wish him well, isn't it great about Jim.* Nobody went out thinking, *Ain't this awful.* Instead, *This is great!*"

It was also gratifying for Gary Richards, CEO of P. C.

Richards, a $100 million GE customer, who years earlier in Campbell's sales career wasn't sure that Jim was ready to be the GE sales rep for his business. P. C. Richards recently published a corporate history, the first one hundred years, and one full page was devoted to Jim Campbell and the phenomenal relations that he continues to have with the company. Campbell's first remark on the page was, "P. C. Richards is the only customer that nearly got me fired."

Campbell admits to some apprehension when he got the job. "But that's the beauty of the GE system," he says. "I'd run both sales and marketing, been to executive education courses at Crotonville, had developed a set of skills, contacts, and networks. You're always somewhat mentally prepared for a challenge or a change. For example, who would have thought that Larry Johnston from sales would be running the medical business in France? And where I had gaps, I had very strong team members to help me."

And so it turned out that Campbell energized and repositioned the business. When GE merged Appliances with the lighting businesses in 2002, he became president and chief executive officer of both businesses, with $8 billion in revenues, twenty-seven thousand employees, and a hundred locations. In 2007, when GE was again under pressure from investors to divest Appliances, Immelt went out looking for buyers but learned that he couldn't make the sale. Several interested parties looked at it but said, "There's no way we think we can run it any better than you can." Says Immelt: "Against tough competitors in a brutal industry, Jim is knocking it out of the park. No buyer would give us the value we perceived it to be worth."

EPILOGUE

Relationships based on trust and candor played a large role in dealing with Larry Johnston's resignation, and they played an even larger role again five years later in a similar situation with much higher stakes. Vice chairman Dave Calhoun, forty-seven, was a fast-rising star and potential CEO successor who ran the $70 billion infrastructure segment, GE's biggest and most profitable industrial business. One Monday morning in August, Conaty got another of those calls that will stay in his memory forever. Calhoun told him he was leaving to work for a private equity consortium of KKR, Carlyle, Blackstone, and Thomas Lee Partners, as CEO of its A.C. Neilsen holding. His departure would be a serious loss to GE, and the investment community would surely notice.

Jeff Immelt and Bill Conaty had both learned a lot from the Johnston-Campbell episode and now instinctively thought "same-day succession." GE had a ready replacement, John Rice, the vice chairman who ran the industrial segment. And of course there was a replacement in the wings for Rice, too. But the best candidate at the moment would be Lloyd Trotter, the senior vice president who headed the consumer and industrial business, a part of the industrial segment. There was only one problem: Trotter wanted to retire. The challenge was to persuade him to stay. It took some work, but Trotter eventually agreed.

GE then announced Calhoun's departure and two bigger moves for both Rice and Trotter as GE vice chairmen. The financial community applauded the moves. Inside the company there was a loud gasp over losing a guy of Calhoun's caliber—to the private equity world, no less—but also loud applause for both John Rice and Lloyd Trotter and the company's ability to have ready-made succession plans at all levels and under any set of circumstances.

These triumphs were the end product of an unparalleled talent management system. What does it consist of, and how does it work? The next chapter takes you through its intricacies.

Chapter 3

A TOTAL LEADERSHIP DEVELOPMENT SYSTEM
How GE Links People and Numbers

The processes, relationships, and interactions that you saw in the last chapter are parts of a unique and comprehensive total leadership development system. This chapter shows how its many components function as a continuous loop of business and social systems. Its underpinnings are candor in conversations, the accumulation of observations through multiple sources and lenses, and discussions of individuals that stretch throughout the year to feed outputs of each component into the others.

Most companies have a rhythm of managing the organization through periodic reviews. Seven are standard: talent, strategy, and operating plans, along with quarterly performance reviews. Many companies add others, such as innovation, risk, or technology reviews. These reviews in combination are what we call an operating system. The problem at many companies is that the reviews tend to stand alone—strategy reviews are linked only to the next strategy review, talent reviews only to the next talent review. They aren't linked with one another, and thus don't integrate and reinforce the knowledge gained in each.

What we advocate is what GE does: using the output from one process as input to another. Whenever leaders at

GE conduct, say, a strategy review, the issues they bring to the surface or conclusions they reach are reflected in reviews of talent, and vice versa. The information and insights are kept top of mind through ongoing dialogue in which leaders continually, and after a while, instinctively, link business with people.

THE GUTS OF GE'S OPERATING SYSTEM

The following diagram is a highly simplified view of the GE operating system. It shows the timing of several major types of reviews throughout the year and their interconnections.

January ⟶	July ⟶	November
People ("Session C")	**Strategy** ("Growth Playbook") plus follow-up on Session C by video conference	**Operations and budgets** for next year preceded by follow-up on Session C

These are the key points to understand about it:

- Leaders commit time and energy to talent. They put people before numbers.
- Reviews are rigorous and robust and linked to one another.
- Coaching and feedback are constant, direct, and substantive.
- Observations are accumulated from multiple sources over time and in comparison with others.
- Dialogue is candid and ongoing throughout the year.

Jack Welch took GE's operating system to a new level and created the culture of forthrightness and candor, and of course Jeff Immelt continues to develop them. But the core values and processes originated nearly a hundred years previously with Charles Coffin, the successor to Thomas A. Edison. Coffin established the principle of meritocracy based on measured performance—a radical approach at a time when businessmen everywhere chose their replacements largely on rough judgments and personal considerations. Each succeeding generation of GE leaders has expanded on the principle.

Welch's predecessor, Reg Jones, was a finance man and one of the last great business statesmen. He focused most of his energy on rationalizing a clutter of businesses that GE had accumulated through acquisition, grouping them into sectors and organizing a disciplined strategic planning process. Yet Jones made a great contribution to talent development with his choice of a successor. He knew that his company needed a different kind of leader in a business environment that was getting ever tougher. The man he picked fit the bill and then some. Jack Welch had worked his way up in GE's Plastics business. He came in with the zeal of a revolutionary, the persona of a pugilist, an unstoppable drive to improve GE's performance dramatically, and radical insights that propelled GE to its leadership in talent mastery.

What most people recall of the early years of the Welch era is the violent restructuring that earned him the unflattering nickname of "Neutron Jack." (Like with the neutron bomb, the buildings were left standing, but the people were gone.) Any business that could not be number one or number two in its field, he declared, would be either fixed, closed, or sold. Several businesses went by the wayside, and GE shed thousands of jobs. Welch also linked compensation more closely with performance by making stock options a bigger part of the package.

But as important to Welch as restructuring was improving the company's talent management. He wanted leaders, not managers. How would this person deal with people and develop them? Did he have the self-confidence to find and develop people better than himself? Could he see what was coming from the outside and deal with it? Finally, he wanted leaders who could put their own near-term interests on hold for the good of the company. To bring these kinds of leaders to the fore, he would have to create a new culture at GE. What he accomplished was nothing less than a revolution that crystallized the company's values and culture into rigorous operating mechanisms and social systems.

Welch used tools such as Workout and Change Acceleration Process (CAP), which he and other leaders formulated at the Crotonville center. Workout was a way to collapse hierarchy and get the voice from the factory floor up to the CEO—and, not incidentally, to get candor into dialogues. People met in groups of fifty to one hundred, including every level from the top decision makers to machine tool operators and assembly line workers. GE brought in outsiders as facilitators—business school professors and consultants. The meetings were initially done off-site, in local hotels or conference centers, and later directly inside each business as candor and trust developed. The concept remains alive today, done more instinctively and informally than as a special event. Importantly, Workout was the opening salvo in Welch's battle to break down typical communications barriers—silo mentalities, the tendency for leaders to pull rank instead of engage in open debate, and dialogue that places harmony over truth. It was an all-out frontal assault.

Bill Conaty recalls the extraordinary flavor of these sessions: "There'd never been anything like it before. There were town hall meetings, basically, with verbal fistfights as people got in the habit of speaking out. You'd have guys from the shop floor presenting with flip charts, showing potential productivity improvements—for example, how much a plant could save if the machines were maintained on the third shift when they weren't in full production. The plant manager would have to react on the spot, saying yes, no, or 'That's a good idea but I need to do a little more research, I'll have an answer next week.'

"It could get passionate. There would be cheers if the leader accepted the idea and boos if he didn't. The facilitators might have to step in and say, 'C'mon, gang, let him finish.' And then the leader would have to explain his decision. The issues all got dealt with on the spot; nothing was left hanging out.

"The dialogue was different in different parts of the country. At the time I worked in aircraft engines at Lynn, Massachusetts, which had the company's most hard-boiled workforce—they frequently voted down union contracts that every other GE union approved. As far as they were concerned, anybody from management was full of it. For instance, if I was making a presentation, I couldn't get my first flip chart up before six hands were up challenging me. It was the resurrection of the Boston Tea Party. It was a Northeast cultural reaction, as opposed to giving a similar presentation in the Midwest. For example, in Cincinnati, you'd give a pitch and people would be totally respectful. Though it was pleasant, it was tough in a different way, because they'd never ask a question. You couldn't get anybody to speak up—until coffee break time, when people would come up one at a time to question you privately. So Welch's upbringing in the Boston area gave rise to the GE town hall meetings to get the straight scoop from the bottom up.

"This was the beginning of his trying to create a revolution from the bottom up, and it was all about simplifying and eliminating bureaucracy and putting voice in the organization. It de-layered a lot of hierarchy. We felt that we didn't need twelve layers between the CEO of the business and the factory floor. Ideally, if you could get that to four or five layers, the communications would be exponentially better, the people would feel like they're more in the game, and we accomplished that. So this was a fearful time for a lot of people who had been trained to manage in a hierarchy versus lead. The ones who couldn't make the transition went the way of the dinosaur."

BRINGING SESSION C ALIVE

Welch's next big move was to radically overhaul Session C. The heart of GE's talent management process, Session C is an in-depth review of each business unit's leadership. It is where the decisions on development, deployment, and retention are made and followed through on. Meetings include GE's CEO and HR director, the business unit manager, and the HR director for that business unit. When they sit down, they have voluminous amounts of information about leaders at all levels. (Formerly compiled in big "books"—binders with data and photographs—this information is now online.)

But the reviews Welch inherited were formalized, stiff, and polite exercises. Poring over the big book that contained reviews of all the talent, leaders would say such things as "Joe Blow is doing a great job for us, should be able to move up to the next level in the organization." Others would rarely disagree or press for more specifics, and the executives would move on to the next person.

Welch brought Session C alive. "He put angst into the system," says Conaty. "He would say, 'Tell me all you know about Joe Blow.' Then he would challenge the response: 'What makes you think that? I don't see it that way. Didn't he just miss the last quarter on his results? And I hear he's a horse's ass who bullies his people.' And boom, all of a sudden, these nice formal books with the page flipping take a completely different turn.

"Oftentimes Welch incited debate to test the person's conviction. If they backed off, he figured they didn't really know what they were talking about. But given a strong enough argument, he was willing to say, 'Hey, look, maybe I'm wrong.' He turned Session C from an event into an institutionalized process that reflected and reinforced GE's core values and culture. And there was no hiding the truth. Sooner or later, opinions would be verified or rejected as more evidence came in." The rough-and-tumble give-and-take made leaders more conscious of their observational acuity.

Behind his tough language, Welch was teaching people the art of drilling down to get at people's core qualities. His searching questions combined the hard facts of business performance with the soft observations of others, gleaned through careful listening. He strove to isolate the real talent of a person from the context he or she was working in, with the aim of reinforcing it and taking it further. In one case, for example, he sent a message to everyone in GE when he prominently gave the highest-percentage bonus in the company to a business unit leader who failed to make his numbers. Why? The leader overcame a terrible business environment better than anyone else in the industry. "Welch enjoyed nothing more than what we called battlefield promotions, which we did routinely in Session C reviews by pulling a future star out of the pack and promoting them on the spot," says Conaty.

Welch also dispersed Session C, moving it from headquarters to meetings at each of the businesses. His idea was that the reviewers would get to see more people at each business, and more leaders in the businesses would become involved in the process. He knew that the more people who could view his intensity and passion on the topic of management development and succession, the faster it would become institutionalized in the corporation. Business leaders across the company were blown away by his probing, questioning, and in-depth challenging of their views on GE talent. "You had this semicrazed, impassioned leader at the top saying, 'I'm taking you up the mountain with me whether you want to go or not,'" says Conaty. "He was role-modeling, building the new culture, and institutionalizing rigor around talent management."

HARDENING THE SOFT SKILLS

The style that Welch built is the foundation of what makes GE's Session C so special. After all, there's nothing remarkable about the agenda itself; it covers the issues that most any company tries to address in a people review:

- Business issues and their external context
- Overall performance and value ratings for all key people

- The succession plan (backups for key jobs), prepared initially by the CEO and the head of HR for each business
- Identifying the highest-potential leaders
- An assessment of diversity in each business
- Nominations for people to go to the top executive courses at Crotonville
- Analysis of the CEO opinion survey results, including a review of progress on employee engagement—the overall satisfaction of people with the employer

Behind the agenda is a singular focus, vibrancy, and thoroughness of discussion. All Session Cs begin with a review of how the business is doing and what the future prospects are. This is then linked to the leadership. As Bill Conaty explains it, "When we go out into the field to do a Session C and the business is encountering some turbulence, we don't say, 'Look, we're out here today strictly to talk about people.' We start with, 'Hey, what the hell is going on lately? What's happening here with the industry dynamics? What's happening with the competition? And what is happening to margins and revenues?' And we'll spend time on that to get a grip, a better consensus up front of the issues, because whatever they are—whether we have a flawed organization concept, a flawed structure, or a major shift in the future needs of the business—they usually directly relate to the people side."

This linkage is the reason GE holds Session C before the strategy session. Most companies do it the other way around, on the theory that strategy must come first since it determines structure. GE knows otherwise. Strategy comes from the minds and cognitive makeup of people—their abilities to differentiate what matters, their understanding of trends in the external environment, their risk appetite, and their skill in modifying a strategy in the face of change. A strategy can only succeed when the right people conceive and execute it. Session C leaders are always on the lookout for past errors in placing people. They're not afraid to confront the reality that everyone makes mistakes; the worst mistake is the failure to remedy those already made. The leaders then deeply search for the causes of the error and develop options that are appropriate for the person and the company. The accumulated data bank of observations about the person and knowledge of the businesses across the company bring precision to making decisions about people—for example, whether a person has to be removed from a job; if a person should be given help with a development need; the job has to be changed to make the best use of the individual; or the person has to leave the company entirely because his values and skills no longer fit.

Jeff Immelt, the current CEO, has added a new element to Session C: the balance and chemistry among the CEO, CFO, and HR leader of each business. His goals are a diversity of thought and characteristics and a willingness to work collaboratively. No business, for example, should have leaders who are uniformly conservative and unwilling to take risks (or the opposite, all risk takers). Nor should it be run purely by hard-nosed types. As Bill Conaty explains, "Immelt is looking for balance between 'hammers' and 'softies,' and the key issue is whether the HR leader is strong enough to face off with a tough CEO and CFO as a true employee advocate without getting rolled." Conaty first argued that this particular focus wasn't necessary, since GE had already done functional reviews. But Immelt said, "Bill, just do it." So Conaty did. "And to my surprise, we found that we had some problems. There were cases in which all three leaders were hammers, so the employees didn't stand a chance. We then made the changes to get the right balance."

The culture of candor and relentless drilling for answers ensures discussions and conversations that spark creativity and improve leaders' judgments about other leaders. What has a leader under discussion accomplished? What are her strengths and weaknesses, what is her potential, what development help will enable her to reach it? These discussions set the tenor for all other leadership discussions in GE. Recall, for example, the meetings after the resignations of Johnston and Calhoun: these were informal Session Cs on the fly.

Session C, along with its follow-ups, is the core of some half a dozen meetings and processes spread over each year that drive the GE system. The two others that play major roles in developing leaders are S1 (now called the Growth Playbook), which is the strategy review held in the summer, and S2, the operating plan review in November, which is combined with a Session C follow-up called C2.

When leaders talk about a business in the strategy review, they engage in spirited discussions of the people whose job it is to design and execute the strategy of the business being reviewed. The same interconnection takes place during the operational review, and also in quarterly performance reviews.

FOLLOW-UP AND RECALIBRATING

Session C has a long tail. As Bill Conaty puts it, "There are three times during the course of the year where the process gets recalibrated, and they're all action-oriented. Stuff happens all the time. The question always asked is, 'What's new since we last met?' Maybe Charlie in Turbines isn't quite what we thought he was. Or a competitor in the aircraft industry is suddenly trying to hire our talent, so we need to put some special retention hooks in a dozen key people. It wasn't an issue back in April, but it's a big issue now in October. So the discussion goes, 'Okay, we need to put some special retention hooks in a dozen key people. Let's just do it.' The proposals are immediately implemented, and those select people know they've received special recognition and that GE wants to keep them for the long term."

The follow-up process to Session C field reviews starts when the CEO, head of corporate HR, and vice president of executive development are riding on the plane after their meetings. The vice president for development would have taken notes in the meeting and summarized them. Working from the summaries, the group focuses on people who deserved special recognition or who might have development needs—for example, the leader who needs to be more demanding of subordinates and less prone to trying to solve issues on his or her own. Or they may decide to accelerate a person's development by giving her experience in the Chinese market, since more leaders will be needed there in the future. They will sharpen their insight into people by comparing and contrasting them in their different stages of development. The summaries of the Session C discussions are sent the next day in bullet form to the business CEO and HR leader for their review and follow-up actions.

Those notes become the basis for update reviews, starting with the Corporate Wrap-up in late May, where the CEO, senior vice president for HR, and the vice president of executive development consolidate all the data on all the businesses from Session C field reviews and determine any cross-business moves the company needs to make. They also put together the Corporate Organizational Vitality Assessment, which aggregates senior leaders into the categories of "top talent," "highly valued," and "less effective," and determine which leaders will attend which top executive-level courses at Crotonville. At the Session C Follow-up, a videoconference in July with all of the businesses, the documents from the field reviews serve as the framework for the discussion and action items: "What did you do about these issues and action plans?" Leaders are asked if anything has changed since April—business environment, key talent, succession plans, or critical retention issues.

Any action items coming out of Session C—for example, sending a person from one business unit to another; taking someone out of a job; changing organization structure; needing to recruit from outside—are reviewed before the strategy session. In November, when the business leaders and their teams meet for the full-day S2 operating review at headquarters, the first ninety minutes of the day is called Session C2, and it's completely focused on people issues, from performance and retention to promotions.

The commitment to identifying, developing, and deploying talent is ongoing. It all comes back to "people first." Jack Welch used to tell his leaders: "I have made more critical operating decisions in Session Cs than I have in actual operating reviews."

INTIMACY IN SUCCESSION PLANNING

The intimacy GE develops with its leaders extends to the board of directors, making their judgments about possible future leaders exceptionally keen. They get reports on the company's overall talent picture as well as on individual leaders. But in characteristic GE form, they get some of their best insights by talking informally and often with and about leaders in the context of the businesses they're running. The CEO and chief human resource officer keep the directors updated on how some leaders below the CEO's direct reports are progressing, and make a point of having as much one-on-one contact as possible. Apart from what they see in the leaders' boardroom presentations about their businesses, they spend a lot of time with them in social situations—for example at dinner the night before the board meeting. They are also required to visit leaders in the field, where they can see them in action. Such firsthand observations deepen directors' insights into the individuals.

Knowing the depth and range of leadership talent, the board doesn't narrow its succession focus too soon. Even during the closely watched succession to Welch, the board kept its options open until the time of the announcement. As succession drew nearer, three strong candidates emerged—Bob Nardelli, Jim McNerney, and Jeff Immelt. Each was expected to carry on leading his business and not turn the succession process into a horse race: lobbying for the job internally or externally would have been the kiss of death. Meanwhile, the board got a closer look at each of them during field visits and other board reviews.

At decision time the board had to factor in their best assessment of the emerging needs of the business. In November 2000, the directors and Welch—whose opinion they weighted heavily—considered in real time the business challenges posed by the emerging external landscape:

- The company was becoming more global, with an increasing proportion of revenues and employment from outside the U.S.
- GE's industrial businesses and financial services had to have the right balance.
- External constituencies representing societal and environmental stakeholder concerns were gaining voice.
- Shareholder activism was on the rise, particularly on issues of compensation and governance.
- Crisis leadership was important (this was before 9/11, which occurred on Immelt's second day as CEO).
- Workforce dynamics were changing, with issues around dual careers, flex time, telecommuting, and diversity.
- Growing an already big company posed a special challenge.

This assessment played a role in their final decision. Another helpful tool was a profile of "the ideal CEO" prepared some five years before by Welch, Conaty, and Chuck

Okosky, the vice president of executive development. While it was understood that no one could meet all those criteria, the list defined qualities to watch for and provided a template to compare people against. You can read the entire list in the Talent Mastery Tool Kit.

Welch and the board knew that when a successor was announced, the other two leaders would almost certainly leave the company. After all, they were in high demand and had ambitions to be CEO. So Welch made it clear to the candidates six months before that the two who were not chosen were expected to leave, and all were to begin the process of passing the baton to their successors. This allowed ample time for the leaders filling in behind the candidates to get up to speed, and for GE to observe how well each CEO contender assimilated his successor. This bold approach worked well. Within days of the announcement, Nardelli accepted a job as CEO of Home Depot and McNerney became CEO of 3M. GE wished them well and maintained positive relationships with both. Meanwhile, each of their former businesses was in capable hands, and the company didn't miss a beat.

CROTONVILLE, THE CROSSROADS OF CULTURE

Like the GE talent management system as a whole, Crotonville is widely admired and frequently benchmarked—and just as frequently misunderstood by observers who think of it as simply a management education facility. True enough, Crotonville is officially called the John F. Welch Learning Center, and offers basic and executive-level courses for rising stars, but that's only one of its purposes. It is a driver for management innovation, change and adaptation, a melting pot to bring people and businesses together—and the central transmitting station for GE culture and values.

Located in Ossining, New York, about an hour's drive

from GE headquarters, Crotonville is the venue for a range of corporate gatherings, including the quarterly two-day meetings of the Corporate Executive Council and the annual company officers meeting. It's where GE introduces major corporate initiatives such as Workout. It's also a place to translate company strategy into short-term actions through exercises geared toward executing ideas to improve business performance. It's also used to bring in key customer teams to work jointly with their GE counterparts to solve real business problems and strengthen relationships.

When GE acquires a company, it often brings the new leadership teams from GE and the acquired company to Crotonville, a kind of neutral ground, to discuss any cultural differences and what is going to be expected in the GE culture. When GE makes the occasional outside higher-level executive hire, sending the person to Crotonville is a surefire way to speed that person's assimilation.

Most of the nearly $1 billion a year GE spends on education and training goes to Crotonville. It's not cheap, but GE considers it worth every penny. (See part IV, "The Talent Mastery Tool Kit," to learn how other companies get much of the same value at less cost.)

The learning part of Crotonville is not what most people think of as executive education. To be sure, there are courses for executives at all levels, from first-time managers to experienced leaders, on topics ranging from leadership development to general business expertise. But these are GE-specific, giving leaders practical and experiential learning about issues that directly connect to the company's priorities. The students are an elite group, a thousand a year out of GE's more than three hundred thousand people, chosen through the Session C process as worthy of the significant investment in their careers.

The courses can produce real-world results. One notable example came out of a study in the late 1990s of what GE's role should be in countries such as China, Russia, Mexico, and India. During the Business Management Course, where high-level GE teams travel to and study GE's prospects in these countries, Bob Corcoran, a class participant from the HR function, made an impassioned plea to Jack Welch and the Corporate Executive Council for a greater presence in Mexico. Welch not only bought the idea but told Corcoran, "Since you're so passionate about Mexico, you get the job of helping us to develop it." Corcoran sharpened his Spanish-language skills, moved with his wife and two children to Mexico City, and spent three years there—doing such a good job that later in his career he was given the leadership role for all of Crotonville.

Some 80 percent of the instructors are senior GE leaders. (The outside instructors are the best GE can find—leading thinkers and experts in such areas as strategy, finance, marketing, and innovation.) Those who teach at the top executive levels are the corporate CFO, general counsel, CIO, head of HR, corporate business development leader, presidents and CEOs of the businesses, vice chairmen, and CEO of the company. These are not casual commitments; the leaders participate at least once a month. They conduct sessions for two to three hours, with interactive dialogue and an open Q&A period, all the while assessing both the content of the programs and the caliber of the participants. At most companies, by contrast, top management's participation is likely to consist of a twenty-minute speech from the CEO on the state of the company, followed by a brief Q&A before he or she heads back to the office.

There's an implicit lesson as well: by putting themselves on the line, the leaders show that they really do know what they are talking about. They are the living, breathing role models that the class participants dream of being someday. Conversely, the leaders get from the participants a better sense of what's going on in the company: Crotonville exposes them to roughly a thousand potential future leaders over the course of a year.

The instructors need to be well prepared, since they get evaluated by the participants, and the feedback is hard-hitting. During the HR segment, the classes get a peek into what happens in those career discussions between the CEO, HR, and their business leaders. They see the importance of candid feedback, and how seriously it is taken from the bottom to the top of the company.

Each senior officer discusses their own area of expertise. The CEO will talk about the broad company picture, getting at strategy and the future direction of leadership. For example, he might ask: "If you were CEO of GE, what would you do differently?" This has huge development value for the class and increases their bandwidth and the connectivity of diverse viewpoints. Meanwhile, the CEO is evaluating the quality of people's thinking and perspective on the topic.

Since the sessions run all day, most senior leaders who are presenting in the afternoon stay for cocktails to talk informally about what is happening at the company, moving among groups and getting deeper feedback that helps them connect the dots. The students get a better feel for who the senior leaders are and how they think, and the leaders get a better feel for the organization at the ground level. These interactions are invaluable linkages between the top of the company and lower organizational levels.

Bill Conaty taught about HR content, of course, and then led the probing and debating of issues. One of his objectives was to demystify the Session C process by explaining how leaders are selected, developed, and promoted, and on the flip side cautioning classes about potential career pitfalls. "Your personal involvement in Session C disappears after the first quarter of each year," he would say, "but what I want to show you is how it rolls out through the year. It is not just a one-off event, but an everyday process."

"I would take them through the entire year," says Conaty, "showing the Session C Wrap-ups in May, the video teleconference follow-ups in July, the C2 process in November prior to the operating reviews, and our intimate interactions with the board of directors throughout the year. The learning for them: how critical this process is in GE, and the importance of the personal inputs they make to the internal resume they fill out at the beginning of each year. It is a living, breathing process, not just paperwork."

PUSHBACK IN THE PIT: THE DYNAMICS OF A MANAGEMENT DEVELOPMENT COURSE

There's no better place to study the soul of GE than in the Management Development Course, or MDC, the first-level executive course and one of the company's core development programs. No less important than the content of the courses is the tenor of the discussions and the socializing that occurs around them. It's a total immersion in the fundamental elements of the GE culture. Classes are held in a commodious amphitheater called "the Pit," with breakout conference rooms nearby. The residence center resembles a first-class hotel, accommodating up to two hundred participants, with fine dining and a top-notch fitness center. Nearby is a casual recreational facility known as the "White House," with an open bar for socializing.

GE runs about ten Management Development Courses a year, placing eighty to ninety people in each class. The criteria for participation in the MDC course are that the participant has either already achieved executive-band status or is deemed to have the potential to become an executive in the near future. The average participant will be in her mid-thirties to early forties, with eight to ten years at the company. About 40 percent of the class is from outside the United States. Typically three or four will be from a given business, though a business such as Financial Services, with its size and scope, will send more. It's a badge of honor—the chosen few are deemed to have significant growth potential and are endorsed by the business CEO and VP of HR.

The students get a good grounding in finance, marketing, and other subjects, but the content is mainly centered around giving people a deep understanding of GE values, leadership, and culture. For example, notes Conaty, "the participants are astonished at the candor of the presenters and the fact that we did not always agree 100 percent with each other. Of course, we were all philosophically moving in the same direction, but we weren't marching there like toy soldiers: we could have differences of opinion, which is valued at GE. They found that really refreshing and energizing."

Thrown together for three weeks, mingling between sessions in class, at the gym, or over drinks, the students become a community. As the sessions progress, they learn to become more and more outspoken about their business and the company. They're urged to push back and to challenge the instructors. Eventually they're not only comfortable with it, they even exult in doing it. Few leave unchanged by the experience.

"One of the greatest things that participants experience is their internal GE network expanding exponentially. They come to the class with a very narrow network. They'll initially gravitate toward the people from within their business, and then it expands during case study breakout sessions and drinks at the White House. At the end of the course it's a cathartic, familial experience, and after they graduate they remain in touch with each other. For instance, I went to this class in 1980 and I still remember who my classmates and roommates were. In fact when I attended, the residence quarters were more like dorm rooms, with three or four people assigned to a suite. One of my roommates who remained a very close friend was Lloyd Trotter, who also recently retired from GE as a vice chairman, one of the top five people in the company. So I guess he was smarter than me.

"By the final week of the class," continues Conaty, "when the CEO and the SVP of HR are slotted on the agenda, the class has been together for three weeks, exposed to all the top leaders in the company, and they're feeling very empowered and self-confident. I would bring along my VP of executive development—I worked with three great ones over fifteen years, Chuck Okosky, Bob Muir, and Susan Peters. We would spend about two hours on content and one hour on Q&A with the group. I always wanted my session to be scheduled in the afternoon, so we could finish and spend an hour and a half having cocktails with them right outside the Pit. By then they were at the point of knowing that we wanted to hear what was really on their minds, and I wanted to be sure they would be as candid as they could. During the session I would say, 'We're serving the truth serum later, so if you can't get it up now, I'm sure you can find a way to do it when we go out for a drink.' They would all laugh and relish the chance to probe us.

"I often brought along some junior HR people so they could get right in the middle of the postsession dialogue. They'd be contemporaries of the people in the class, and could add peer-level perspective to the dialogue. When the session in the Pit ended and we got upstairs, the circles would form—you'd get a drink and, swoosh, you got twenty people, thirty people hanging around you. Then we'd move around, we'd try to make sure we made contact with everyone in the class. In these dialogues, they would speak on a much more personal level, typically about ideas for improving their businesses in particular and the company as a whole.

"We wanted to empower them to speak their mind. For example, one common complaint was lack of clarity about promotions to executive band. Someone would say, 'Bill, you mentioned that the businesses have control of how many executive-band slots they allot, but our leaders in our business tell us that it's you in Fairfield who do this.' Others would chime in—'It's the same in my business.' Then we're off to the races. I say, 'Look, it's easy to blame headquarters and most people will buy it, but it's not true. You can go back and tell anybody that's not the way it works. And you've got an obligation to push back on us if we're doing stupid things and demotivating people that we're trying to energize.'

"Others might tell us about a leader they think is great and deserves more recognition from headquarters—or one who they think is a horse's ass. They were incredibly grateful for the attention, and all these discussions expanded our corporate database of knowledge regarding people and leadership—both the good leaders not getting enough recognition as well as those who, in their assessment, we needed to keep an eye on.

Conaty recalls that "when Welch used to take his turn onstage, he would always stir the pot. He was a master of body language; he had a scanner on every person in the room whether they knew it or not. If somebody was rolling their eyes, he'd say, 'You don't seem to believe what I'm saying.' The whole class would turn, and suddenly some classmate was on the spot. The participant might say, 'I hear you, Jack, but y'know, the stuff that you guys talk about here at Crotonville just doesn't work that way in my business. My boss is kind of Neanderthal and he just doesn't get it; he doesn't believe in this stuff.'

"Welch would be right on him, saying, 'I don't want you here thinking you're a victim. You've got a choice. Fix things by changing how the game is played, because you've got an obligation to push back on the system when things aren't working.' I remember one guy who kept complaining, and Jack finally said, 'You know what I'd do if I was you?' After he got people in the class all on the edge of their seats, he said, 'I'd quit. There's no way I could work in the kind of environment you're describing.' This guy thought that Welch was going to stand there and take a beating. He was expecting him to say, 'What business are you in? Who's your boss? I'm going to go talk to him.' Well, no way. If you can't take what we're talking about and use it to influence or persuade, then you ought to get out.

"And the rest of the class loved it, because it's always the guy that was dominating the Q&A and feeling that he knew more than the teachers. You normally pick out that kind of person within the first three days and ignore most of what they have to say, though I will say there are a lot fewer in the classes these days than in my early GE years."

Interacting with GE's rising stars is an enormous time commitment, but the payback far outweighs the disruption to everything else on leaders' plates. The evidence is clear: the time spent nurturing talent creates an intimacy that pays off in the performance of the company. "Over classes lasting three weeks, we get a great look at people and they get a great perspective on the top leadership of the company," Conaty says. "We may spot someone in the class or at cocktail hour who is genuinely sharp; we store that in our memory bank and that expands our knowledge for Session C discussions. Prior to visiting the class at Crotonville, I would talk to other senior leaders during lunch hour back at headquarters and would let them know that I was going to Crotonville that afternoon to address the MDC class. I would ask who had already been with the class, what did you think of them, and what's on their minds that I can address and add some value. Those discussions over the years just got progressively better—for example, 'dynamite class,' 'really animated,' 'one of the best we have seen yet.' We would often say, 'I don't know how we are going to top this class,' only to find that the next one was even better."

Immelt initiated a new course in 2007 called Leadership-Innovation-Growth (LIG), which brings intact senior business leadership teams to Crotonville to learn as a group and apply the lessons to their current business issues and challenges, for example, balancing short-term results and long-term growth. At the end of the session each business is charged with writing a "letter of commitment" to Immelt detailing the results of their learning and an action plan for improvement. This keeps the spark of enthusiasm from flickering out when people get back to their desks. "It's obviously a huge investment to pull a handful of leaders from the same business unit off the field," says Conaty, "but the effort has paid off by helping them apply their learning to the business as a unified team. For example, the senior leadership teams from the Aviation, Healthcare, and Energy businesses might come together to learn from a top business school professor and Omar Ishrak, the president and CEO of GE Healthcare Systems, on the topic of market dynamics and analysis. Working as a unit and in breakout sessions, the team would capitalize on what they'd learned to make their business more productive and competitive."

Presenting at Crotonville is itself a learning experience, as exemplified by Bill Conaty: "It certainly improved my game. When I did my first presentation to an MDC class back in 1993, I got unfiltered feedback on what they did and didn't like about the presentation. At first I was ticked off. But when I thought about it, they were right; I had been way too cautious in my answers. After that, I couldn't wait to get in front of these groups and really have at it and say, 'Okay, let's go, what's on your mind—any observations, any rumors, any questions, any anything? Nothing is off-limits. Here is your big chance to square off with me.' "

Crotonville also serves as a retention hook. Those chosen to attend an executive-level course, knowing they are considered among the company's best and brightest, would never dream of leaving the company at that point, or anytime soon after finishing.

EVERYDAY VALUES

Just about every company has a stated set of values. GE has working values—the kind that actually influence how people deliver results. They are a part of everyday language: "He's got GE values" is as routine a statement as "He did a great job." People don't get promoted if they don't exhibit them, and all leaders are compensated partly on how well they live them. Performance—getting results—is viewed as the ticket of admission; it's expected as a matter of course. But leadership values determine whether a person will rise in the organization.

It wasn't always the case. Recalls Bill Conaty, "When I started at the company in 1967 I don't ever remember anyone saying, 'Here is what we are expecting from you.' Sure, there was a code of ethics and dos and don'ts, but they were neither aspirational nor inspirational. Later in my career it became clear that if you're going to have a performance culture, there's got to be a very well understood set of company values to keep people from going off the rails ethically or behaviorally."

In 1993, Welch commissioned a corporate team to construct a set of values that were actionable. The finalized values were put on a laminated card and distributed to every GE employee. They articulated what behaviors would be tolerated and what behaviors would not. They made it crystal clear to all employees what was expected of them and what they could expect from the company. Integrity, of course, headed the list; Welch made it plain that one strike took you out. A more distinctive value was Welch's concept of "boundarylessness." It may have mystified outsiders, but it was clearly understood within GE. Welch meant that there should be no boundaries that prevent sharing information and collaborating across silos, organizations, and levels—all the way down to the factory floor. Boundarylessness, he stressed, was what it took to make the best decisions quickly, and it put the greater good of the company ahead of turf protection. It also applied to the unhampered movement of people from business to business, which is essential for giving leaders a variety of development opportunities. You don't hear the word much anymore because there's no need for it: boundarylessness is part of the culture.

To make sure GE's values were taken seriously, says Conaty, "Jack made a huge deal out of it at the annual global leadership meeting with the top five hundred leaders in the company" and did a survey of employees to see how well they were being acted on. Welch called it the CEO survey, to give it some weight, and made a point of asking people to respond. One more way of reminding people that values are as important as numbers was to make the results of the CEO survey part of the Session C agenda, where each business would highlight the pluses and minuses and explain what they were going to do about the minuses.

GE also included values in an analytical tool that was part of the management assessment process: a simple four-block matrix, with performance on the horizontal axis and values on the vertical one. That made the message clear and simple: If you don't have the values and you're not delivering the results, you're leaving. If you've got both values and results, you're bound for glory. If you've got the values but you're having problems with performance, GE tries to help raise you to the top right quadrant of the matrix with additional training, more resources, or a job restructuring.

The toughest category to confront, says Conaty, "was the bottom left—'I'm cranking out the numbers, and to hell with your values; as long as I get the results, I'll never get fired!' This was the group Welch identified as Type IV managers—informally, we called them the kiss-up, kick-down crowd. We used Session C feedback, as well as 360-degree performance appraisals for evaluations, to locate this crowd. We gave them fair warning to change their ways but ended up dismissing about a half dozen leaders in the mid-1990s who just didn't believe we were serious. Welch made a big spectacle of it at one of the big reviews to explain why there were some 'missing soldiers'—that is, people who had been removed. You could say there was a little intimidation in this, but if you didn't believe in the importance of values before that meeting, you certainly did afterward."

Today the values are so ingrained in the culture that it's almost unheard of for a leader to be removed for failing to live up to them. Indeed, shortly after Jeff Immelt became CEO, he recast and simplified them to reflect more contemporary challenges. The new ones fall under the four umbrella themes of "imagine," "solve," "build," and "lead."

CONCLUSIONS

The GE talent management system is a complex mixture of software and hardware. Yet when you boil it down to the key elements, the resulting list is relatively simple. Most important, it's actionable and customizable: you can begin to think about how you will achieve these in your own organization, in your own way.

- **A formalized evaluation mechanism** (Session C) that is followed through (Session C2). This is central to building a company's talent. Others around the world have emulated and adopted their own variations.
- **The pursuit of accurate knowledge about individuals.** It comes not only in formal meetings and evaluations but continually. Leaders get to know their peoples' natural talents and hone their judgments collectively through the cross-verification of multiple observations through multiple lenses.
- **Timely, constructive oral and written feedback**, delivered throughout the year. This is how GE breaks the curse of the typical evaluation, so often an unsatisfying and even useless event in many companies. There are rarely surprises in the formal sessions.
- **Connections between people and numbers** in every review and linked to causes and outcomes.
- **Self-evaluation.** Every year, every leader must cite one or two crucial personal development needs and an action plan associated with addressing them.

- **The responsibility of leaders to develop other leaders.** How well they do this influences their promotion prospects and compensation.
- **The practice of GE values.** Leaders can't get ahead unless they live by them.

Call the GE system "humanistic" and people who don't know better will look at you oddly. Yet in the end, that is one of its great strengths. You can't get more humanistic than paying careful attention to the development of individual human beings. The next chapter will show you exactly what we're talking about.

Chapter 4

HOW
INTIMACY PAYS OFF
Nurturing the Careers of
Mark Little and Omar Ishrak

With their cumulative knowledge of individuals, GE leaders are not just familiar with their people: they know them intimately. In this chapter we'll see two examples of how the rigorous intimacy built into GE's talent system works in practice.

Our first story is about a man who found himself in a job that suddenly became bigger than he could handle. Most companies have a simple way of dealing with this kind of problem: they get rid of the leader. More often than not, it's a terrible waste of talent. Success is almost never a straight line. Indeed, often the greatest talents are those who progressed through twists and bumps. A setback tests you, and your response to it tells a lot about your character. If you learn from it, the experience toughens your emotional strength and your ability to deal with unknowns and adversity. So when talent masters see a recognizably talented individual stumble, they analyze the reasons for the failure, judge his response, and redirect him so his talent can develop. Sometimes they discover that the problem is not with the leader himself but with the fit between his talents and new challenges posed by a change in the business or its context.

A MIDCAREER REBIRTH

"It was the worst thing that ever happened to me," says Mark Little, today the leader of GE's Global Research Center, his voice husky. "I still get passionate speaking about it." In 1995, at the age of forty-one, he'd been made a company officer—vice president of engineering at GE's Power Systems group, a $5 billion business that included all power generation. He not only was a stellar technologist but also had proven in several P&L jobs that he could run a business. That put him among the top 125 in GE's pyramid of leaders, and he seemed destined to rise higher still.

Then Power Systems missed its numbers—not once but three times in a row, a serious failure in any company but nowhere more so than in Jack Welch's GE. Little's many talents had not disappeared, but the business needed specific expertise that he didn't have. His bosses split the job so a more experienced executive could step in and solve the problems, leaving Little to run a smaller portion of the technology function. "It was all the emotions you would expect," Little recalls. "I was hurt, I disagreed with how they came to that conclusion, and I was just really pissed." Worst of all, Little suspected his career at GE was over.

But it wasn't. Today he's the senior vice president in charge of the corporate R&D center, one of the company's top twenty-five executives. The details of how that came to pass reveal how a talent master balances solving a business problem while preserving its precious talent.

GE recruited Little as a research engineer in 1979 from Northeastern University, where he was just completing his master's degree. Talking with him, you come to see that he was a man who started his career with more talents than he realized. Indeed, he allows, as a youth "I didn't know what I wanted to do. I had some sense that science and math were good for me, but didn't really figure it out until after I got my master's degree."

He worked for about a year in GE's Turbine business in Lynn, Massachusetts, and then—with the full support of his bosses—took a leave to get his doctorate at Rensselaer Polytechnic Institute. But when he returned to GE, he realized that the Turbine business wouldn't offer the kind of advanced research work that he had imagined himself doing. He asked to go to the industrial side as a design engineer instead, with the idea that it would offer broader challenges. Again, GE obliged: they had already spotted him as someone with exceptional talent, a keeper.

Little continued to pursue research, but not long after he came back with his PhD, his bosses chose him to take the Management Development Course at Crotonville, an honor accorded only to people GE saw as having high leadership potential. At the end of the four-week course (these days it's three weeks), much to his surprise, his class voted him "most likely to be a general manager." As he advanced through a series of engineering jobs, the idea of managing grew more and more appealing. "I let them know I was interested," he says. "When I got my first management role, leading a group of ten engineers, it was a great opportunity to work in a cross-functional capacity, and I loved it."

In 1989, thoroughly enjoying management, he asked to be considered for a P&L job. It didn't take long for the Power Systems leadership to find him one that they thought he could handle but which also would challenge him. The call came from Dennis Donovan, then head of HR for the business, and soon he was in Schenectady, New York, as product line leader for the generator business. "So I went from being a highly technical guy to running a P&L for the first time, which was really exciting. I became intimate with the corporate operating system and got to see the bigger picture."

Another call came from Donovan in 1994, this one completely unexpected. "Dennis told me that the engineering leadership of Power Systems needed a change and that the business leaders wanted me to become vice president for engineering. They felt that I could bring teamwork and focus to it." Though the job as VP of engineering for Power Systems would take him off the P&L business track and back to a functional role—"an interesting twist," Little calls it—he was elated. Utilities were investing heavily in new plants at the time, and Power Systems was hot, with the best top- and bottom-line growth of any GE industrial business.

When Jack Welch himself called Little, it became clear that he was one of GE's rising stars. He'd made it through the executive band, which includes the top five thousand GE executives, and into the senior executive band—the top five hundred executives at that time. That's where Welch and Conaty would get deeply involved in following an individual's career, watching carefully during Session Cs and operational reviews. They had readily agreed with the business leader's recommendation to make Little a GE officer. With this job change, Little would join an elite group of top GE leaders, about 125 at the time, and would be front and center in most corporate meetings that involved Power Systems.

"ON THE EDGE OF PROFESSIONAL DEATH"

"And then the wheels came off," he says. Power Systems' flagship product was the F turbine, huge 200-megawatt machines that sold for around $40 million each and earned their owners a handsome return in service fees. Six months into his new job, the rotors began failing in customers' plants.

These were major technical failures, the biggest GE had experienced. "It was an enormous loss of face in the marketplace and over the course of several years caused very big financial losses. We were shipping replacement turbine rotors around the world, getting Russian aircraft because they were the only thing big enough to carry them; we had our customers shut down for months at a time. It was just absolutely horrible. The *Wall Street Journal* was writing bad stories about us. I remember going to a GE officers' meeting at Crotonville and everybody's saying, 'Geez, you're never going to sell another one of these turbines.' "

At about the same time, the business was heading into a cyclical downturn. The business missed its financial target again, and GE replaced its leader with Bob Nardelli, who had been doing a great job reviving the rail transportation business. (Nardelli later became one of three candidates in line to replace Welch as CEO, then served as CEO of both Home Depot and Chrysler, and is now operating in a senior leadership role with the Cerberus private equity group.)

Nardelli came in with optimism and excitement about bringing Power Systems back to glory. But business continued to lag behind the projections. "So we became a financial train wreck at the same time we were still dealing with this worst-ever product problem. We missed our financial plan twice more in a bad way.

"We went down to GE headquarters to see Welch. I remember this as clear as day—it was right after he was back from open-heart surgery—and we were telling him then that we were going to come off our financial plan. He yelled and screamed at us, and we left that meeting thinking, 'Okay, we lived through this, that's the worst that could possibly ever happen to us.' And we came back to Schenectady and said, 'Okay, now we're going to build ourselves back up.'

"And then, maybe three months later—I'll never forget this one either—it was, like, seven-thirty on, I'll say, a Wednesday night and I was in my office with Steve Bransfield, vice president of operations, when Ron Pressman, the vice president of Power Plants, came in white as a sheet, saying we're off our financial plan by another hundred million bucks, which at the time was huge. I said, 'That can't be right,' but, sure as hell, it was, and we had to inform Bob. So Bob lost confidence in the whole staff and, well, it was just the ugliest thing you could possibly imagine."

No one was blaming Little for the problems, but circumstances had turned his stretch assignment into mission impossible. Nardelli reasoned that the problem with turbines called for the best expertise available, and Welch and Conaty concurred. In the spring of 1996, Nardelli brought in Jon Ebacher, a gas turbine expert, to run the bigger and more important part of Power Systems engineering. Ebacher had spent more than two decades working on state-of-the-art gas turbine technology in GE's Aviation business and was head of Aircraft Advanced Technology Operations. He had built a reputation as GE's go-to guy on technology issues around the company; among other things, he had been lent to GE Appliances to solve a serious refrigerator compressor problem and sent to Motors to fix design and productivity issues.

Nardelli asked Little to remain and run the smaller steam turbine engineering function. "So I was now going from running the whole engineering function to running a much smaller piece of it. I could understand it intellectually," Little says. "But I hated it emotionally and deeply—and I still get bad feelings thinking about it."

Solving the business problem created a people problem. Conaty recalls: "We had just promoted Mark to officer and then had to quickly sidetrack his career. It would have been logical for him to leave. It's embarrassing and demotivating to lose what you have earned, and usually it means your chances of getting back on a promotional fast track are diminished. Beyond that, you can't brush aside the psychological damage—the diminished self-confidence that undermines your ability to lead.

"But we loved Mark," Conaty continues. "He was a brilliant technologist and he really understood business. More importantly, he had the ethics and the values we believe in, so we did everything we could to show him that we wanted to keep him in the company."

ENCOURAGEMENT FROM THE CEO

Nardelli reassured Little that he still had a future and reported that Welch and Conaty wanted to see him at GE's headquarters. They knew an encouraging message would be more credible coming directly from them. Says Conaty: "Unless you feel like you've really got that intimate support from the corporate office, most GE leaders won't buy into it. In the GE system, we say the top six hundred people are ours—they're corporate assets. While your immediate performance, recognition, and career are driven by the business you're in, your real career and your future is more in the hands of the CEO of the corporation."

Little left the Fairfield meeting having heard the message, but he couldn't quite accept it. "I had enough trust in the system to know that these guys meant what they said," Little explains. "And that mattered one hell of a lot. Still, I was embarrassed and uncomfortable to be there in the first place; I frickin' hated it. So I figured the job change was probably not going to work for me."

He nevertheless hung in. "I wanted to stay and at least get through a part of it," he says. What's more, he had some money coming in the next year under GE's Long-Term Incentive Plan—compensation in addition to base and bonus that pays out after three years. "After that, I could do what I wanted to do."

He kept his internal turmoil to himself and his family. "It was an awful time emotionally for me, but my focus was entirely on making sure that the team that I was leading—and it was still a pretty good-sized team—felt that we were actually going to make something terrific out of this.

"And I worked hard to make sure that Jon Ebacher was comfortable coming in, that everything was easy and smooth for him. I had a lot of friends in the business and I wanted to be sure that they weren't thinking that he was any kind of a bad guy. There was never one ounce of bad blood between us. And I know very well that teams respond to that."

Observing Little in Steam Turbines, Nardelli and the corporate office were impressed with both the quality of his work and his maturity in the face of adversity. And as he built his track record, Little gradually gained enough confidence to ask for a line job. When one opened up as head of Power Plants, Little screwed up his courage to approach Nardelli. "Having felt on the edge of professional death, it was an emotional moment for me to say to Bob, 'Hey, I'd like to have this big job.' It involved all the new products in gas turbines, steam turbines, hydro turbines. We built all the power plants all around the world."

Nardelli judged that Little had both the technical background and the business leadership experience needed for the job—a powerful vote of confidence from one of the strongest operating leaders in the company. Welch and Conaty had kept their eye on Little and were quick to agree. It was a stirring story of triumph: a leader comes back from the brink of career death to run a significant P&L business. What impressed everybody the most, says Conaty, "was the way Mark showed his leadership characteristics and values in handling the setback."

"I'll never forget how joyful that was for me," Little says. "It was a rebirth."

For his part, Ebacher acknowledges that sharing the overall engineering responsibility with the man who'd previously had it all was awkward at first. But when he arrived, he says, "Mark welcomed me openly and sincerely and made me feel that a good working relationship would be the outcome." After Little got the P&L job, Ebacher was given the entire engineering organization. "We were both rewarded for our efforts," he says. "We continued to enjoy a terrifc working relationship that allowed us to leverage our mutual skills to address emerging business growth opportunities."

The new Power Plants job didn't lack for challenges.

"We were losing a couple of hundred million bucks at that time," says Little. "The aftermarket services segment was the darling of the business, making lots of money. We were the dog part. So we set ourselves a goal to get profitable by the year 2000, which nobody had any idea of how we could possibly meet that target.

"But the F turbine problems were on their way to being solved. I remember going down to Fairfield in the early days, when I still had the engineering job, and having to explain to Jack Welch how these beautiful turbines were breaking down left and right. It wasn't just one thing, it was a set of things that were really tough to figure out. He told me, 'What I need you to do is get all the resources you can possibly get, spend whatever money you need, but just make sure this thing comes out the back end so that our customers will say, "Geez, it was a lousy problem, but this is the best company in the world to have this happen to because they will fix it." '

"And that is exactly what we did. We stuck with these customers, we supported them in every way we could. We suffered a lot to do that, but at the end of the day, they came out exactly with that feeling. Along the way we got to do great global acquisitions—for example, successfully integrating the major French business we acquired. We did that all before the market really turned up, so we had capacity and a great set of people to help us execute. And then at the end of the run we got the wind turbine business, which was a train wreck at the time, and now it is a glorious GE business.

"When the market turned up, particularly in the United States, we got gigantic share, we got price up, we got our cost down. We had everything going any way you could want it to in a business, and we took advantage of it in the strongest possible way. We got profitable in 2000, and in 2002 we made $4 billion of operating profit. We became one of the most profitable parts of the company. Today we have an installed base that is really the core of the Energy business unit's profitability."

AN UNEXPECTED PROMOTION

Little went on to run bigger and bigger P&L pieces of the energy business. Then in 2005 GE offered him an unexpected promotion to head of the Global Research Center (GRC), where most of GE's top PhD scientists work. It gave Little a moment of anxiety: back to staff? But GE does not move leaders without a great deal of care and thought. Finding the right fit is paramount, and no one was a better fit than he. Functional and line leadership at GE are not as far apart as they are at most companies. Jeff Immelt regards staff heads as business players, on equal footing in the corporate system with the line leaders. Now Little would be part of GE's inner circle, the dozen or so top executives who report directly to Immelt. And the job would put him at the center of Immelt's vision for GE's future.

The R&D center was in the midst of a major turn in focus under Scott Donnelly. In the past it had functioned like most such organizations, where businesses would come shopping for useful ideas and products. But Jeff Immelt, who assumed the CEO role in 2001, felt that GE's future lay with technological innovation that would yield solutions to some of the world's greatest needs, from clean energy to abundant water to better health care. GE's mission, he declared, would be "redefining what is possible." He committed $100 million to upgrade the center facilities near Schenectady, New York, and Bangalore, India, to open new centers in Shanghai, China, and Munich, Germany. (There is also consideration being given to a center in the Middle East.)

Donnelly managed all of these improvements and also upended the old operating model. He brought a customer focus to it, strengthening the business input into the center's activities. One thing that helped bring the businesses closer to the technology was a new Crotonville-type residence center overlooking the Hudson River, adjacent to the research labs near Schenectady. Business leaders could take their staffs and work with the technologists on issues related to their businesses; customers, sometimes in conjunction with business teams, could see and touch what was going on in the R&D center. Says Conaty: "The facility brought a new sense of pride to GE scientists and technologists—they could strut their stuff and show their wares. It really fires them up to see GE business leaders bringing their entire team there to explore new technological possibilities. They say, 'Boy, we've got these big business leaders coming in here today. And we've got to make sure we show them that we're on track with what they need to improve their businesses.' "

So Donnelly had done a great job, but GE wanted to put him in charge of a big P&L, Aircraft Engines, to test his full potential in the company. The bare recitation of facts in executive changes rarely hint at the forces and factors that determine them, and the story behind Donnelly itself illustrates the many things GE leadership may have to take into account. The first non-PhD to run the center, he originally wasn't interested in running it—he was hoping for a P&L. Conaty and Immelt, however, felt that he was the right person to lead the center through its shift, and advised him that if he did an outstanding job, they would then find him his big P&L job.

So Donnelly's moment had arrived—and he balked. Says Conaty: "He's still a young guy, and we tap him for the Aircraft Engines job, a huge P&L—and he didn't want to go! 'Yes, I always wanted a P&L,' he said, 'but, you know, really I think I'm of more value to the company here at the R&D center.' I can't tell you how many discussions I had with him. But eventually we persuaded him that both he and the company would gain if he made the move. And that's how it turned out. After a successful run at Aircraft Engines, Scott left to become COO at Textron, and has since been named chairman and CEO.

"This is all part of the development process at GE, and we never feel bad for long when one of our executives lands a big number one job outside the company."

Normally Donnelly's successor at the GRC would have come from the ranks of R&D, and Little would have moved to a bigger P&L job. But the changes Immelt had in mind required rethinking the central criteria for R&D. He wanted the center's mission to be solving the world's most essential and difficult technical problems—for example, energy, water supplies, and environmental problems. He also wanted it to be proactive in conceiving products that could open up new segments for growth. To do this, it would have to partner even more intensely with the businesses. That would require a leader who could talk easily both with technologists and with business leaders, and who could think broadly enough to make GE technology the underpinning of the growth strategy Immelt had laid out. Of the several candidates considered in the reviews that spring, only Little met all these benchmarks—and he met them in spades. His technical credentials were impeccable, and having run the largest profit center in GE's industrial businesses, he had huge personal credibility with the businesses.

Under Little's leadership the GRC is meeting Immelt's goal of becoming a powerful driver for innovation and growth. "It's probably the most intellectually stimulating job you can possibly have," Little says, "because you're trying to link high-end technology with real-world business challenges and issues. Our technical teams are deeply engaged in every great new thing that happens across every business in the company. We bring technical depth and know-how depth. And it's a lot of fun.

"If you're a technologist in this kind of a culture, you

would typically be in a situation where the business guys are giving you direction and you'd be reporting to a business person. Coming in as a business person is just psychologically quite significant in our culture. So I don't look at the business leaders with awe. I come with the understanding of the sorts of issues that these guys deal with, and I had a strong relationship with them as a business equal before coming here.

"So I never felt a loss of affiliation with a business when I went to the GRC. What I felt is that I gained a dozen more businesses."

Would the CEO and the top HR leader of *your* company hold the hand of a guy two levels down whose boss decided his job was too big for him? No, we didn't think so. In many places, even his boss wouldn't reach out for fear of catching the failure germ. Why, then, did Jack Welch and Bill Conaty bend over backward to encourage Mark Little and try to restore his confidence after his fall from grace?

First, GE recognizes that great leaders are likely to emerge stronger from setbacks. Second, GE really knows its top talent. The discipline and rigor of the GE operating systems focuses people on top talent, giving them multiple looks at them during the course of a year. Many people, not just his boss or the director of HR, knew what kind of leader Mark Little was and everything he had done through the reviews that took place during the year (Session C, operating, budget, long-term strategy reviews), as well as meeting him personally at Crotonville and other GE global leadership meetings around the world.

Says Conaty: "Mark wasn't just a name on our list but a guy we knew thoroughly. We knew what he was going through. We tried to put ourselves in his shoes and said, 'How would we feel if this was happening to us?' And since we thought that this was a great guy with great GE values, we wanted to sit down eyeball to eyeball and tell him that we're serious about wanting him to remain in this company and continue to grow and develop, and that we're going to be supportive. If he had just got that from within the business, without that personal touch from the Fairfield headquarters, he would have been gone."

BRINGING AN OUTSIDER INTO THE CULTURE

Even the best producer of homegrown talent can't meet all of its leadership needs internally. The trick is to pull out all the stops to help the newcomer succeed. A great many organizations bringing in a new leader are satisfied to sign the papers and put him to work. If all goes well, great. If it doesn't, they fire him. By contrast, the senior leaders at GE recognized that any outsider joining their highly institutionalized and close-knit culture would need careful sponsorship, and they were open to having him challenge their sacred cows. When they hired Omar Ishrak for his specialized knowledge of the ultrasound business, the whole system swung into action to "GE-ize Omar," coaching him and educating him in GE practices and culture—in short, doing everything necessary to replicate a GE career experience, including building intimacy and trust as fast as possible.

FILLING A LEADERSHIP GAP

In the mid-1990s GE Medical Systems had a problem. Overall, the business was among the company's stellar performers. Its X-ray, MRI, and CT Scan businesses—called "modalities" in Medical Systems lingo—were leading their industries, meeting Jack Welch's demand that any business must either be number one or two in its field or fixed, closed, or sold. But one modality, Ultrasound, lagged badly, ranking far below the leading players in the industry. Most of the GE leaders who tried to turn it around were corporate audit staff graduates, high-potential, fast-track leaders who had had intensive financial and leadership training. They would typically finish their program and move rapidly through a series of challenging management assignments. But Ultrasound confounded them all; despite their talent and training, the domain expertise of the business was outside their range of knowledge. After a number of misfires, GE decided it needed an expert in ultrasound technology, someone known to the industry. It was time to search outside for the right person.

Omar Ishrak, then at Diasonics, a small maker of ultrasound machines in the San Francisco Bay Area, had a deep understanding of his industry, was both a technologist and a businessman—a techie who could speak in non-techie terms—and had a winning personality. Above all, he was driven by a passionate sense of purpose: he wanted to build the number one ultrasound business in the world.

Ishrak's passion made him an unusual candidate. Unlike most outside hires, who were most interested in how soon they could move up and take the boss's job, his focus was the business itself. "How serious is GE about making Ultrasound number one in the industry?" he asked. "Because we've got a lot of work to do if you're going to do it, and I will need a lot of support from you guys."

He was wary about joining a giant company, however. He'd worked for one before and found it too bureaucratic and not committed enough to the ultrasound industry. But he could see that GE was deadly serious in its intent, and he got assurances that he'd be allowed to do his job as he saw fit. Says Ishrak, "Jack Welch and the management team in general made it clear that I was being hired with a clear charter to do what I needed to."

LAYING IT ON THE LINE

Ishrak had a good idea of what was wrong with GE Ultrasound even before he started, and he laid his views out bluntly. The products were too expensive, laden with unnecessary bells and whistles, and the Medical Systems sales force didn't understand how to sell them. Selling X-ray, CT, and MRI machines usually involved bringing in a customer to show how they worked. Ultrasound was different. The companies that specialized in ultrasound equipment took it to the customers and often engaged in head-to-head competition. "You take your system to a site and you demo against a competitor: you do one patient using your technology, they do one patient using theirs, and the comparison makes for a dramatic kind of event," Ishrak explains. "People use psychology and it's an intense day. But GE was expecting to fly people into Milwaukee, show them the machine, and get an order, which just wasn't reality. The salespeople got outsmarted in no time. The specialist ultrasound companies just ran rings around them.

"The basic assets were all there but weren't being used correctly and weren't being pointed in a direction that could turn the market upside down. I had the sense that previously there had been committees and meetings of people and no one was really sure; someone wanted to do a market survey, someone wanted to do this or that, and no one got anything done. I didn't hesitate. I said, 'Hey, this is what we must do and this is the way to do that.' " Bold criticism from the new kid on the block, but people listened respectfully. "It seemed that everyone was kind of waiting for someone to say that. And they gave me full support."

During his first six months at GE, Ishrak's peers in Medical Systems provided an important support network. "I felt a little lost at first in this big structure, but I quickly found that I could learn so much from the other modalities, including the fact that those businesses were so good. CT Scan, for example, was a profitable $600 million business, while Ultrasound was a $130 million business losing money. It was pretty obvious to me that I needed to find out how those businesses succeeded. And when I went there and asked questions, my peers were friendly, supportive, and really explained their businesses to me. They were very helpful, all of them, in really wanting me to succeed, giving me really good advice."

He also had a good mentor in John Trani, CEO of the business, who helped Ishrak to sharpen his grasp of finances, cost cutting, and productivity. Trani saw that Ishrak was great in product development. What he had to learn was how to profitably sell Ultrasound, understand the multiyear product plan and how it would evolve over time. His business acumen developed quickly.

With its rough-and-tumble candor and constant drilling and iteration, the GE culture takes some getting used to. As Ishrak entered into the managerial and social processes, including GE's rigorous review sessions, Trani coached him on how to work in the system. "When you go into a meeting with Jack Welch or through a strategy or operations review, it is like going into a championship game, and you better be ready," Trani explained. "It is never a love-in, and sometimes it might be a little bit of a war. And you have to learn things, and put things in a context that maybe you had never thought about before. Over time, Omar learned to step up his game."

One seemingly small thing was mastering the GE business language. "I had all these ideas and they were probably correct, but I didn't really know how to communicate them in the GE language. I knew what had to be done, but John helped me frame it in the right language. It was more than simply grasping the lingo. The language gave a business context and a systematic view to how initiatives could be done, and it clicked with me."

The rigor of the GE processes worked well for Ishrak, whose nature and personal views about how business should be run were in line with the way GE operated. He says, "It was extremely useful just going to the different meetings and being part of the operating mechanisms once a quarter, once a month, and hearing how the other businesses operated, getting feedback from John and questions when I presented. That marriage of industry expertise, together with process discipline, rubbed off on me."

Attending a four-week executive development session at Crotonville gave Ishrak the chance to build relationships outside the medical business and to see the breadth of GE. In those classes, he was part of a team whose members were from different GE businesses. Charged with undertaking a project they would ultimately present to Welch, the team traveled to various GE sites. He credits that experience for expanding his knowledge of GE and helping him "appreciate how systematic GE is."

Support from the very top was nonetheless critical for someone with big, ambitious plans that challenged the status quo. At the first corporate review Ishrak attended with the medical and corporate leaders in attendance, Welch put his arm around him and said, "I want you to meet my friend Omar." The message was not lost, and Welch reinforced it for some time in subsequent reviews by pointedly calling on Ishrak for his views on one topic or another. Welch challenged Ishrak too. "In the reviews he would ask me very pointed questions that were difficult for me to answer in the beginning. Things like, 'Are you looking at the cost correctly? Are you giving your sales leader a dedicated sales force? That's what he wants.' "

BUCKING THE SYSTEM

It didn't take long for Ishrak to make a difference at Ultrasound. "Almost within two weeks of joining, I knew the top five things that had to be done. It would take two to three years to get the costs down and the optimization right, but in the meantime we had strong products in Japan and India. They were very good products, the kind of products the rest of the world was craving. But the fascination in Milwaukee was with a product built in the United States, which actually was too expensive and not quite optimized.

"The Japanese product was extremely good. I immediately recognized its value, fixed it up a little bit, and started to sell it aggressively around the world. This drove immediate growth and immediate wins within the business. And then I fixed it up more and sold it in the United States as well, which upset the market a little bit, which helped us," he said with typical understatement. Ultrasound was in the black by the end of his first year there, the first time it had made money in years.

The second big change took longer, and depended heavily on support from both Welch and Immelt, who took over Medical Systems in 1996. This was a complete redesign of the sales organization. Medical Systems had one sales force that sold all of its products, from X-ray and CT to Ultrasound, but the salespeople did not put a lot of effort into Ultrasound products: they weren't very popular, and the selling proposition was hard to understand. Ishrak knew from his experience at Diasonics that ultrasound customers were used to salespeople from niche companies with deep, specialized knowledge.

He wanted to create a separate, or parallel, sales force of people with the best specialized talent he could find in each country. Further, he wanted to coordinate their efforts across the globe. "I wanted Ultrasound to be a very focused business, with dedicated salespeople and dedicated business functions, to take on those companies who were expert at this," he says. "We needed to position the products correctly and get the Japanese team in particular, as well as teams from Korea, India, and the U.S., working together to look at the global market in parallel, as opposed to just a U.S.-centric approach."

But the idea of a parallel sales force ran into internal resistance. It challenged the very basis on which other health care modalities were organized and had achieved great success. They had a centralized sales force, which leveraged economies of scale and gave one face to the customer. Ishrak's model was to forgo the economies of scale in favor of giving local Ultrasound general managers more flexibility.

Their speed and responsiveness, he reasoned, would expand distribution and grow the top line.

Welch supported what Ishrak was trying to do. Says Ishrak: "He sensed this, even without me saying anything, and he really pushed it. I didn't actually find out how much he pushed until later." So did Immelt, with his background in sales. "Jeff helped me enormously, first by encouraging me, validating that that was the right strategy, and second, with right organizational structure, and third, by pushing the overall business to seek out and get the right talent across the world and have them report directly to me." That was critical, because often the local leaders wouldn't hire people who might be their competitors, who were equals in rank, and who sometimes earned more than they did. "For them to be hired required encouragement and intervention from Jeff. He himself made convincing calls to many of these people we wanted to hire."

The parallel sales force would in fact be a strategic coup. Now GE could not only outsell its competitors at the ground level but, finally able to match the small competitors' agility, also outgun them with heavy artillery they didn't have. "We would be using GE's financial clout and scale in the global marketplace intelligently, in step with a precise view of the ultrasound industry," Ishrak said. "We'd be targeting what we wanted to do and exercising our muscle, as opposed to going out there and just guessing and trying some new stuff and throwing money at it. It was a very precise strategy, and it couldn't have been done without Jeff Immelt's support, especially globally, because no one would have done it on their own."

Ishrak compared his situation at GE to his competitors in much smaller ultrasound manufacturing operations. Such a small competitor trying to set up a distribution organization in China would face all sorts of hurdles, including a lack of knowledge about the cultural and legal environment confronting him and whom to trust.

"At GE I could go into China and have a whole army of people and an office to work in," Ishrak marveled. "I'd know which distributor was good, which was bad, how to vet them. I'd have a legal team through which I could get things in place straightaway. I could figure that piece out and then I could get help from the local team to get it in place, with confidence that we weren't doing something really bad. A small company can never do that. And recognizing that and leveraging that, without losing the ultrasound expertise, really was the key to success here."

By Ishrak's third year on the job, Ultrasound's revenues had more than doubled to $300 million.

LEARNING FROM A MASTER

As Ishrak's focus shifted from straightening out the products to putting his parallel sales organization in place, Immelt's skill in sales and marketing became increasingly important to him. Immelt could help Ultrasound both at the strategic level and on the ground. "There was always pressure," Ishrak recalls. "There was always the question, 'Why do you have three engineering teams? Put them into one and you'll save money.' Or 'Why do you have this little outpost in India?' I would say, 'I need engineers close to the Indian market.' But they would say, 'That's not worth it, you know. Consolidate them in Milwaukee and you'll save a ton of money.'

"Jeff helped me push back. He understood it, was very intuitive about it, and had a keen sense as to how to present that sort of thing within GE. He helped me articulate how duplication provided speed, and speed in the end provided margin, and that would make more money and more leverage than just cutting costs. He helped me optimize that equation as to when to take cost out and when to duplicate and get speed."

Immelt had a lot to teach about salesmanship, and he did it by spending time on the job with his protégé. Some of the most intensive learning came from what Ishrak calls "the informal time" spent observing Immelt on the front lines. "He spent two days a year going out in the field with me. That may not seem like a lot, but if you take the demands on his time, it is—two days a year dedicated to me and the sales team.

"We'd go around the U.S. and visit customers. Much of the learning came from just watching as he quizzed about how the business was operating, not so much in a review, but more informally: 'How does this thing work? What do these customers want? How different are they? How does the sales process work? How did the demo work?' I saw the interaction back and forth, the bonding with the sales team on the ground, the CEO of the business talking comfortably to an applications person doing a demo. And Jeff was also always coming up with ideas. He was always thinking about how can GE do something which other people cannot."

Ishrak also met customers with Immelt. "We used to visit maybe eight, nine customers from city to city, a whole variety of them, all kinds of different disciplines, talking to the users, to the sonographers, all the way to the CEO of the hospital. Just watching him do these swings and learning along with him was a huge thing for me. Since then I do that myself in the U.S. and around the world, a mix of bonding with employees, with salespeople, and with customers. And at the same time, providing value because I could do things I realized that the local salesperson cannot do. So that was pretty important."

GE executives are famed for their ability to distill the gist of a proposition in a single page, and Immelt coached Ishrak in that skill. "He gave me great insights as to how to pitch—how to simplify a case and present a concept with four bullet points of six words each. He would pull out these three or four little phrases, which really captured the essence of what you're trying to say, and then you can speak to it."

What could be called Ishrak's apprenticeship at GE lasted through the four years, during which Ultrasound went from almost nothing to generating significant revenues and profits. "After that it could stand on its own feet, and I was much stronger as a leader," he says. "I understood GE and knew how to fit comfortably within the system."

So it seems. The man who wasn't looking for promotions was made a vice president and officer of GE in 1999 and became president of Clinical Systems in 2005. Healthcare Systems, which he took over in 2009, is a $12 billion business whose mission is to develop innovative technologies that improve clinical performance and make care accessible to more people around the world. In 2007, Ishrak was also added to Immelt's elite Corporate Executive Council, comprising the top forty leaders in the company, who meet quarterly at Crotonville to discuss overall company operations and strategy. Needless to say, even the most robust talent master company must always be calibrating between the best in-house talent and the best world-class talent wherever it may exist.

CONCLUSIONS

The power of intimacy. Leaders at GE make every effort to pinpoint a person's true talent and potential. In the culture of intimacy and trust, they can dig for the root causes of performance, good or bad, and sharpen their judgments by comparing observations. Welch, Immelt, and Conaty knew what Jim Campbell's Achilles' heel might be as head of the appliances business, and when Dick Segalini said he would make sure that Campbell succeeded on the operating side, his word was golden. Mark Little stayed with the company despite a disappointing job change because he trusted the reassurances from Welch and Conaty; Welch and Conaty persuaded Little to stay because they knew him well enough to see his underlying talent. Omar Ishrak learned quickly that he could trust peers and superiors who knew his strengths to help him even though his ideas challenged some entrenched beliefs and business models.

The power of social processes. Talent management comes to life through GE's social processes—that is, through the formal and informal discussions in which leaders push for candor and rigor and connect people and numbers. Masters use social processes to make business and talent a continuous loop, using outputs of one review as input to another, and to keep talent top of mind between formal meetings. Over time leaders accumulate observations through multiple lenses and test their judgments. That depth of knowledge gives them the confidence to act decisively when speed is needed, as GE did when Larry Johnston and later Dave Calhoun resigned, or to "pull the trigger" on leaders who no longer fit.

Intensity of talent development. Leaders at GE consider it a major part of their job to develop other people's talent. They spend time and mental energy on it regularly, not once in a while. They give candid, constructive feedback on a timely basis, focus on the positives in the person, and try to figure out how to build on them. Assignments are carefully chosen to stretch and build talent, and people are often moved from one business to another to broaden and challenge them. The result is a huge pool of leaders prepared to take positions in a range of businesses.

Continuous learning. GE expects its leaders to keep growing. Despite its emphasis on learning through experience, it spends considerable resources to provide other kinds of stimulation. Leaders are exposed to thought leaders from outside the company and senior leaders within the company at Crotonville for the express purpose of expanding their perspective and deepening their understanding of the business and its external context. Leaders are expected to create an annual plan for their own development and to follow it.

It's easy to see why GE is so widely emulated: it is a model of comprehensive talent management. But notice that we don't say *the* model. Of the many other successful models out there, none are more different than that of Hindustan Unilever, the subject of the next chapter.

Part II

The SPECIAL EXPERTISE of TALENT MASTERS

While talent masters share basic principles and building blocks, each has its own emphasis and in some cases its own tools and techniques. Each of the following four chapters takes you inside a company whose practices we found unusual and useful. Most have been developing their mastery of talent for a long time. They've gained varying degrees of recognition for what they've done, but outsiders generally don't have a clear understanding of their specific approaches.

Hindustan Unilever (HUL), Procter & Gamble, Agilent Technologies, and Novartis stand out for the way they shape particular types of managers: leaders with a uniquely intense commitment to developing other leaders at HUL; global leaders with deep consumer insight at P&G; general managers grounded in technical expertise at Agilent. Their wide range of practices can suggest valuable ideas for your own pursuit of talent mastery—for example, the "management trainee contact book" that HUL uses to accelerate talent development. But keep in mind that principles matter more than mechanics: rigor, discipline, and candor are the foundation of talent mastery.

Chapter 5

BUILDING a TALENT PIPELINE to the TOP
Hindustan Unilever Starts at Day One

U nless you knew him by sight, you wouldn't imagine that the dapper businessman sitting next to you at a restaurant in the small south Indian town of Salem is anybody notable. He is listening attentively as a young manager describes recent work. From overheard snatches, you infer that the young manager is brand-new on the job. The conversation is cordial but intense. The senior executive listens closely and often asks pointed questions. Sometimes he seems satisfied with the reply. At other times he offers advice or probes for more information, drilling down with the seasoned familiarity of an old hand at the business. As you finish your dinner and leave, they are still talking earnestly.

Had you recognized the businessman, however, you might wonder what Nitin Paranjpe, the CEO of mighty Hindustan Unilever (HUL), Unilever's $3.5 billion Indian subsidiary and an increasingly important contributor to its global strategy and success, is doing in this out-of-the-way place talking to some kid. But it's the sort of thing Paranjpe does five or six times a month: he visits young sales managers, many of them management trainees who are HUL's up-and-coming future leaders in the field. So do all HUL senior managers, who spend 30 to 40 percent of their time "growing leaders," as they put it, to meet the company's future challenges.

"As chairman I used to go to virtually every single management trainee induction program and spend an evening there," says Vindi Banga, chairman of HUL from 2000 to 2005 and until recently a member of Unilever's global executive committee and now a partner at the private equity firm CDR. "I also used to travel in the field all the time for two reasons. One, there's no better way to find out what's going on with the business than with customers. Two, I met many of the trainee sales managers. Senior people have to cut through the hierarchy to interact with junior people, either on the job or in training programs." Paranjpe continues the tradition.

No other company we know of recruits and trains people from day one with the explicit aim of growing leaders able to reach the highest levels. And in no other company we know of do senior managers work so directly with those rising leaders. HUL believes that this is the most important way to build and sustain an organization, repeatedly renewing it with fresh energy, perspective, capability, and creativity. "There is no better investment than improving the quality of your future leaders," says Banga.

Most companies look for bright graduates, put them to work long enough to show their capabilities, and then try the promising ones out in leadership roles. This wastes irreplaceable development time for those with potential. Just as the first three years of life are pivotal for a child's development, so the first three years of a career are pivotal for a leader's development. HUL believes that leaders are born, not made; it sees leadership as a specific competency that it can identify and develop right from the start. Dr. A. S. Ganguly, who led the company throughout the 1980s, often told reporters and rivals who marveled at the company's consistent leadership excellence, "You cannot make leaders. All you can do is look for, find, and polish leaders." By the time people are in their early twenties, they will show visible—if subtle—signs of their leadership potential. HUL zeroes in on those signs. Over decades it has developed techniques for spotting and developing raw leadership talent with a dual emphasis on the qualities it describes as the *what* and the *how* of leadership. The what of leadership is getting things done. The how is acting in a way others will admire and want to follow. HUL wants its leaders to have both qualities in abundance.

Starting with the critical first three years, it puts promising leaders in a special development pipeline that leads all the way to the top. Of the approximately nine hundred people it hires every year across all levels, the most important for its long-term future are the thirty-five to fifty young men and women it recruits to join its Business Leadership Training (BLT) program. The difference between the future leaders and other hires, says Paranjpe, is that "we do not recruit these potential leaders for the first or second job they will do. We recruit them with an eye to whether they have both the intellectual capacity and the leadership capacity to go, if not all the way, then pretty much all the way."

HUL makes senior managers, individually and collectively, responsible for spotting and developing these high-potential leaders from recruitment onward. A sophisticated, capable HR department supports the process, but line management leads it. HR and senior executives at HUL invest three and a half days a year for every management trainee. The close attention does not come at the expense of meeting business objectives. To the contrary, guiding and mentoring expands leadership capacity, strengthening performance at every level of the organization and improving leadership transitions. As a result, the senior leaders have fewer fires to put out. The virtuous circle of apprenticeship and mentoring continuously builds and renews organizational muscle as successive generations of leaders progress from apprentice to mentor.

Some of that time is spent on new graduates who have not even been hired yet. This responsibility, in Paranjpe's words, "is too important to be delegated solely to junior people." Recruiting is the most critical phase in a talent management process, and senior leaders, with all their experience, insight, and cognitive bandwidth, are better equipped than junior managers to spot leadership talent when they see it.

RECRUITING RAW TALENT

Competition for graduates of India's elite business schools and technical institutes is so intense that many companies cannot secure a place on campus on designated recruiting days, when students go from room to room meeting representatives of India's top companies and Indian divisions of global multinationals. While other top companies offer jobs on the spot to well-credentialed students, HUL takes its time in vetting them. It selects management trainee candidates in three stages—group discussion, preliminary interview, and final interview—cutting many hopefuls each time. But HUL's mastery of leadership development has given it an extraordinary competitive advantage in recruiting India's top management graduates, many of whom call it "the dream company to work for." Job seekers only have to log onto HUL's website to see that its CEO and management committee members rose quickly: all are still in their forties.

HUL has refined a singularly powerful tool for assessing candidates. It brings several applicants at a time together with HR people and senior managers to discuss a specific business issue in groups. This is an absolutely unique innovation in our experience. The discussions bring out whether individuals "have it all"—not only the functional skills but also the judgment, integrity, and temperament required to make good decisions and build and maintain relationships. In particular, they put a spotlight on getting things done in ways others will admire and want to follow.

To understand how it works, imagine that you are a

bright, accomplished second-year MBA student interested in working at HUL. You've been short-listed (after rigorous scrutiny of your comprehensive questionnaire) and invited to participate in a group discussion that goes on up to an hour with others who may be friends or rivals. You can't shake the thought that the discussion will be judged like a debate, and that you'll be expected to score points against the other students. You want to best them all in the quest for a great job—but at the same time you don't want to lose your friends over it and you'd like to stay on speaking terms with everybody.

As you take a seat in a seminar room, you wonder if you should have accepted the immediate job offer a big consulting firm made after your one brief interview with it this morning. Even if you get the job at HUL, you'll be training for fifteen to eighteen months, far longer than anywhere else.

A well-dressed man in his forties comes into the room and takes a seat. Another man and a woman join him. They all seem to be on very friendly terms and highly placed. You can't put your finger on it, but there's something about everyone's body language. The forty-something man is leading the meeting. He welcomes everyone and introduces himself and his colleagues. You were right about their being higher-ups—he's second-in-command in HR. The others are senior leaders in sales and marketing.

No time to focus on that now. The meeting leader is moving right along and saying, "We never waste an opportunity to learn from the best young minds. You've all been superbly trained and you've all done extremely well in your studies. So we'd like to tell you about a current challenge in our business and get your reactions and suggestions. It's the toothpaste market in Mumbai and other major urban areas. How can we increase market share for Pepsodent in this very competitive sales environment?"

Before you know it, you're staring at a slide summarizing the toothpaste market and trying to think up a good answer.

Concepts from marketing lectures flash in and out of your mind, but you're drawing a blank about how to apply them to this problem. Your pulse goes up as you rack your brain. The summary slide shows a lot of toothpaste use by middle-class and affluent consumers. How could more of them be persuaded to use Pepsodent? You start to follow that train of thought, but you also see that the chart shows relatively little but growing use of toothpaste by low-income consumers, the majority of the population. The HUL motto, "Doing well by doing good," pops into your mind. The motto wasn't part of the presentation, but if more of Mumbai's ordinary working people developed the habit of brushing their teeth with toothpaste, that could be a win-win-win for them, India, and HUL. But how would you get that rolling, and how would you put Pepsodent at the center of it all? Would HUL want to give away a lot of valuable product to seed the market?

The brief period for reflection is over, and the HR leader wants responses. Should you jump in with your half an idea before anyone else can speak? Too late. Another candidate is talking authoritatively about urban advertising and costs per thousand impressions. It's a pretty good spiel. You glance at the marketing executives. No reaction. These guys are as cold as ice.

The HR leader says, "Okay, good, thanks. What other thoughts do people have?" Self-doubt creeps in and you wonder if you should try to dream up some specific ideas for a toothbrushing education campaign before mentioning it. The HR leader looks around the room, but everyone seems a little cowed. Except the guy who spoke first; he's bursting his buttons to say more.

Oh well, you figure, it's now or never. You take a deep breath, catch the HR leader's attention, and explain your idea. Out of the corner of your eye, you see the two marketing executives exchange a look. Was it a sign of approval? You can't dwell on that; another candidate is suggesting how to get community groups and charities to partner in the campaign. The rest of the ninety minutes passes as quickly as the best seminar you've ever taken. You leave the room excited, hoping HUL will short-list you for the interview.

The quality of applicants' thinking and interpersonal style comes out like sunlight as HUL leaders watch the discussion unfold. This person is a lot of hot air. That person is incisive. This other person is really creative, doesn't have the answer, but can open the minds of others. Another person is only for himself and does not care what other people think. Yet another shows a knack for building consensus around the best solution. The candidates can't dodge the challenge of showing who they truly are as people, and they can't fake it. Equally important, having multiple HUL people in the room ensures that nothing significant, no matter how fleeting it may be, goes unnoticed or misinterpreted—an encouraging smile from one candidate to another, a crestfallen frown, a self-satisfied smirk, a condescending sneer.

As Banga puts it, recalling his experiences as a job seeker and a senior manager, "The group discussion is an opportunity to look at how you think on a topic and how you interact with others. Do you dominate the conversation? There's a tendency to be first to speak, which is important, it shows initiative, but only if you have something to say. The right share of voice is also important. Were you too domineering? Did you allow others to come forward and make their point as well? Were you building on what others said, or showing off how smart you are?

"It's very important how individuals build consensus and foster teamwork. Do they hector other people in a direction? Or can they both lead through the power of argument and, just as important, be willing to be influenced by someone else's good reasoning? People who are individually brilliant but cannot work in teams get weeded out."

Every candidate who survives the cut after the group

discussion has two rounds of interviews with four to five HUL people in total, including executives from HR, one or two direct reports to the management committee, and a member of the committee itself. Based on a review of all the data on the candidate, especially his or her leadership behavior during the group discussion, the HUL executives decide who will handle which line of questioning. To test functional skills, one HUL manager may bring up the topic of the group discussion or introduce a similar business issue. To explore leadership skills and interpersonal style, other managers may ask about the candidate's most significant achievement and her take on aspects of the group discussion.

The final interview includes putting the candidate under pressure. The interviewers push a topic to see if there is something the candidate is sensitive about, testing for maturity. The most important issue at this stage is whether the candidate has the right values to fit into the culture of the company. "You look for consistency in response and intellectual honesty," Banga said. "You look for people who don't get swayed and say, 'Yes sir, no sir, three bags full sir,' people who have their own internal convictions."

On the rare occasions when time pressure does not allow for a group discussion, HUL relies on multiple senior managers' assessments during interviews.

Members of the management committee make the final hiring decisions, informed by multiple observations from senior people. If it seems like a lot of trouble and expense to have so many people involved in recruiting—senior people at that—it is a pittance compared with the cumulative cost of bad hiring. HUL rarely makes a job offer it has cause to regret.

LEARNING FROM THE GROUND UP

Before they're formally hired, all future leaders have to prove themselves in action. Some highly promising prospects go into a summer internship program where they can show and develop their abilities by tackling business problems. Paranjpe recalls what he learned as a summer intern in 1986. "I spent two months in the most backward districts of Maharashtra working on the sales van, selling soap village to village. I was also asked to come up with a strategy to improve rural reach at reduced cost." The combination of daily work on the front line and the intellectual stimulus of developing the strategy made the summer a memorable experience, and also gave Paranjpe a taste of the learning opportunities HUL offered.

All BLT participants go through the training period of fifteen to eighteen months. The program accelerates their career development through a series of stints supported by a tutor (an experienced manager who reviews and evaluates progress in each stint), a coach (a very senior manager in the functional area who is an anchor through the training period), and a mentor (a member of the management committee who reviews progress periodically). Each stint puts the hopeful leaders in the front lines of the business's battle for competitive advantage and challenges them to prove their mettle in demanding jobs.

Leadership opportunities arise in "core stints" in a future leader's area of specialization. "Cross-functional stints" show how the different functional areas in the company link up; an "international stint," across Unilever's global operations, gives them experience in different cultures. Then there's the "corporate responsibility" stint. HUL has for several decades sent every future leader to work in rural areas of India. Banga, for example, sold products in farming villages in the central Indian state of Madhya Pradesh in 1977. Ten years later, Paranjpe did the same in a remote area of the northern state of Uttar Pradesh near the Nepal border. Those rural locations are great learning crucibles and highly relevant to the futures of both HUL and India. Seventy percent of India's one billion people live in more than 625,000 small farming villages, so rural economic development is a high national priority. HUL has made a motto of doing well by doing good, and improving the quality of rural life with more access to consumer packaged goods is one way of doing it. Another way is its Project Shakti ("Strength"), where HUL extends microcredit financing, along with coaching and other support, to village women who become local franchisees for its products. Enormously popular and expanding, the program now includes tens of thousands of women entrepreneurs, many of them illiterate, in more than a hundred thousand villages. HUL also contributes financial and management support to small enterprises and infrastructure projects through its corporate responsibility program.

On the brand and product side, the late-1980s launch of Wheel, a low-price detergent, made loyal HUL consumers out of tens of millions of low-income women in rural India who wash clothes by hand in ponds and rivers and in buckets beside wells and pumps and could not afford other product offerings. Parent Unilever has capitalized on HUL's expertise in rural India for its global growth strategy. More than 50 percent of Unilever's sales growth now comes from Developing & Emerging (D&E) markets. Finally, doing well by doing good in rural India holds tremendous appeal for the young people HUL most wants to hire as future leaders. They tend to be from at least relatively well-off backgrounds, and going to live and work in poor farming villages can be quite a shock for them. But the great majority enthusiastically embrace their assignments, which build intense esprit de corps.

For future HUL CEOs Banga and Paranjpe, the time spent working in rural India was formative. In his stint in Madhya Pradesh, following orientation week with other trainees, Banga spent two weeks shadowing a veteran salesman to learn the basics. He then worked on his own in a vacant territory for eight weeks. Managers visited him during this period to see how he was doing, but otherwise, in his words, "I ran the territory completely independently and had specific sales targets I had to achieve." The next step was to work with a sales supervisor for two weeks watching what he did. He then became a full supervisor for seven salesmen—another eight weeks—and went on to a series of cross-functional stints where he was given analytic and strategic projects in addition to his managerial duties. After all this he was given independent responsibility for a sales area in eastern India covering both urban and rural markets.

Paranjpe, who followed much the same path ten years later, notes the value of working from the ground up. "Selling soaps to shopkeepers in remote villages gives you valuable lessons," he says. "You start listening to the market, you empathize with the problems that salespeople face. These are lessons no B-school can ever teach you." The later stages develop managerial skills rapidly. "Managing a sales force of five hundred to eight hundred village franchisees suddenly gives you a large line leadership responsibility," he says. Salespeople's counterparts in other functional areas also get early leadership opportunities and challenges, whether working with factory supervisors implementing a pilot program to boost productivity or leading IT and finance project teams.

COACHING FROM THE TOP

Senior leaders accelerate the learning experiences with coaching, assessment, and on-the-spot feedback. Each young leader has a "Management Trainee Contact Book" in which senior leaders record their feedback following a visit to the trainee's site. The book becomes a written (now electronic) record of how the young leader is growing. It may take a lot of rough travel for senior leaders to reach some of the more remote locations, but they do it eagerly, in part because they themselves personally benefited from it.

Consider Banga's eight weeks on his own in a vacant sales territory, after one week of orientation and two weeks shadowing a salesman. "Various people came and met me: the sales supervisor, the area sales manager, the general sales manager," he recalls. "Whoever met me had to put an assessment in my contact book. So I got instant feedback on what I was doing right, which was encouraging, and what more I could do and what to concentrate on. Typically senior visitors would spend a whole day and evening. There was a lot of discussion around dinner and a drink. In some ways that was the most valuable time, from seven to eleven in the evening."

Paranjpe, who went through similar experiences in Uttar Pradesh, recalls one big lesson he learned. His regional sales manager had spent a day with him in the very small town of Chutmalpur. Looking over the accounts, the manager spotted a math mistake. At the end of the day he wrote in Paranjpe's contact book, "You are doing great things, but you need to be more rigorous. Sales have been lost because of faulty order booking." Of that comment, Paranjpe says: "What he wrote twenty years ago is engraved in my mind. It was specific, not vague. The lesson I carry from that today is the trouble and care that people took, and how valued I felt during these visits and how important it was to the company."

Usually these one-on-one contacts with senior managers go all the way up to the management committee and the CEO, who are particularly valuable to future leaders as role models. Besides the general sales manager, Paranjpe's senior visitors in the field during his first sales stint included Dr. Ganguly, the CEO, and Sushim Datta, then HUL's number two executive and two years later Ganguly's successor as CEO. "Dr. Ganguly [a biochemist who joined HUL's R&D department] spent the whole day with me, first in Allahabad going from shop to shop inquiring about our brands and business. That's when we came across a paanwala with a small kiosk. Vendors of snacks and other impulse items, paanwalas are not merely small-time merchants but also important social links in Indian daily life. The small paanwala mentioned to Dr. Ganguly that he'd been selling our products for decades and asked if we could give him a window display, which would increase his sales. Dr. Ganguly said, 'Yes, Nitin, that's a good idea. Why don't you do it?'

"Later in the day we visited a small village called Jasra near Uttar Pradesh's border with Madhya Pradesh. Dr. Ganguly asked me why Lifebuoy soap wasn't doing well in Jasra. Commerce between Indian states was then rather tightly regulated, and I gave him a glib answer about stock coming over the border from Madhya Pradesh. Dr. Ganguly was quick to point out that I should investigate the issue and not accept things at face value.

"Four months later, I had my confirmation interview. Dr. Ganguly always handled the interviews himself, and he had only two substantive questions for me. Had I reached a deeper understanding of why Lifebuoy sales were poor in Jasra? And had I honored his commitment to put up the window display? Thankfully, I had done both, but otherwise it would have been the end of me, I am sure."

In that moment, Paranjpe says, "Dr. Ganguly demonstrated the importance to the company of following through." One kiosk window in itself could make no difference for the company. But "that senior people follow through with junior people, and do not just leave things as a comment, makes all the difference in the world."

By spending time with as many future leaders as possible, not just the obvious stars such as future CEO Paranjpe, senior management keeps its compare-and-contrast sense honed to a razor-sharp edge. One who visited Paranjpe soon after he became a sales manager was Banga, then in the middle of his rise to becoming HUL's youngest-ever CEO at age forty-five in 2000 (until Paranjpe set a new record by a few months at age forty-four in 2008). Banga's description of meeting Paranjpe illustrates the penetrating compare-and-contrast ability that HUL's methodology produces:

Nitin had been working in the sales operation in east UP in north India with huge rural potential for five or six months when I went and met him. I spent the day with him and his team in the marketplace, and then through the evening over dinner. I wanted to figure out what he had learned and what he was like as a person.

The first thing that struck me was that he already had a very good understanding of how our whole business model worked. Usually with new people, I had to spend a lot of time explaining why we did things in certain ways. But he had already figured out many of those whys himself. In fact, he had moved on to the next stage. He was thinking about what could be improved and what challenges might be blocking us in one direction or another.

He had not stopped there. He had already started experimenting with a couple of franchisees to increase the frequency of distribution in the villages in the area, balancing increased revenue against higher cost of distribution. This addressed the problem that rural consumers only bought when they had cash in hand from selling their crops and so on, and our franchisees could not afford to extend credit to them. But because rural people are basically self-sufficient in food and shelter, they often have higher annual disposable incomes than low-skill urban workers in India, and more frequent sales calls meant that our products were available to the villagers on more occasions when they had money to buy things they needed.

So I could see that he was thinking deeply about business issues and had creative ideas. And that he was not just someone who talked a good game; he was willing to take a well-considered risk to grow the business.

Finally I noticed the way he interacted with the rest of the sales force. The profile of the sales force was that there were a few young people, but many more seasoned veterans. Over the day and a half I spent with him, I saw that he had a very good manner about being with them. He was respectful of their age, seniority, and experience, but it was quite clear from everybody's body language and the chemistry in the room that he was the leader. The look in the eyes of the sales veterans and the tone of their voices showed me that they saw Nitin as their leader and liked him in that role, that even though he was in his early twenties and doing his first job, they did not think of him as just a trainee passing through.

Let us point out some lessons here.

- Note how Banga implicitly compared Paranjpe to both the other twenty or so young trainee managers of that year and the scores of other trainees he had met and assessed in years past. Second, the basis of comparison was both quantitative and qualitative, both what and how.

- Paranjpe's impressive sales results and his ideas for improving them showed that he had integrated the details of his first job into a big-picture understanding of the business. He was looking at the business with an external focus on the needs of retail customers and end consumers alike, and taking action to develop others—the essential mark of a leader. Equally important, Banga's assessment of qualitative information, such as his observations of body language, was so well developed by repeated observations in similar situations that it became as hard and reliable as a sales quota number.

- Because Banga was only one of many senior managers who met Paranjpe during this time, he and his colleagues could jointly calibrate their well-seasoned judgments against each other to produce a precise, three-dimensional picture of Paranjpe's current leadership performance and long-term potential. They could do the same with all the other trainees, assembling a comprehensive record of each individual's performance and particular strengths and weaknesses.

- Through continuous practice, HUL senior managers essentially develop a sixth sense for leadership potential.

This final lesson is the most important of all. "It is remarkably easy to spot people who are real leaders," says Banga. "They stand out because of their results and the way they do their jobs. There is only one key to this: senior people must cut through two, three, or more levels to spend time with junior people."

Well, it's remarkably easy if you pay close attention. In fact, it becomes intuitive. People develop intuitions about things and people they've been deeply involved with over a long time. All the while, the subconscious or unconscious mind is accumulating information, including bits whose meaning may not become clear until some later time when they click together with other information. HUL's leaders have developed their intuitions through lengthy, intimate, and repeated involvements with their protégés and each other. Effectively they've built vast internal databases that they can access in a heartbeat.

PASSING MUSTER

Probation ends in a confirmation interview with an executive member of the HUL board of directors. Approval of the trainee by his or her coach, tutors, and mentors is a prerequisite. If confirmed, the person becomes a full-fledged manager. If not, he may wash out of the program, but more will likely get added training and learning opportunities; the probationary period might be extended. HR, the steward of HUL's leadership development system, ensures that assessments are objective and deep, and that no promising leadership talent is overlooked.

Freshly confirmed managers immediately go into leadership

roles, which include more cross-functional and cross-divisional experience. Besides broadening their talents, this keeps them from becoming the prisoner of a narrow boss. Though the managers are expected to show early successes, they have some leeway to develop at individual paces and along individual paths. Conversely, the initial placements have enough headroom so that even the ablest people cannot outgrow them too quickly.

Senior leaders continue to act as coaches and mentors, carefully watching the pattern and speed of growth. "One year can be a flash in the pan," Paranjpe says. "Over three years we see enough—not just the performance track record, but also the behaviors and other leadership qualities—to form a view of how far and fast an individual can go."

HUL continues to compile multiple what-and-how assessments of young managers during their first three years on the job. After that, senior managers as well as immediate bosses assess the leaders' results and compare them with those of their peers and predecessors.

What and how factors, performance, and potential together determine whether a manager becomes what HUL calls a "lister"—someone with the potential to grow to a very senior level in the organization. Managers can become listers as early as the fourth or fifth year after the confirmation interview, as Banga and Paranjpe did, or as late as the eighth year. Managers who are selected as tutors, coaches, and mentors are generally high performers, and many of them are listers. Their performance in those roles is probed along with their other accomplishments. Says Paranjpe: "If I get feedback from a few trainees that such and such a person is not accessible or helpful enough, that manager could get dropped. To be on this list has to be an aspirational thing for our managers." Leaders who fall from the list can get back on if they improve their development of the employees normally reporting to them. Otherwise they must accept that they have reached the limit of their rise within HUL.

Once a year each functional member of the management committee prepares to discuss the managers in his or her area with the rest of the committee in what Paranjpe calls "a collaborative dialogue to calibrate individuals." Leaders are placed on a color-coded matrix that gives focus to the dialogue, categorizing them as top, middle, or lagging performers. The dialogue is candid and the questioning is rigorous. For example, says Paranjpe, "one member of the committee may say to another, 'Do you really think this guy belongs in the green box? You may think he's great, but I think he's terrible when he works with other functions. His collaborating skills are awful; half my team complains about him.' If someone is in the red box, we ask, 'Is he truly in the red? Has he received enough feedback? Does he know that if he's there for one more year, he will be moving on?' That's the conversation. We do a calibration across people and across functions of who is really doing well, who can develop further with some inputs, and who can't."

The CEO and the management committee collectively look after the top one hundred jobs across the company, "which we have identified as 'hot jobs,' because of their scale, complexity, or strategic relevance," says Paranjpe. A "hot jobs/hot people grid" shows what proportion of these jobs are filled by listers and how many up-and-comers will join them soon. "We want to make sure the best people are in the most important jobs for current operating success. But management also has a responsibility to give the hot people the most exciting, complex, challenging, and value-adding roles, because that helps them develop and progress further."

If you had such a list in your organization, would you use it to produce a 100 percent match between hot jobs and hot people? HUL doesn't think that's a good idea. A 100 percent match leaves no room to move leaders as they develop. HUL thus likes to see an 80 to 85 percent match, Paranjpe said, "and if it is less than that, we feel uncomfortable."

Finally, the management committee meets twice a year

for a four-to-five-hour discussion of the top fifty managers below them in the company. These are people who are in the sweet spot of high performance and high potential. In the year's first meeting the committee reviews their individual what-and-how leadership measures. Six months later, it finalizes career planning and decisions about next assignments for each of them.

Wait a minute, you say—a four-to-five-hour meeting on fifty people averages out to six minutes a person, tops. But here's intuitive-level information at work. Everyone on the management committee knows all fifty through frequent informal interactions. It takes little time to sift out collective information and achieve a consensus. They can efficiently ratify judgments and plans about the up-and-coming managers, leaving time for longer discussion of difficult cases.

Because the top fifty are all big producers, the difficult cases hinge on qualitative rather than quantitative matters. Qualitative information emerges as one member of the management committee relates how he saw a particular manager handle a specific leadership challenge, and other executives offer concordant or discordant perspectives. The executives probe each other's impressions to find the common truth in them, step by step establishing and confirming an accurate, reliable consensus.

In these discussions, Banga stresses, "the most important thing is the manager's integrity." Paranjpe adds details: "Character and integrity determine whether a person should go to a higher leadership position. First, I don't want to spend sleepless nights worrying that someone's actions will compromise the company. If you have to keep an eye on someone, that individual cannot go to a higher level. The other reason we emphasize character and integrity is that they shape a person's capacity to connect with others authentically. Charisma and talking well are useful leadership qualities, but they are not enough if a person cannot connect authentically with others to build consensus and teamwork.

"You only develop a feeling for people's character and integrity when you know them and see how they deal with problems. Do they take accountability for issues? Do they own up to big problems? Or are they the sort of people who in a difficult situation start transferring pressure down and blaming others?"

To illustrate this, Paranjpe mentions "a very high-performing manager, with nothing in the written record to indicate that you had to look over his shoulder." Yet as the committee discussed this manager, misgivings began to emerge. "No one could put a finger on exactly what might be wrong. No one had a concrete example to give, and yet we were not comfortable. We spent an hour and a half on whether there was any basis to our feeling. And we didn't get it. We said, 'Look, today we don't have a basis, but we have a feeling. It is unfair to this individual if we leave it at a feeling and drop him. Equally it's unfair to the company not to pursue this.'

"We decided that over the next six to twelve months each of us would interact with this manager. If no concrete basis for our misgiving arose, we would give him a clean bill of health. But if there was anything at all, then that would be that, and irrespective of performance he couldn't go any further."

Note the unwavering focus here on what matters most to the future of the company. Note too how senior managers take personal responsibility for gathering the soft data, their own multiple observations and impressions, that they can jointly calibrate to produce hard facts about the manager in future meetings.

GREAT CHALLENGES GROW GREAT LEADERS

Underlying HUL's talent management system is the belief that leaders must have tough assignments to grow. The toughest, trial-by-fire jobs go to those with the most promise, even during management trainees' probation.

It would be hard to imagine a more challenging assignment than Banga got as a trainee doing a cross-functional stint at HUL's headquarters in Mumbai. One day then-chairman T. Thomas called him into his office along with two other trainees. Thomas said that he had chosen them to demonstrate his idea that HUL could accelerate rural development in India. The young men were each to go to one of three farming villages near the small town of Etah in a remote part of Uttar Pradesh. They were to stay in their respective villages for two to three months, devising and piloting projects to improve the villagers' lives that could be scaled up across India. Thomas would visit them a couple of times to see their progress.

Banga says, "Thomas told us, 'Use your imaginations to the full. You can do anything you think will help your assigned village. The only thing you can't do is spend the company's money. You each must make your way with the resources you find in yourself and in your village.' And that was it. We were out of his office."

At first the experience was "like being on Mars" for Banga, a city boy from a well-off family. HUL had a milk products factory in Etah, and the factory manager had arranged that each trainee would have a place to sleep and a family to eat with in his assigned village. "That was the extent of the support structure. That and a little survival kit of first-aid stuff, bedding, mosquito net, and flashlight." Dropped off in the middle of the night in Sirsabadan, a place of around fifteen hundred people, Banga found the next morning that the conditions were so primitive that the villagers took care of all personal hygiene in the open. He also had an ethnic divide to contend with, because he was a Sikh in a community that had no experience of Sikhs.

Over the course of the first month, Banga broke through his own personal barriers, made himself comfortable with living as the villagers did, and spent hours talking with them about the village, their families, their work, and their aspirations and concerns. One of the biggest problems he observed in the village was the lack of any covered drainage, so large pools of standing water collected everywhere and became breeding areas for insects. Having earned an engineering degree before his MBA in marketing, he knew that it would be relatively simple to build drainage pits to address the problem.

The villagers were skeptical, he recalls. "They said, 'Who cares about the water on the ground? It's always been like that.' They couldn't make the connection between the standing water and its health impact. Finally I persuaded the village headman to let me show him how it would help." Banga, the headman, and one other villager dug three drainage pits, circular holes about ten feet deep and about six inches in diamater, around the village well. Then they filled each pit with small pieces of brick and gravel to prevent it from filling up again with silt and sand. He did this around the well where there was a lot of collected water in a very public place.

Overnight the area around the well was transformed. The villagers started telling one another to go to the well to see what had happened. Banga and the headman then called a village meeting. The headman spoke first about the benefits to them and their children of building drainage pits throughout the village. When it was Banga's turn to speak, he made it clear that they would have to do the work themselves. " 'It's very easy,' I told them. 'I'll show you how to do it. But I can't do it for you, and I don't have any money to pay for it. You have to do it for your own village.' They saw the wisdom of that. Earlier I had gone around the village and made a site plan of where the drainage pits should be. And then people who lived in a particular lane would build a drainage pit for that lane, and I would supervise. This occupied about four weeks, after which the whole village was completely transformed in terms of its level of sanitation." Banga followed this with a similar effort involving the village school, which was badly dilapidated. The village headman had a small development fund at his disposal to buy the paint and brushes. Banga and the headman started the cleaning and painting, then turned the work over to the villagers. The school went from being the worst to the finest building in the village, "in better shape than the richest farmer's house," says Banga with pleasure.

When Thomas arrived, he was duly impressed. He had chosen the villages for this experiment personally, and he had the "before" picture vividly in his mind. He was so impressed with the results of Banga's leadership that he asked him to head up a rural development project reporting directly to him, rather than go on to a normal next job in sales and marketing. Banga demurred because he was engaged to a young career woman who needed to be in one of India's big cities for her work. Thomas flew into a rage, and Banga imagined that he would be fired. But he had shown that he was too valuable to lose, and he soon found himself assigned to a brand marketing job in Mumbai. He had, understandably, gained enormous confidence in himself given the hurdles he had to overcome. He had also learned the leadership lessons of a lifetime about listening to people, understanding their needs, and winning their support for an important project—one of a leader's most valuable skills.

A daunting challenge of a quite different sort came four years later in the early 1980s, when Dr. Ganguly, Thomas's successor, sent Banga to work at Lever Brothers in London. Banga arrived expecting to be assigned to a job immediately, but—echoes of Sirsabadan—he learned that he had to find that job for himself. The lone Indian (indeed the lone Asian) manager in Lever Brothers at the time, he met all the marketing managers in what was essentially a series of auditions. "After about a week I was offered the job of senior brand manager for a medium-sized brand. I said I'd love to do it. The annual plan discussion for the brand was supposed to take place in three weeks, and my new boss, an Australian, said he would do the presentation because I'd just arrived. I insisted on doing it myself and worked day and night for the next three weeks to construct the plan, and presented it to the entire marketing department on the due date. It was a hugely important thing. In one stroke I made an impact on everybody and was accepted."

Two years later, Ganguly called Banga back from London and gave him the most high-pressure, high-leverage job in the company: heading up Project STING, which stood for "Strategy to Inhibit Nirma Growth." Nirma was a low-priced detergent invented by an entrepreneurial chemist, who began selling it village to village in 1969. As a cottage industry, Nirma did not have to pay the mandated minimum wage and was exempt from a variety of taxes and regulations that affected HUL, including restrictions on discount pricing against smaller competitors. HUL did not even have a low-price product it could consider discounting. Worse, as Nirma grew, it began to threaten its top laundry brand, Surf. By 1985, Nirma was so successful with consumers throughout India, and not just in rural areas, that it was outselling Surf three to one in volume. Wheel was launched by Banga's team in 1987 with a product formulated to be superior to Nirma and offered at the same price. When it was launched, it had strongly negative margins. A cross-functional team created a new business model to deliver positive margins within eighteen months.

Though Nirma had a sixteen-year head start, HUL had resources that would help it catch up. One was the on-the-ground experience its leaders gained in rural India, which gave the company sharp insights into Nirma's customer base. Over the years, Wheel overtook Nirma and became the biggest brand in Unilever's global portfolio.

Then came a career setback. After the global stint, Paranjpe was brought back and put in charge of HUL's laundry business. Arriving in the midst of an intense battle between HUL and Procter & Gamble, he was for the first time unable to meet his sales growth targets. He had been a lister from early on, and although he still had the how of leadership behavior and potential, he did not have the what of leadership performance. Paranjpe remembers the time when his boss, the managing director of HUL's home and personal care business and a member of the management committee, called him in and said, "Irrespective of any leadership potential and behavior you demonstrate, your recent performance does not put you in the top bracket. You need to be dropped from the list."

Paranjpe responded to his boss by saying, "I cannot argue with the decision, and in many ways I feel good about it, because it is objective, it is transparent."

Off the list, he nonetheless remained head of the laundry business and under heavy pressure to get the business moving forward. On reflection he concluded that he had been slow to realize that the business required structural change and that he "needed to do a lot more to galvanize and realign the entire organization." He went to work doing that, while making sure he "didn't transmit the pressure down and create panic." He got the business's growth on track, and two years later the management committee not only put him back on the list but made him executive director of home and personal care products—and a member of the management committee itself. Three years after that, with the what and how finely balanced, he was made CEO.

CONCLUSIONS

As successive generations of leaders progress from apprentice to mentor, HUL's virtuous circle of leadership development continuously builds and renews its organizational muscle. It's an invisible, qualitative social process, but its specific elements can be pinpointed:

- The special pipeline for leaders from recruitment onward
- Consistent focus on the *what* and *how* of leadership

- Senior managers' joint calibration of their frequent direct observations, evaluations, and mentoring of future leaders
- The attention to coaching by managers at all levels
- The always-demanding approach to individual leaders' development paths, with significant leadership opportunity and both cross-functional and cross-divisional experience in the crucial first three years of a future leader's career
- Growing great leaders with great challenges

Like West Point, which produces not only generals but an unmatched officer corps, HUL pursues excellence in leadership at every level of the organization—including a succession of superb CEOs. Fast-developing leaders provide enormous competitive advantage in fast-changing markets, and HUL gets younger and fresher every year without ever losing the benefit of deep experience.

The next chapter features a company that has a long history of developing truly global leaders. P&G is world class when it comes to brand management and consumer focus and has a pipeline of leaders who get special attention, including global assignments that stretch them to their limits.

Chapter 6

DEVELOPING CAPABILITY and CAPACITY THROUGH EXPERIENCES THAT MATTER
How P&G Develops Global Leaders

Companies that adapt to a changing world constantly update the qualities they want in their leaders. Procter & Gamble has always been a forerunner in talent development, and its decade after decade of success reflect in good measure its strength in choosing leaders attuned to their times. Marketing prowess has been a constant, but the company continually fosters added skills.

When A. G. Lafley became CEO in 2000, he saw that his company's big growth opportunities would come in the world's developing regions, and tuned its talent processes to focus on strategy, innovation, and market and consumer insight. The leadership "gene pool" had to keep pace to realize that future. Global perspective has always been a core strength of P&G leaders, and today global assignments are increasingly woven into the tapestry of P&G's leadership development processes. Indeed, a global assignment (or extended global experience) is one of the key thresholds that P&G uses to develop a person's capability and capacity and to prepare them for higher office. When in 2009

P&G needed a successor to replace Lafley, it had one: Bob McDonald, a homegrown leader whose global experiences and accomplishments gave him the ideal preparation to take P&G forward. And when Dick Antoine retired from his job as global head of HR, Moheet Nagrath, a longtime P&Ger who himself had lived in many parts of the world before moving to Cincinnati, brought a decidedly global bent to the development of the next generation of leaders. Under Bob McDonald, P&G continues to grow leaders with deep consumer insights and who understand innovation and appreciate the value of experiential learning in global assignments.

No amount of visiting can match the experience of living in unfamiliar places. The immersion in myriad things that are new and different tests a leader on many levels and provides enormous opportunities for growth. By breaking people out of their comfort zone, it develops personal sensibilities, sharpens judgments, and provides an unmatched opportunity to build relationships with a wide variety of people from different backgrounds and cultures. It expands both capacity, which is the ability to get more of the same work done, and capability: achieving more through doing a higher level of work. Finally, it fosters the kind of collaboration and working across boundaries that is one of McDonald's goals for increasing the power of P&G's global organization.

As Lafley reminds us, talent development is not only about developing and growing leaders but also testing the best with complex and challenging stretch assignments that will reveal which ones have CEO potential. "Running a tough country like Korea, Indonesia, Russia, or Nigeria, or a tough business that we're not winning in, or a newly acquired business we don't understand, or a chronically underperforming business—all of these are stretch assignments," he says. "But we have to be careful not to blow up very good people with very strong potential by moving them a 'bridge too far,' and subjecting them to more challenge, complexity, and difficulty than they were ready for."

Here's how P&G pushes them just far enough. You'll meet two people in particular who show how carefully chosen assignments can greatly accelerate the development of high-potential leaders.

THE WAGER

Dick Antoine was catching up with several leaders of P&G businesses gathered for the company's annual November strategy meeting when he spotted Deb Henretta making her way toward him. He hadn't seen Deb since she'd taken the assignment in Singapore five months earlier, and he was anxious to hear how it was going. Many P&Gers are eager to take an assignment abroad, but getting her to uproot her family from Cincinnati had been a hard sell. She finally agreed to put in an eighteen-month stint—short for an international move at P&G, especially considering the resources it consumes and the time it takes for the leader to adapt. People are usually in those assignments for three to five years. Antoine, then head of HR, and Lafley, then CEO, were willing to bend because they knew that her ties to the Cincinnati community were unusually deep. She had three school-age children, two of them teenagers and one of them already in high school, and she was strongly committed to the plethora of corporate and advisory boards she served on.

Besides, Antoine had a hunch that she'd stay longer. He had seen many P&G leaders resist such assignments only to discover how much they learned from them. Many ended up wanting to stay as long as they could. He had a feeling Henretta would be one of them. "I'll tell you what," he said before she left. "If you want to move back to Cincinnati after eighteen months, I'll buy you dinner. If not, you owe me one."

Henretta was totally at ease as she approached Antoine during the cocktail hour at that November strategy retreat. She greeted him warmly, then paused before asking, "So where do you want to go to dinner, Dick?"

Henretta had discovered that she loved running Southeast Asia. What's more, her children were happy in their new schools and the entire family was enjoying traveling and learning about such a different part of the world. She had grown in ways she couldn't have imagined. Before long she was running all P&G product lines for fifteen Asian countries, including China, and becoming a candidate for bigger roles in P&G. Four and a half years later, she still has not requested that return ticket.

EARNING A CRUCIBLE ROLE

P&G has for decades produced leaders who are great general managers with a particular bent for either brand or category management. To move up, they have to demonstrate expertise in consumer insight, drive innovation, and be "globally effective," meaning able to lead in cultures other than their own. Other companies regularly scout P&G for high-level leaders. Among its alums are Microsoft CEO Steve Ballmer, former eBay CEO Meg Whitman, Intuit founder Scott Cook, Boeing CEO Jim McNerney, GE CEO Jeff Immelt, and the recently appointed CEO of archrival Unilever, Paul Polman.

P&G regards choosing the right assignments for leaders as a crucial part of building its leadership DNA. A mix of assignments, or "accelerator experiences," gives leaders both depth and breadth of experience, so they can develop the capabilities to lead a large, complex, global organization. Each assignment is not just a reward or a call to duty but also a learning opportunity and a test, a basic element in sorting, sifting, and selecting leaders who have the mix of skills, personality traits, relationships, judgment, and experience to prepare them for greater responsibilities. It is a balancing act between the needs of the business and the developmental needs of the person.

Henretta was chosen for the Singapore assignment largely because of her success in an especially tough job, one of P&G's so-called crucible roles: reviving the global baby care business, which had been trailing Kimberly-Clark for fifteen years. It seemed a risky move at the time, because she was new to the business; all its previous leaders were old hands, many of them manufacturing people. But Antoine thought otherwise. "It was one of A. G. Lafley's really good assignment planning moves," he says. "A.G. saw that P&G was heavily focused on big customers such as Walmart and not enough on the consumer. He thought Henretta could bring the needed consumer focus to the job. She had been in the laundry business, and like a lot of other people at P&G, her entire background was in marketing and brand management. She was on our watch list of high-potential leaders. Not only that, she was a mother of three kids, so she understood the consumer and knew how to talk to mothers."

Lafley got it right. Henretta transformed the baby care business. The commercials changed from technical advertisements to messages about love and all the emotions mothers feel for their children. She brought the business to a tie with Kimberly-Clark, and it's stayed there ever since.

Brand equity, market share, and profit are standard measures of a leader's success. But it's equally important to observe how the person has grown. What skills and capabilities has she demonstrated? What are her strengths? Which ones should be expanded? What areas does she need to improve? Some talents might be deepening. What new ones might have just emerged in the recent past? Observing these developments, not just performance numbers, is essential to assessing a leader's potential to move higher.

Part of how P&G defines potential is the ability to move into a leadership role two levels higher because it's more of a stretch. That narrows the field. How many times have we heard a leader say, "I've got a great number two person"? That person might be fine in the number two role or as a successor to the number one person in that department or business unit. But he is not a high-potential leader if he's unlikely to move beyond that.

Henretta had been president of global baby care for close to five years when P&G started thinking about what assignment she needed next. Lafley and Antoine thought she needed more "runway," that is, more opportunity for personal growth, to increase both her capability and her capacity. Anyone with hopes for high-level P&G positions such as vice chairman or CEO has to have three "experiences": responsibility for managing multiple brands in one country; responsibility for one business across the globe, such as laundry or personal care; and a job living in a different country. (In the case of those working at one of P&G's European companies, that means living outside Europe.) Henretta had only one of those boxes checked, so they were trying to find her an assignment that would check the other two.

The first international opening that came up was leading Northeast Asia, based in Japan. The opportunity confronted her with tough choices. "My children were settled into their extracurricular activities," she says. "I was feeling extremely good about my global business unit job. I had been running the global baby care business for about five years and had become a real expert. To be honest, I really liked my team and the business I was working on."

She also had outside commitments. "I had a network of friends and professional connections that I knew would be very hard to keep connected with in the same way. I was on several community-oriented boards, including Cincinnati Children's Hospital, and involved with advising several universities such as St. Bonaventure, where I received my undergraduate degree. All these activities are an important piece of who I am, since I believe it's important to give back to the community and the schools that helped me get my start." Henretta and her husband agonized but ultimately made the decision to go to Japan. And then, after all of the deliberating and adjusting, her boss decided to leave the company, and the plan was put on hold—Lafley didn't want her leaving the baby care business at the same time for fear that they'd lose the progress they'd made. "The movers were coming to my house literally the next week," she says. "It was incredibly disappointing. I mean, there's no other way to put it.

"But there's nothing like having something taken away from you to make you want it even more. And it had the same effect on my family." A year later, when the job in Singapore opened up, Henretta was ready for it. It didn't bother her that it was a lateral move by conventional wisdom. When Lafley first went to Japan, he had gone from managing the company's North American laundry business, the largest single regional business in the company, which was some 20 percent of the company's business, to managing 5 percent. Here was one of the company's top leadership candidates at the time taking a move that looked like a smaller responsibility. And yet he'd become the CEO.

Still, she wanted to be sure that the particular job was right for her. "There are three worlds at P&G: the global business units, the functions, and the go-to-market organization. I was passionate about the GBUs—building global brands, doing strategic thinking, working the innovation pipeline. And I was quite concerned that those things were not really going to be the focus in the new job."

Several P&G board members spent time talking with Henretta about why they thought she should take the job. They had grown substantially in their own international assignments, and they thought she had just the skills and capabilities for the job. Because Asia was a developing market, Henretta would remain in charge of the GBU portions of the portfolio in addition to taking responsibility for the operations work. She could leverage what she was good at and confident about, while picking up new skills in operations and the go-to-market world.

When Lafley sat down with Henretta, he surprised her by saying, "Deb, you know that assignment probably won't be more than three years." They were talking past each other, because she was trying to angle for something less. "I knew the family could do two years of anything, even if we didn't like it and it became a hardship. But the three years was sort of pushing me over the edge." Her desire for a short stay took an ironic twist when she discovered how much she liked the job and the location. "I'm now entering my fifth year," Henretta said in late 2009. "This past year has really been at my request because my children have loved it so much. My son got halfway through high school and basically said, 'Mom, if you get pulled back to Ohio, you'll have to leave without me. I love it here, and I want to graduate from the Singapore American School.'

"So imagine me now, after having made a huge stink at the beginning, having to ask to stay. And of course I lost the bet with Dick. We had a lovely dinner with our spouses here in Singapore."

FINDING THE DISTINGUISHED FEW

Henretta had been with P&G for about twenty-five years when she made the move to Singapore. As is typical of P&G, her leadership potential had been spotted after she was about five years into her career. While P&G is highly selective about its recruits, it doesn't put people on the leadership watch list right away. Leaders at the senior level are expected to spot potential in those working several levels below them, and high performers with promise to go higher are brought to the attention of higher-level leaders through a well-developed formal talent review process.

It's a bottom-up system that starts at the second or third

level of the company with people who have been around for about five years. Names get passed to the next level, and they work their way to the top, on a business, functional, and corporate basis. Let's say people in baby care in Japan are doing a talent review in that country. They would give the global baby care business unit the names of the five or so top people working in Japan. Each function would also gather names to send to the corporate function. Of course there are overlaps, because somebody who works in the supply chain in baby care might have his name on two lists, for baby care as a whole and for the supply chain function.

Under Lafley and Antoine, P&G had numerous forums for planning assignments and revisiting succession plans, one aimed at general managers, for example, and another for those deep within the business functions. Three times a year a portion of the top forty or so people in the company—those who led businesses, countries, or functions—came to headquarters to talk about their top leadership talent, including how well each person's attributes matched up against P&G's critical success factors. The CEO conducted the discussion. The group reviewed the talent for half the businesses in, say, month four, for the other half of the businesses in month eight, and for all of the corporate functions and countries in month twelve.

"After a few years of tinkering, we finally got them to be very efficient," Antoine says. "While we have roughly a hundred people on the agenda, we really focus on about thirty. We know these people so well that if no change is needed, we might just put the person's picture up on the screen. Regarding the thirty we do focus on, we zero in on one or two items that really matter about that person. We don't have to spend time reading resumes to catch up on their background. And this review was sacrosanct. It was never subject to being taken over by some other agenda item deemed to be more important."

They experimented with talent reviews in larger groups and found it helped leaders get familiar with high-potential talent outside their business unit. But there was a downside: it sometimes inhibited frank discussion. Lafley and Antoine brainstormed over how to make the discussions more reality-based.

"This candor thing is what we struggled with the most," Antoine explains. "You don't want to trash somebody's career in front of so many people, but you also don't want to be talking about how great the person was only to find out later that they've got warts growing out of their ears."

The solution was to add a session with the CEO, the head of HR, the vice chairman of that business, and the HR person for that business. Those four people began having meetings after the talent reviews, where they could say, "Okay, let's talk about these very top people. Who are they, how are they doing, and what assignment plans or interventions do we need to make?" They could be more candid because they weren't affecting the thinking of some forty other people. And because they knew the people well, they could make suggestions such as "Why don't you consider some coaching for this person?" Moreover, it was easier to identify leaders who needed to move on. People were added to or dropped from the list of the company's very top talent, and that information was subsequently reported to the board.

McDonald and Nagrath have since enhanced the talent review process, increasing the time and attention spent on it.

PROBING FOR TALENT OUTSIDE THE FORMAL TALENT REVIEW

Talent is always on the radar screen at P&G—in strategy reviews, innovation reviews, financial reviews, visits to country units or business units, and in-house training programs such as P&G's General Manager College. The strategy reviews include the head of that business, of course, usually with his or her CFO and a few other key people, and then a handful of the seniormost leaders in the company, including the CEO. Afterward, the corporate leaders often talk informally about how the business leaders handled their strategy review from a leadership standpoint.

Almost all the leaders do a good job, but occasionally someone leaves the senior leaders scratching their heads. If something isn't clear, the CEO obviously will try to help, but the fuzziness can raise questions: What does that say about the president of that business? What does the fact that her report wasn't focused say about her leadership style? What does it mean that the person didn't address one or two key issues that are causing problems within the business? That's how the strategy reviews inevitably have a leadership element to them. Senior management takes note of the people who brought new thinking to the business and those they have to keep a sharper eye on.

Lafley turned the strategy process into a powerful coaching tool by introducing a novel practice—one we recommend other companies adopt. He reviewed each leader's strategy document ahead of time and provided handwritten comments to the presenter before the meeting. The feedback might be, "I don't understand how this will address our number one competitor killing us on pricing" or "Boy, I think you really hit a critical item here." It is a way of coaching the leader, and the CEO learns something about the person from how he or she responds.

An increasingly important attribute is the ability to run an innovation program. P&G has a long history of creating breakthrough products and new brands such as Tide laundry detergent and Pampers disposable diapers, but when Lafley took over, it hadn't been developing many big hits and was struggling to meet earnings expectations. He concluded that P&G had been trying to do too much too fast and needed to return to its roots. He made innovation the central aim, with the consumer as the focus. Now innovation reviews are routine. Business units scrutinize their portfolios and plans at least quarterly and present them to the senior management team once a year. Full of give-and-take, the sessions are a rich source of information. The chief technology officer and CEO can easily observe who's good at leading an innovation program and whom they should worry about.

Talent is also observed in financial reviews. It's pretty obvious who sets an aggressive budget and who sets a budget she knows she can easily meet. And when the CEO and head of HR visit countries and businesses to discuss results and challenges, much like GE's operational reviews, they finish every session with a review of the organization's talent. They come away with fresh insight into each country or region's talent, and an overall deeper knowledge of the global talent pool.

McDonald uses P&G's General Manager College, designed to help prepare up-and-coming leaders for future challenges, as another way to get to know top talent better. One of two programs that newly promoted general managers participate in, it is taught by P&G executives, at times paired with an external partner. McDonald takes it seriously, so much so that he himself teaches the program's leadership module and sits in on other periods. Nagrath attends the entire week. "The most important thing I try to achieve in those sessions frankly is just to get the individual leaders to be introspective about their own leadership and to be more deliberate," McDonald says. "I tell them, 'If you don't remember anything else, please remember this: the larger the organization you lead, the more deliberate you have to be about your leadership. Think about the movie *Hoosiers,* where Gene Hackman pulls out the tape measure and has the basketball team he's coaching measure the height of the basket and the length to the free throw line.' I ask our P&G leaders, 'Would you be that deliberate or would you have just stood up on the bus on the way to the Hinkle Fieldhouse and said, "The court's the same size, guys, so get over it and perform well"?'

"We talk a lot about character, which I define as putting the needs of the organization above your own needs. The best leaders at P&G are those who take care of the organization. So while we're an organization that cares about results, and everybody who succeeds here gets good results, we also care about *how* you get the results. We talk about leadership beliefs and we try to get them in touch with their own stories so they can deliberately use those stories to lead.

"Regular attendance at these sessions gives Moheet and I valuable insights into people. It's also a great opportunity for us to learn about the issues leaders are facing in different parts of the world."

Even job postings provide information about a leader. If his subordinates are constantly posting or volunteering for jobs outside his business unit, there may be a problem. And 360-degree feedback is another. "It's important to use every opportunity to observe and evaluate people, whether it's a formal assessment, an informal dinner, having people in my home, being in their home," McDonald says. "When I get leaders in front of me and I ask them to tell me what the organization will look like in 2015 or 2020, it becomes relatively obvious who's thought about building organization capability and what capability they've thought about building. Our knowledge of the individual leaders in the company is pretty deep. And having spent a week with each one of our general managers through GM College, I know those people pretty doggone well."

How much time does a CEO of P&G spend on people? "Somebody once asked A.G. that question," Antoine says. "He thought about it for a minute and said, 'About 40 percent.' I was sitting there thinking that sounds a little high, but I didn't say anything. I went back and looked at his calendar over a six-month period and found he was not far off. It was 38 percent."

FROM "WHOM DO YOU KNOW" TO "WHO IS BEST"

Computerized employee database systems are not uncommon now, but P&G was far ahead of the pack when it created its own in 2003. When he requested funding for it, Antoine had been heading HR for several years and was highly trusted by Lafley, whom he worked with in Japan in the pre-CEO years. Nagrath led the project, and by 2005 it was up and running, initially in the United States and then globally. It's now integral to P&G's talent management.

(GE's HR team had built a similar all-employee global database a few years earlier. Bill Conaty recalls that when he proposed the project to Jack Welch with the title "HR Simplification Plan," Welch snapped back, "That's an oxymoron!" But Welch approved the $12 million project, which was successfully completed, and jokingly now takes the credit.)

P&G's global database captures all the pertinent information about each of its leaders and displays it on a screen during talent review sessions. Leaders input some of the information themselves, listing, for instance, skills and experiences such as language capability. If the person under review is married, they might note he needs an assignment where his spouse can get meaningful employment. If the spouse is another P&G employee, his background information would be there too. It also shows the person's assignment, compensation, and performance histories imported from other HR systems.

The database is linked to P&G's scorecard, which is a way of evaluating leaders on both hard and soft performance measures. "Scorecarding makes performance management more metric-oriented and easier to track," says Nagrath. "It's performance under a microscope."

The scorecard measures all general managers, presidents, and vice chairs on two dimensions: quantitative hard numbers (market share, sales volume, profit, and so on) and qualitative capabilities that help build the organization such as innovation, leadership, and strategy. That information is hardwired to P&G's performance rating process, which in turn is hardwired to the compensation process. The company has been using this system for several years, so leaders can look back to see how a person has done over time, even if it's across different assignments. "Sustainable performance is especially important," McDonald explains. "When you evaluate a general manager over a rolling five-year period, it's easy to see which leaders were building clocks and which leaders were telling time."

The scorecard includes an innovative metric P&G created: the leader's enduring impact on the business. Brands, for instance, take a long time to build yet can be destroyed very quickly. P&G started to track what happens after the leader moves on to her next job. When the very best managers leave a job, things get better. In other cases, things get worse regardless of who goes in behind them. That leads senior management to ask some pointed questions.

When P&G started making such information transparent, behavior started to change. And in some instances it came back at them. Antoine remembers a specific promotion when people came to him saying, "Hey, I seem to remember that things didn't go too well after Charlie got promoted from his last two jobs. What's going on here?" Antoine sums it up: "We held them accountable, and they held us accountable." McDonald adds, "At some companies, this kind of looking back is done anecdotally, when people make comments like, 'You know, Joe wasn't as good as we thought he was,' but meanwhile Joe has moved on and no one does much about it. We act on the information."

The database has made a notable difference in the quality of decisions. "It gets away from the 'whom do you know' system," Nagrath says. "It used to be when you needed to replace the general manager in France, you'd say, 'Who do you know that speaks French?' The boss of Western Europe or the head of that business would say, 'I know Joe and Susie.' But there might be eighteen other really good candidates out there that they just didn't happen to know. And if virtually all the leaders you knew were from the U.S., guess who got promoted most? Leaders from the U.S.

"The system suddenly opened it up to everybody. You input the criteria and within seconds you get a list of people. And then you can say, 'I've never heard of so-and-so, but on paper he looks great and we should learn more about him.' When you have access to data and people all over the world, your options widen. And our employees appreciate it because it's more of a merit-based system. You can talk about the old-boys network—that's just another way of expressing the 'whom do you know' phenomenon."

HR facilitates the search, but the line manager is responsible for finding the right person. For jobs below the top 300 leaders, which are managed by corporate, a manager typically calls the head of HR to say, "We've got some bad news here: Pierre is leaving." HR pulls three candidates from the system. Then the phone calls begin. What do you think of them? What do you know about them? This is where leaders draw on their knowledge about who is ready for something bigger or needs an international assignment, so people get the opportunities they need to keep expanding.

The scorecard helps spot those who are most deserving based on the pattern of their performance. "We're looking for general managers whose results stand out, who can perform year in, year out in different environments," explains Nagrath. "Say we're looking at several general managers to fill a position as president. We can see that for the seven years a particular person was a general manager, she on average had the highest results of any general manager in the pool. That makes the decision to promote her ahead of everybody else almost irrefutable. It's also useful in succession planning when the board can see that the leader not only met the short-term goals while she was in the job but also built a business that continued to produce good results after she left."

LAYERS OF LEARNING IN ASIA

Even the most thorough tracking systems and most thoughtful assignment planning cannot predict whether a person will grow in a new job, and in what ways. Virtually all companies track performance, but masters of talent use close contact and a wide lens for viewing how the person is responding to the new situation. Deb Henretta's business results were good; she met the targets. But it was evident early on that she wasn't merely tapping an existing set of skills in a new location. Rather, she was learning on many levels, which is evident in her description of her four and a half years in Asia.

"From the start I was running multiple countries of Southeast Asia, including India and Australia, each with differences of culture, religion, regulations, politics, economics, and infrastructure. I got to know a country and culture firsthand. I had traveled a lot when I was in baby care, and I always tried to get out with consumers and customers, but when you're swooping in for a visit all you can get is a peek. Having an international assignment gives you a comprehensive understanding of another culture and a different way of doing business. It helps you grow intellectually.

"Because of the time difference and the physical distance from Cincinnati, and also because of the nature of the job, I feel like I truly run a business out here. I hadn't realized how protected you are when you're working in Cincinnati, because there are so many staff people to support you. You have a lot of resources. I certainly have a large staff out here, don't get me wrong, but you're on the front line with the media if something goes wrong, and with governments when you need a partnership or you've got a customs problem or they change the laws and you're trying to figure out how to manage efficiently within that change. You're a little more on your own, and because of that, you have to develop coping mechanisms. And you're forced to find a network of people who can help you. It isn't ready-made.

"Many developing countries are eager to increase their economic standing and are seeking partners to help them develop economically, and they don't have a lot of bureaucracy to get in the way of that. So I find myself interacting with governments and coming to understand how they work and what they're trying to accomplish in terms of their economic development, even with some of the more developed countries, as we look to set up R&D centers and move people around within Asia. It helps me see who they are as a people and what types of products or positionings might be important to them."

Asia is full of unexpected challenges. If it's not a cyclone, it's a mudslide. If it's not a mudslide, it's a coup. If it's not a coup, it's a government getting nervous about a product ingredient. Henretta had to develop a sense of calm to take such things in stride and the personal confidence to deal with them. "At one point we dealt with an earthquake in Indonesia. It was people first—you've got to locate all your people, including the visitors there, and you've got to make sure that the buildings are structurally sound. You kind of go through your whole business continuity plan to get through that."

NEW SKILLS, NEW MENTAL HABITS

Henretta found herself dazzled by the speed of change in the developing world. Her metaphor for it is a visual memory of Vietnam. "When I first started going five years ago, the streets were crowded, but they were crowded with bicycles and scooters, and if you saw an occasional truck on the street it was an unusual sight. And now in places like Ho Chi Minh City, it's largely cars and trucks on the road. I have pictures from Vietnam from the first year I was out here to now going into the fifth year, and you can see the amazing progress in those pictures.

"Maybe I should have been embracing change more in my previous job, but you certainly can't *not* do it here. And it makes you more forward-thinking. I've become more interested in putting the foundational pieces in place out here, both from a business strategy standpoint and also from a people and organization capability-building standpoint. So it's really helped me focus on building something that will continue to generate good business results for the company long after I leave, or at least I hope it will." She adds that her experience in the baby care business probably laid the groundwork for a longer-term view: "A business that has been declining for the better part of ten years can't be turned around on a dime."

A key part of embracing change is learning to think on your feet—making judgment calls even when you don't have all the information you'd like to have. "I'm much faster at making decisions I used to agonize over," Henretta says, "because crisis situations have forced me to make more immediate decisions. In my previous assignment, having a tendency to be a bit of a perfectionist, I was wanting 90 percent of the facts and understanding on the table before I made a decision. Now I make decisions on 80 percent of the facts. I've swung ten points the other way."

Lafley and Antoine understood the challenges and saw Henretta's growth. "One of the biggest things any P&G leader has to learn when they get outside the protective cocoon in Cincinnati is dealing with ambiguity and the lack of data," Antoine says. "In the developed countries there are data to cover almost anything. On the other side of the world, there's some data and a lot of intuition that must be developed. Henretta also had to expand her scope. She'd been running P&G's largest business with some $9 billion in sales in about eighty countries. In Asia she has only fifteen countries, but she has virtually every product line."

Henretta built her own support system in Asia through roundtables and involvement in the Young Presidents' Organization. "When I was in Cincinnati, I had a dozen or more global business unit peers who were sitting in the same building in the same city as I was, and if you had a knotty problem, you could bounce things off them. Out here I had to rely on external relationships. The first time you go through something like an earthquake, it's of great value to have a bunch of other company heads who have been there, done that. For instance, when a coup broke out in Thailand and the airport shut down, there were lots of phone calls between the executives out here running Asia: 'What are you doing to get your people out? How are you thinking about it?' We got some good suggestions, and we were also able to help others." In 2009, she was asked to join a multidisciplinary planning committee tasked with developing the blueprint for Singapore's future—another opportunity for her to expand her capacity and capability.

She also adjusted to differences in organizational capability. "In Asia by and large we are working and operating with a much younger organization of people than what you typically work with in the developed world, so you have to put a lot of time and energy into building capabilities. And it begins with the fundamentals of the business, the way P&G thinks about the business, and things like the fundamentals of brand building. Much of the early Asia years have been white-space expansion, bringing the main P&G categories into brand-new countries, where P&G has had no sales in the past. But the challenge in the early days of coming into a geography is easier than what I would call the middle period, when you're trying to make sure that what you've put out there is actually building the business. I've found that we needed to go back and do a bit of remedial work on building the fundamentals so the brands and the business will last for decades. A lot of that is teaching people all of the things that the Cincinnati-based folks know how to do instinctively.

It's in the DNA of those folks, given the schooling they're getting, the experiences they're getting through internships, and so on.

"When you go into places like Vietnam or Indonesia, you're not necessarily finding talent that has all of those fundamentals in their DNA. What you're getting is an incredibly eager, passionate, ready-to-learn group of people. But a lot of that teaching and training in the fundamentals has to take place before you can take the business to the next level.

"Culturally there is a greater sense of hierarchy here, that what the boss says is what you do. And so getting people to be comfortable asking questions or pushing back was something I had to adjust my style to. In the U.S., if you put an idea out there, you might get a whoosh of pushback and 'Let me tell you the fifteen reasons that isn't going to work.' Here you kind of have to pull the devil's-advocate position out of people. So you have to make time in your leadership approach to do that."

BREADTH AND DEPTH

For Melanie Healey, who joined P&G in 1990 and is now group president of North America, going global meant leaving Brazil, where she was born and raised by her Chilean mother and British father. Her career began when she graduated from the University of Richmond and landed a job with Wisconsin-based S. C. Johnson in Rio de Janeiro, where S. C. Johnson and other well-known consumer goods companies, including Unilever, Colgate, and Johnson & Johnson, had entrenched positions. She did a rotation of several months in each business function before being assigned to brand management. A few years later, when she got married, she took a job with Johnson & Johnson in São Paulo, where she became a marketing manager.

P&G was conspicuously missing from Brazil in those

years, but in 1990 it prepared to make its entry by buying Phebo Soap, a $120 million family-owned company. That move piqued Healey's interest, for two reasons: first, because of P&G's reputation as being number one in marketing and brand management, and second, because it was a company known for growing talent. She wouldn't have to leave to keep learning and growing. When a friend from Johnson & Johnson joined P&G in Brazil, Healey soon followed as one of P&G's eight local hires in brand management.

With seven years of work experience, Healey was not the typical P&G new hire, but she had something the company needed: on-the-ground knowledge of the Brazilian culture and market. Some thirty-five expats were charged with growing the business in Brazil, and while they knew everything about P&G, they knew little about the specifics of Brazil. "It was a wonderful opportunity to learn from these very experienced people, who had opened the market in several other countries," Healey says. "And the sense of camaraderie really helped. We formed great relationships among our team from day one as we figured out how to make our mark on the Brazilian market." Healey led the introduction of Pampers Uni, a low-cost entry into the disposable diaper market that shook the local industry leader from its perch.

Her next assignments, running bar soap and then Downy fabric softener in Mexico, put her brand and marketing management to the test in a completely different venue. Mexico was P&G's fifth-largest subsidiary, and the brands were well established there. "The point of that assignment was to learn how to operate in a more typical P&G environment as well as to experience a different culture," Healey explains. "Those three years in Mexico City were great for learning how to operate when P&G resources are at your fingertips. I also learned a new language and came to know a new culture. And then there was the devaluation of the peso in December 1994. That kind of thing happens about every other year in

Brazil, but the 1994 devaluation was a big one. I had to manage through that."

After Mexico came an assignment in Brazil, then another in Venezuela, and then in 2001 a move to Cincinnati. Healey has had several promotions during her nine years at P&G's home base. Over time, she realized that she was learning something more than the familiar lessons as a result of having lived in Brazil, São Paulo, and Mexico. It's what she calls peripheral thinking, which is analogous to peripheral vision. It's a hypersensitivity to subtle changes at the fringes of your environment. Some people call it street smarts, which is apt in her case. "I had developed a little bit of a survival instinct in Brazil, because as a child, I'd go off on my own to get the bus to school or wherever, and your chances of being mugged on the way to the bus were pretty big. You'd be watching every movement, every person's body language. It wasn't exactly paranoia, because you had to have pretty good self-confidence. You had to figure out what was happening around you and watch to see if something was a little bit different. Even as an adult in places like São Paulo and Mexico City, I had to think almost cynically about what could happen to me."

This mental agility translated into instinctive business behaviors. "When something happens, whether it's a competitive move or someone pitching a new product idea, I pick up on it pretty quickly. I can very readily put myself in the shoes of a competitor, an employee, a subordinate, a boss, and look at things from their perspective and react. When I'm in a meeting, I watch the body language and I can tell whether the person really believes what they're saying or just feels compelled to say it, or whether there is a conflict between two players. I can figure out the truth of what's going on in the business or the organization.

"Because of this peripheral thinking and having been in environments that have different constraints, I can see more possibilities. When people in one country say something can't be done, but you've seen it done in three other countries, you can try to help them look at it from a different angle. The developing world is so vibrant, upbeat, and optimistic. They're so eager and hungry to learn. That attitude is precious."

As Healey's varied assignments expanded her breadth of thinking, increasing levels of leadership responsibility deepened her understanding of her business. "In fem care for ten years I was able to develop incredible depth in that category and strong instincts about what worked and didn't work. I learned how to ask the right questions, which is important when you're turning a business around or launching new brands or managing a function, which is what I did a lot of. I was able to get deep into R&D, manufacturing, the financial health of the business, so I got to know all the levers I could pull. It was also a different business challenge. In Brazil, my assignment was to build a brand from scratch. In Mexico, I was building on a strong base and business momentum. But fem care had lost a lot of share and was in pretty bad shape. It needed a turnaround to restore top-line and bottom-line growth, and the organization had to be reenergized.

"Now, as group president for P&G North America, which is 40 percent of P&G's total business, I'm back to breadth versus depth. The North American portfolio is huge, with 123 different brands and subbrands in twenty different categories. I'm charged with the sales force, the supply chain and logistics teams, external relations, marketing, media. I'm committed to training and to formal and informal mentoring as well. It's impossible to know everything about everything, so you learn to tap into the organization to figure out what is absolutely critical from a helicopter view, and where you need to go deep.

"At the end of the day, it's that accumulation of different experiences that feeds the capability, and in a sense it amplifies your capacity too because you learn things quickly and can do things faster because of the experience. On that, it's important to surround yourself with great people, people who complement you. The concept I use is casting for a play. I think about who is the best person to play a particular role. Who has the relevant experience and talents to really help? Jack Nicholson and Tom Cruise are both great actors, but I wouldn't put Tom Cruise in *One Flew over the Cuckoo's Nest,* and I wouldn't cast Jack Nicholson to star in *Top Gun.*"

UPDATING THE GLOBAL NETWORK

As they work in different businesses, geographic regions, cultures, and markets over the years, many P&G managers keep up their relationships with former colleagues and bosses (who often become mentors). These global networks help them adapt to new environments and business challenges. Now P&G is institutionalizing them, using social technology to better connect P&Gers around the globe and leverage the learning those relationships provide.

McDonald himself is its champion. "I remember the shock I had in 1991 when I suddenly became responsible for people who weren't in the same geography I was in. Remember Tom Peters's book *In Search of Excellence,* where he talked about managing by walking around? Well, you can't walk from the Philippines to Korea, so you've got to find a surrogate for connecting people. We now have our own internal Facebook and our own internal YouTube, which is consistent with the way people socialize today and with what they'll need to be effective global leaders in the future.

"How do you get an organization of 127,000 employees in eighty countries to feel small and reachable? One way is by working with different people. In each assignment, you get to know a lot of people from other parts of the world, and as you move across different roles, you keep crossing paths. You develop a critical mass of peers who have international experience.

"The other way is through technology. For example, we've

started doing worldwide webcasts from various locations in the world in real time. I recently did a town hall meeting in Brazil, which was uploaded to the company website so employees could access it. Meanwhile, the GMs sitting in the audience were communicating back with their organizations in real time, talking about what was taking place on the stage to an organization that might be two thousand miles away. The GMs are given Flip cameras, so they can do on-the-spot interviews and capture reactions for the people back home. Employees can also reach out and ask questions. It's visual, and real-time.

"These connections are a great foundation for broadening people's knowledge base about the global consumer and global competition. We're also discovering that they allow us to deploy our new strategy deeper and more quickly than we ever could before. And the biggest surprise, which really shouldn't have been a surprise, has been that they help people connect to our purpose—touching and improving lives. The more people feel connected with that purpose, the more fulfilled they feel on the job and the more motivated they will be."

THE BIG PAYOFF

P&G's strengthened leadership bench left the company well prepared when A. G. Lafley announced his retirement as the aftermath of the financial meltdown was ravaging many companies' strategies and leadership. Every CEO in the company's 172-year history has been promoted within. It's a great tradition, but one that can be dangerous if tradition is the only point.

Lafley and the board approached the succession decision with one overarching goal: to choose the best person for P&G at that point in time. The search started early, as Lafley made talent planning, including CEO succession, part of his ongoing agenda with the board. Directors started tracking candidates soon after Lafley took office, and they got to know them better by visiting them periodically on their own turf. "We put a lot of horses in the race and let them run until we were ready to make a decision," Lafley says. The list shortened as the planned retirement date neared, but a handful of viable candidates remained.

When the decision point was a couple of years away, Lafley and the board worked with their own HR experts Antoine and Nagrath and with Bill Conaty to refine the criteria for the CEO job. Integrity, character, and values were absolute essentials, and all of the candidates met that test. The remaining criteria were based on scenarios looking forward five to seven years that helped to pinpoint the issues the new CEO would have to contend with and therefore the skills and traits a leader would need to take the company forward. Consumers' needs were changing and widely varied, and so were opportunities for growth. In developed countries, the economic downturn was pushing consumers toward lower-priced products. Meanwhile, economic growth in emerging markets meant that hundreds of millions of people were gaining the wherewithal to improve the quality of their lives. P&G needed a leader who understood the complexity of meeting diverse consumer needs through both innovation and cost.

McDonald stood out as a candidate well equipped to build on the company's momentum and consumer focus and take P&G to a new level. In June 2009, he was named chief executive officer, and on January 1, 2010, he became chairman as well, completing the handoff. A West Point graduate who joined P&G in 1980, McDonald expected to spend his whole career in Cincinnati. Instead he developed his leadership skills in a series of assignments in Canada, Japan, Belgium, and the Philippines—where he saw firsthand how P&G products affected people's lives, sometimes providing affordable health and hygiene benefits that were truly transformational. P&G's restated purpose—"to touch and improve more people's lives, in more parts of the world, more completely"—

follows directly from McDonald's global experiential learning, and he has already started down that road. After bringing the cost structure in line with the economic downturn, he announced a new initiative to have one billion additional consumers using P&G products within five years—in China, India, Brazil, Africa. With people such as Melanie Healey and Deb Henretta in the pipeline, P&G is poised to make his vision a reality.

CONCLUSIONS

Developing talent through experiences expands capability and capacity in the four major components of talent: personal traits, skill mix, relationship building, and judgment about people and business. It was a smart decision to provide Deb Henretta and Melanie Healey with assignments in which they could grow exponentially in all four areas in a short period of time. This is learning by doing, and no book or classroom teaching can substitute for it.

- **Personal traits.** Healey developed a quick sensitivity to changes in key variables, and the ability to read the social dynamics of a group. Henretta came to see past cultural differences to extract an individual's real meaning. She learned to restrain herself from making conclusions before hearing all sides of the story. Healey and Henretta have shown unmistakably the most important item in talent—the inner drive to learn and then convert learning into their DNA.
- **Skills.** In America Henretta ran one category. In Singapore she is running all categories in fifteen countries, places with different cultures, consumer behaviors, and distribution channels. This kind of experience expands cognitive bandwidth in deciding strategy, allocating resources, and developing competitive advan-

tages. Healey had a breadth of experiences in South America and Mexico, then deepened her knowledge and insticts in one of P&G's businesses. She learned to drill down to the important details and trust others' expertise.

- **Relationships.** Henretta's job in Singapore posed a challenge. She had to develop relationships with the executive, legislative, and regulatory agencies of fifteen governments and deal with all kinds of regulatory constraints and logistical impediments. She is now a key player with the strategy and planning committee of the government of Singapore. Her capacity to deal with the broad business of P&G has grown manyfold. In Healey's first days with P&G, her relationships among the team members and with constituents were key to breaking into the Brazil market. Later, her relationships with former colleagues and mentors helped her transition to new cultures and address different business challenges.

- **Judgment.** When the scope of Healey's job outstripped her expertise, she had the good judgment to assemble a team whose capabilities complemented her own and whose expertise she trusted. In Henretta's Singapore assignment, ambiguity is a constant. Information is seldom timely, often not accurate, and generally incomplete compared with what she was used to when working at P&G headquarters. It's a great challenge to judgment to know what information to use, which sources to trust, and whose recommendation and opinion should be given higher weight. Similarly, assumptions about consumers, competition, and national trends are always subject to change, and judgment is required to know which old rules of thumb to discard and which new ones to develop. Such a dynamic environment is a huge crucible of leadership development.

. . .

In every company we've seen so far, it's a given that the leaders being developed are general managers. That's not the case for companies in fields such as science and technology, where specialists don't get many opportunities to develop general management skills. In the next chapter we'll see how one technology company has created a new breed combining both disciplines.

Chapter 7

CREATING a NEW BREED of GENERAL MANAGERS
How Agilent Turns Technologists into Business Leaders

O ur increasingly specialized world requires top business leaders with specialized knowledge. The need is clearest in science- and technology-based industries, and in financial services with its ever more sophisticated mathematical tools. But leaders in industries you wouldn't necessarily think of as expertise-based also need specialized knowledge. A hospital chain CEO, for example, has to know the ins and outs of public policy to work well with regulatory agencies. A case in point is Kaiser Permanente CEO George Halvorson, who has all but made a second career of writing and advising about health care policy. Retailing CEOs, whose companies face fast-changing consumer tastes and proliferating market segments, need deep merchandising expertise and a solid grasp of logistics.

Most companies have long relied on leaders whose specialty is managing—that is, general managers—to take care of business. General managers develop their skills by running profit-and-loss centers, learning from experience in a way that no management course can provide. But it's hard for managers who aren't grounded in the discipline of an expertise-based company to lead it effectively. They may not be able to identify salient business issues because they can't probe their subordinates to get to the real causes of operating or competitive problems or recognize a breakthrough idea. They aren't equipped to make the best decisions about strategic direction, resource allocation, goals, and key hires.

Companies led by domain experts have their own problems: the leaders rarely know how a business makes money. They get promoted within the silos of their functions or specialties, where there are no P&L opportunities to develop managerial skills. Bringing in seasoned general managers from outside runs up against the first problem we described, and also makes CEO succession planning problematic.

Bill Sullivan faced this dilemma when he took over as Agilent Technologies' CEO in 2005. His company was full of experts but shy on general management talent. How he squared the circle is an invaluable lesson for any company facing the same issue.

BUILDING BENCH STRENGTH

Sullivan knew exactly what he wanted to do. Spun off from Hewlett-Packard in 1999, Agilent included a mixed bag of technology businesses. The centerpiece was the one that made scientific and technical measuring instruments, and Sullivan would focus entirely on them, shedding all the other businesses. His aim was nothing less than to make Agilent "the world's premier measurement company" by matching its scientific and technical expertise with management smarts, including sharply focused strategies and marketing skill. It was a bold plan, but Sullivan had just the right leadership qualities for it, and would play a large role in executing it.

The key to his plans would be what he called "a best-in-class general management bench" made up of leaders with both top-notch technical abilities and outstanding managerial skills. This rarity in the technology sector, he saw, would give him a powerful competitive advantage. He began by reorganizing Agilent from a functional structure to a decentralized one, with each business unit responsible for its own P&L. The P&L structure would develop the kind of leaders he needed, and it would make Agilent competitive in other ways as well. While a functional structure has certain cost advantages, today's global markets require lightning-fast decision making, which is difficult in functionally organized companies. Silos such as marketing or finance report to the CEO, who then must integrate the decisions made by each silo. By the time a decision goes up and down the elevators, the opportunity may be lost, or the crisis escalated beyond salvaging. Further, the company is dependent on a CEO who may not have the ability to do everything.

Sullivan's views on leadership also made him a natural-born master of talent. A key part of his plan was to put leaders front and center in developing other leaders. He decreed that Agilent's division managers would be responsible for building organizational capability and holding their direct reports responsible for doing the same. This would be every bit as important as delivering financial performance, and would get substantial weight in calculating their compensation.

Sullivan, who spent his career at HP and was Agilent's COO before taking over, combines the exactitude of a technologist with business acumen and the hands-on, proprietary manner of a small-business owner. His key top leaders shared his mind-set and also brought outside perspective to their jobs. Adrian Dillon, the chief financial officer before he became Skype's chief financial and administration officer in June 2010, was an economist by training who had been CFO of Eaton Corp. Ron Nersesian, president of the Electronic Measurement Group, is an engineer who worked for HP most of his career but left for a few years to head marketing and then serve as vice president and general manager for an oscilloscope manufacturer before returning to Agilent. As Agilent spun off its unwanted businesses, Sullivan, Nersesian, and Dillon reviewed the leaders of the businesses that would stay, looking for those who had what it would take to execute the changes required in the new model. Several were removed and replaced either with top talent from other companies or by people brought up from below.

Sullivan's premise was that the raw material existed within Agilent and that the people needed to be found, nurtured, educated, and coached. But the new leaders would need to acquire a lot of general management skills in short order. Traditional classroom training wouldn't do the job: the executive education and development programs most companies use are more often than not superficial and narrow.

Sullivan asked Agilent's Leadership and Development Team, headed by Teresa Roche, to design a customized set of learning programs that he called the Enterprise Curriculum. It included a basic three-day course for all new leaders and an ongoing series of programs tailored for leaders at different levels. Sullivan and other senior leaders spent considerable amounts of time taking part in them, and coaches led the participants through business simulation exercises that ground them in the realities of the topics.

Two Agilent programs are especially worth mentioning, because they're directly linked to building capabilities that help a person become a general manager. One teaches leaders the essential skill of balancing the many conflicting demands of a business by making trade-offs, such as top-line growth versus bottom-line growth or cost cutting versus customer service. The integration of these items in a fast-changing world is what makes a general manager effective. But making trade-offs is not the sort of thing you can master by watching PowerPoint presentations. Sullivan's programs get the leaders' hands dirty by putting them through intensive real-world exercises, working in teams with plenty of coaching, and using real company data to develop their decisions.

Equally important to general managers is a solid understanding of how to analyze customer needs and segment markets. This is typically a weak area in companies like Agilent.

WHAT MAKES A GENERAL MANAGER?

The hallmark of general managers is business acumen—the ability to see and understand a business in its totality. The other fundamentals for a general manager at a minimum are:

- Understanding how the business makes money relative to the competition and perceived opportunities

- Seeing the business as whole, positioning it ahead of others in relation to the speed and character of change on the outside, and making strategic bets that will position the business for the future

- Knowing who the customers are, what the segmentation is, and what customer behavior is

- Choosing the right set of business goals and being prepared to manage risks

- Developing and continuously maintaining competitive advantage, including building new capabilities and shedding those no longer relevant

- Delivering both short- and long-term business results

- Working with people who are expert in a wide variety of disciplines and drilling deep into the issues they raise and solutions they propose from the perspective of the business as a whole

- Developing alternative solutions by changing assumptions on the issue at hand

- Generating and allocating resources across the business as a whole and balancing both the short and long terms

- Mastering the numbers to deliver quarter-by-quarter results

People in most scientific companies selling to scientific customers are technology-driven. They often lack a feel for the customer and the ability to do market segmentation. Agilent's programs begin with an outside expert who explains the art of market segmentation. The executives go on to learn about needs in Agilent's markets and how the company can meet them. Like the program on trade-offs, it's hands-on work with lots of coaching. Sullivan recruited a boutique consulting firm specializing in market segmentation to work with the nascent general managers in creating actual new market segments for their businesses. In other words, the firm not only teaches them to fish but also helps them hook the first one.

COACH IN CHIEF

Because he was creating a leadership bench with unique characteristics, Sullivan needed new ways of measuring their performance. Assessments at Agilent are based on three criteria: strategic direction, financial results, and the success of leaders in building what Sullivan calls organizational capability. This last one is uncommon—most companies base performance assessments just on financial results and the execution of strategy—and by itself signals the importance Agilent attaches to developing leaders.

To get as much input as possible, the assessments are also informed by a semi-annual employee audit focused on leadership effectiveness in such areas as customer orientation, speed and timing of decision making, and decisiveness. "We look particularly at speed of decision making bringing things to closure in a clear transparent way," says Jean Halloran, Agilent's head of HR. "We recently added a few questions that are aimed at leaders' progress in bet placing and risk taking in the area of innovation. And that's become a very powerful indicator of how leaders are doing."

Senior officers and HR review business heads twice a

year, and once a year they do a deep dive into business leaders' performance, which is the basis for setting compensation and rewards. But the individual division heads review their general managers themselves. "The line of accountability for organization and leadership development stays squarely on the shoulders of the business presidents," says Roche. And while they use the metrics HR has designed for the whole organization, they can add other metrics and tools that they think will be particularly useful in their areas.

Sullivan, however, has built a parallel social system with himself at the center, and he often works outside the bounds of formal assessment processes. "He likes that we give him tools and bring in thought leaders to shape his thinking," says Roche. "But unlike companies that rely only on very defined talent review calendars, Bill just makes it a part of conversations." He makes a point of wandering through the businesses to listen, ask questions, and triangulate judgments. "You've got to see what's happening in people's own backyard," he says. "That's one reason I spend so much time on the road. You want to see people in front of customers. You want to see how they engage with their own people. And you just learn a lot by visiting the divisions and talking to the people. As a result of all this, it's an ongoing dialogue." Sullivan is in fact coach in chief. He role-models the rigor and follow-through he expects throughout, and his lessons percolate down.

Sullivan's social system reflects his hands-on style, and also unease about judging people through formal processes. Too often, he says, these rehash performance evaluations without digging deeper. "You really don't have a discussion of how this individual is able to deal with ambiguity, how are they able to build the team, whether the results are really their results," he says. "It's very easy to get locked and loaded on somebody, particularly if that person has got a good track record for a couple of years. But is that person still the right person with the right skill set to take you into the future?" Sullivan fosters intimacy, though he doesn't use that word.

No less important than assessing is stepping outside of the

processes to reassure and encourage people. For example, says Sullivan, "it's amazing, even at the executive level, how much difficulty people have setting absolute measurable *clear* strategic intent and content of strategy. Anytime that I get an organization where it's not clear what they're doing, it's obviously a point of discussion. Sometimes they're afraid, they're trying to guess the right answer. Some of it they don't know because it's a complicated problem. And sometimes—in most of the cases—they just need a little nudging saying it is okay: 'These are the top three priorities, that's what you're going to do, and let's get on with it. Don't agonize, and we'll talk about it again next time we have a discussion.'

"You've got to have an environment where people know that it's not incriminating to talk about the strength and weaknesses of an executive. I'm a firm believer that you've got to be able to take personal risk. You've got to show passion to be able to drive people." Whenever he talks about strategy or assesses plans, people, or financial performance, he is maniacal about asking about the development of organizational capability: which leaders are being developed and in which way, what new skills need to be developed and which need to be deemphasized, who is coming along to be a leader, which people need to go to specific leadership programs. He integrates all these questions, and his interest as a role model is followed by others. It is a slow but steady and sure way for building the general management leadership culture of the future.

At board meetings, Sullivan gives an assessment of each executive who reports to him, focusing on how well the person has built organizational capability and how well he or she has set strategic intent. "We tell the board that two-thirds of the compensation is based on performance and the other third is based on building organizational capability by building the leaders of the future." (Agilent measures results and compensation every six months because, says Sullivan, "I always thought you get weird things happening when you just have these yearly targets.")

But he always puts the numbers in context. For example, the financial meltdown provided him with a teaching moment for his directors. "The easiest thing for a board or anybody to measure is the financial results," he says. "This year everybody missed their numbers, right? I went in there and gave my own assessment. I said, 'Look, the results missed by $1 billion.' We missed the results, but here's what happened: we organized the company in terms of identifying the three high-potential senior vice presidents to run each of the businesses. I pointed out the organizational capability decisions that Ron Nersesian had made—and he had to make some really tough decisions. He combined into larger divisions, which means there were a bunch of winners, a bunch of losers. He managed through that superbly.

"The process forced a more open dialogue and gave the board a more balanced view of what the leaders had achieved. And they were very, very supportive."

DEVELOPING OPPORTUNITIES FOR PEOPLE

Ron Nersesian, president of Agilent's biggest division, the Electronic Measurement Group, is equally impassioned about building leaders. "Developing other people's talent is the whole company at the end of the day," he says. "Our products all are time-perishable. We might have a product where we could charge $100,000 for it three years ago, and now we're struggling to get $20,000. When you look at the profitability of that product, even with the experience curve, you see the profit or the gross margin going from $80,000 to close to zero. So it's a very, very dramatic swing.

"Products perish. The only thing that stays is the institutional learning and the development of the skills and the capabilities that we have of our people."

Growing people, Nersesian adds, is often about making sure they have opportunities. "If you don't develop opportunity, you don't develop people. All you have are diminishing assets, which are products and solutions, and you have people who are leaving, and the company basically goes down. So it's a never-ending quest to make sure that we develop those opportunities for people." He adds, "I am always looking and scouting informally in the organization, interviewing and talking with folks, assessing them versus opportunities that are there."

There aren't many companies where an executive would reach two levels down to give close personal attention to a manager unhappy in his job. But Nersesian did just that when he noticed that Niels Faché was growing restive. A native of Belgium, Faché was an engineer with academic interests. "But I had that entrepreneurial bug," he says. "I was always attracted to the challenging and the adventurous." While doing postdoctoral work, he took a job at HP Santa Rosa, California, in 1990. There he saw an opportunity to commercialize a circuit simulation program based on technology he and others had developed at the University of Ghent. After he returned to Belgium in 1991, he pulled together a product development team of researchers and PhD students at the university. Organized as a company named Alphabit, the enterprise was spun off from the university and signed an agreement with HP. Its first product, released in 1994, grew to become the market leader in its segment, and when HP offered to buy the business and hire him, Faché accepted gladly. "It would let me go beyond R&D, allow my team to get more product responsibility, and build closer relationships with the customers," he says.

Faché then worked as a first-line manager in product planning and marketing for a variety of its businesses, and was put in charge of software product planning. He liked the job at first. "I put a new road map in place, and it was exciting," he says. But once the work went into the maintenance mode, it lost its allure. "Everything was about making line extensions. It was no longer aligned with my intensity and drive."

By 2003, four years after Agilent was created from HP's

measurement businesses, Faché began to think about striking out on his own. He told the HR manager about his restlessness. She sent word to Nersesian, who was then vice president of the Design Validation Division, and he decided to take a closer look at Faché, who was two reporting levels below him. "What I discovered was that this is a person who was entrepreneurial, action-oriented, and had a drive for speed and results. In this long-term planning role, he was mismatched.

"So I created a new role for someone to explore who could we merge with, who could we acquire, what type of partnerships could we form, and put him in it, effectively bringing him up a level to report to me directly. Working with him in this role, I had a chance to test him and grow him and understand even more clearly where his strengths were."

Nersesian took charge, much like a sports coach bringing along a promising player. He even went so far as to accompany Faché on a trip to Korea, where he was to look into a potential partnership. There he discovered that his protégé needed coaching in setting high-level strategic goals. The negotiations began to bog down as Faché focused on the technical details of which products might fit and which might not. "He didn't have any of the skills on how to negotiate and how to win over this partner," says Nersesian. "So I stepped in, sort of leading by example, and said, 'Let me start with the relationship.' "

Says Faché: "One thing I learned from Ron and appreciated was his strategic focus on priorities and the ability to simplify a situation to its critical parameters. When we engineers deal with a problem, we tend to be extremely analytical and risk-averse, so we go into these decision-making processes that take a long time—it's our comfort zone. Ron immediately starts synthesizing the issues: what is the opportunity about, what do we need to do to make it attractive?"

In a meeting with the company's CEO and a couple of their top executives, Faché watched as Nersesian painted a picture of a win-win situation, talking about such things as values, Agilent's approach to partnering with other companies, and the complementary capabilities of the two companies. "And then the technical details and issues became second-order," Nersesian says. "Anytime there was an issue it was like, 'Hey, we know we're both working together to make this happen,' and we would compromise to get to where we needed to go."

Faché recalls vividly the lesson he learned: "It was one of my best career experiences. We had to come to an agreement with this company. Instead of getting stuck in the details, we worked out a memorandum of understanding in a two-hour meeting and dealt with details afterward. It required around-the-clock work, but we got through it because we had this high-level agreement that became a context for the companies to work with. It was very exciting and rewarding—we had never before launched a partnership in such a short time."

After just six months, Nersesian concluded that Faché was ready for a considerably bigger job that needed Faché's brand of technical expertise, and made him head of the mobile broadband division. Faché calls it "a leap of faith" on Nersesian's part. Though he'd had managerial experience in different functions over the years, he had suddenly gone from being a first- and second-level manager to being general manager of a division with the biggest problems in the company. "The largest number of people I managed previously was sixty. This organization had four hundred people and revenues of almost $300 million, and it was really broken. It had its own culture and was very isolated. It did not have good relationships with the CEO, the sales force, and one of our partners. People were nervous about their positions."

Faché was understandably nervous about his own position and wondered whether Ron hadn't made a mistake. "Driving change is hard in that kind of situation," he says. "It can be demoralizing and lonely. You question yourself, you face opposition. After the first month I declared our new strategic intent, which would be more on R&D than manufacturing. Not everybody on my direct staff was comfortable that I knew enough about the business to do this—this went back to the Agilent culture, which was that you needed to be in the business twenty years to know what to do."

But Nersesian felt that Faché had the drive and energy to get the job done if he got some help in making judgments about people. He coached with care. For example, Faché would check in with Nersesian as he went about reshuffling and replacing leaders in his organization. "I knew that he was such a very good judge of leaders that I didn't make decisions without talking with him," says Faché. "He was always there to provide moral support. But he wanted me to get my own feel for those decisions, so that while he was always there to help, I maintained ownership." He also got help from Agilent's HR staff. "There was always someone there when I needed a neutral party who understood the issues and could chat about situations involving people or help in structuring a change management program."

Faché grew in the job, developing a new understanding of leadership under Nersesian's tutelage. "I'm very driven and competitive, and my own synthesis guides my decision making. At the same time I have learned a lot about the importance of relying on others and empowering leaders in the organization. Ron has guided me with concrete suggestions and ideas while allowing me to maintain strong ownership."

In addition to what Nersesian taught him, he says, he recently got a lot of help from reading Stephen Covey's *The Speed of Trust*. "I realized that building a high-trust organization requires being aware, listening to feedback, and constantly taking the time to reflect. You can never spend enough time in the change management process to get that organizational alignment, because it will take a while before you know if the change will take."

The Mobile Broadband has gone through a major transformation but the work is still in progress. Agilent has combined it with two other divisions in the Electronics Measurement Group. Faché is now GM of EMG's external business development. Says Nersesian with a touch of pride, "Now Niels is able to run a major business. He is a tested P&L GM. He's on the executive level, a vice president, and he's doing a super job."

A TALENT MANAGEMENT ENTREPRENEUR

CFO Adrian Dillon made major contributions to Agilent's transformation in the eight and half years before he left to join Skype. Unusual for a CFO, he turned out to be a sort of entrepreneur of talent management, using his position at the center of the company's information flow to spot, develop, and deploy it. (This is something that CFOs everywhere might want to think about.)

Like Nersesian, Dillon kept an eye out for talent that got overlooked or lost. His venue was the performance matrix (with performance on the horizontal axis and values on the vertical one) used in the formal evaluation processes. It's natural, as he points out, for executives reviewing a matrix to focus their attention on the upper right corner. But giving short shrift to the other areas is a recipe for wasting talent. Take an individual who has been stuck in the lower left for some time—a "stable," doing steady but unspectacular work. In many organizations—perhaps most—that person would have no hope of being promoted. But in a company like Agilent, one leader or another would likely have had occasion to notice he had some potential—they saw it in an encounter, or heard good things from other people.

Then, says Dillon, "we would talk about him, asking, 'What's the problem? What does he need?' Maybe it's 'Well, he's really good, but he does not have executive presence and he won't shut up.' Okay, then, have we gotten him a coach? Maybe he ought to be thinking about how he communicates to his boss, as opposed to a colleague. And I've seen people move from the lower left to the upper right as a result."

Dillon recalls one especially gratifying example, an accountant who had been a "stable" for years before Dillon arrived. "He was very quiet, almost withdrawn, doing what we call the global infrastructure operations accounting and controlling." Then came the transformation of Agilent from a diversified technology company to a pure play in measurements, with its attendant downsizing of infrastructure and churn of leadership. "We needed somebody for a new job, keeping track of the investment commitments, savings commitments, the pace of doing all of that restructuring, and ensuring that we got the savings and would know when we succeeded. We said, 'Let's take a chance on this guy because he's a superb controller and we think he's got potential. Let's see with a little bit more light of day, a little bit more exposure, whether he's able to rise to the occasion.' And he just blossomed. He worked well with the functional leaders in establishing and tracking the savings goals and costs and reporting to the executive council once a month on how we're doing. He visibly gained confidence, and the confidence of others."

The man's startling progress emboldened Dillon to place a bigger bet on him: he put him in charge of investor relations. "And in two and a half years, he went from not having a clue about how to do it to absolutely mastering it—absolutely being a superb representative of Agilent's senior leadership with investors, communicating our strategies, communicating our results. Not only that—and this is how you tell when you got a good one—but taking the feedback and the questions and comments of the investing public and turning that back to Bill and me and saying, 'Here's what they're thinking, here's what they're worried about, and here's what they want to see in order to have more confidence that the operating model is robust, or that our strategies do make sense.' Only the best in an IR job would do that, as opposed to just being a mouthpiece.

"And so he became a player at the table. As a result, we've moved him higher again. Our recent acquisition of Varian, Inc., will move our bioanalytical business from being about 45 percent of the company to nearly 60 percent. I've just asked this person to become the group CFO for that combined business.

"Here's somebody who five or six years ago was just one of the masses of midlevel finance managers, and today is going to run one of the three groups that constitute Agilent and the one that's the fastest-growing and where we're pinning our hopes."

BUILDING ORGANIZATIONAL CAPABILITY

Dillon arrived at Agilent in the midst of the 2001 high-tech bust, and his first priority was to deal with the consequences. But as he drove cost cutting and reorganization, he was building for the future: the Office of Finance Reengineering he organized was also charged with people development. Says Dillon, "One of the things I wanted to do was to establish a more formal program of campus hiring and recruitment to ensure that we got enough young fresh blood so that we all didn't grow old together, just reinforcing our old ways. We kept that going even through the darkest days of the recession, and we've kept it going through this one as well—though with far less resistance, because its value has been proved."

He set up an honorary group called the CFO Club to coach by example in a big way. Every year the finance staff leaders would identify twelve people from the organization who exemplified the best leadership characteristics. "Anyone could qualify, from somebody who'd just joined us out of college to a group CFO. By identifying and celebrating these folks—and then everybody else watching as they got the promotions and the development opportunities—people began to say, 'Oh, that's what he's looking for,' and they began to emulate those characteristics. They'd identify that this person is able to challenge the status quo, this one really takes care of his people and communicates honestly and candid and frequently, this one thinks strategically and is willing to take risks. You can read about these things in a book, but it's when you see the person that you really understand the leadership characteristics we're looking for."

Dillon next started what he calls his leadership organizational review, designed to focus on high-potential leaders—the ones destined to be among those who are effectively in high-leverage decision-making positions.

The review centers on a classic nine-block matrix with performance on one axis and potential on the other. (For an example, see page 273.) "On the performance criteria, 1 is doing steady-Eddie work, 2 is doing really good work, 3 is redefining the job. On the potential criteria, 1 is what we call stable, 2 is promotable, which means that they are promotable up at least one level—or if not up, because that might not be available, able to take on a bigger, broader responsibility within the same band—and 3 is high-potential, which means they're capable of at least two levels or more from where they are today. We do that in the form of, literally, an org chart, where you have people and you have a discussion of here's who they are, how long have they been in their position, what is their performance and potential ranking, some sort of a summary of what do they want to be when they grow up."

Dillon and his fourteen or so direct reports conducted the review each August, going over what each has put together about his or her people. The group evaluated each leader's direct reports and the people one level below that. Then the leaders went back to drive the process through their functions.

The matrix is a classic evaluation tool, but it's also one of those formal processes that can lead evaluators astray if they don't know the people in question well. For example, says Dillon, "some people are put in 'stable' because they self-select. They love what they're doing. They have a balance in life and they're not mobile at the moment. Someone else may have unlimited potential and aims to become a CFO but is green. We will have an explicit conversation about what kind of experience he has, what kind will he require in order to realize what he wants to be in the future at Agilent, or if not at Agilent, somewhere else."

The leaders are also expected to have clear ideas about their succession candidates. "We ask if they know folks not in their function but whom they are aware of through participation in my monthly staff meetings. Could any of them take the job? This is to encourage cross-fertilization, which is something that I feel very strongly about."

A month later they meet again in Dillon's staff meeting and spend most of the day going over the matrix. As is typical, the focus is mainly on the upper right box, the people who are highly promotable and great-performing. But they also take pains to look in the other quadrants for high-potential or promotable people who are not at the top level of performance— say, because they are still early in their jobs. "We talk about them," says Dillon. "What are they doing well, what are they doing poorly? If they want to be this, what can we do? We learn more about what people want, whether they're mobile, where they're located. And through that we learn more about each other. And then some magic occurs."

The magic is a change in the social process that opens leaders' eyes to the possibilities in switching people from function to function. In the early days, says Dillon, people at Agilent—as in most organizations—resisted cross-fertilization. "They were a bit parochial, a bit defensive, and quite possessive," he says. But as people became more familiar with the idea, they began to see the upside. Leaders came to realize that it offered them new sources of talent—or a way to move out people who didn't fit in their businesses but could do well somewhere else. "The evidence is that it has now been driven throughout the organizations of the different functions," says Dillon. "Now we have a group of people who are constantly trying to steal each other's best people, and provide opportunities within their own group to get that fresh blood." The people being moved also welcomed it when they saw that it offered new ways to gain experience. "It doesn't always have to be up; it can be across. And by going across you can get up faster than if you just waited in your silo for the next person to retire or move on. That's when people really started to get excited about it."

To help the magic along, Dillon includes moving people around among his metrics for building organizational capability. "We set a target that we have to move 50 percent of folks who we identify as being high-potential and ready now within the next twelve months. We measure ourselves against that on a quarterly basis. Finally, we do this process of comparing the folks and updating that twice a year.

"At the end of the day, what I'm trying to do is build a team that's more of a repertory company than a collection of world experts. It's people who may not be able to do the job as well as the current incumbent, but could if they needed to."

A DESIGNATED CHANGE AGENT

Thanks to a mentor at Eaton Corp., his former employer, Dillon had an epiphany nineteen years ago that changed his management style—and his life. "My career is sort of composed of two halves," he says. "I started out life as an economist and as a forecaster. And I became a very good economist and a very good forecaster with a national reputation for the quality of my forecasts. And part of the characteristic of an economist and forecaster is that you have to have the courage of your convictions, because by definition, nobody can predict the future very well. You can't be just part of the pack. When you're wrong, if you're insightful and if you identify early why you're wrong, you can retain the confidence of the people because you're providing additional insight. All of that's by way of saying that I became one of those guys who was willing and able to take risks to say that the emperor has no clothes—to say, 'I don't think we should be doing this because of this'; data-based, but also wrapped in a theory or hypothesis. Or 'I think we should be doing something else.'

"So I became sort of a designated change agent. Whenever somebody smelled a rat or a problem and people didn't want to put it on the table, they'd kind of send me at it. And through doing that I was able to develop my relationships with businesses and with people and to move up very quickly in my career to strategic planning and treasury and pension fund management and capital structuring management, and then, ultimately, to the vice president of planning and development. All on the basis of being, if you will, the smartest guy in the room.

"Very early in my tenure at planning and development, we were evaluating an acquisition and I was about to hold a review meeting. As we're about to start, my boss wanders in. He says, 'Don't mind me, I'm just going to sit in the back and listen for a while.' So we had this very good, very efficient meeting, where I called it to order and asked for the reports from the individuals. And then I said, 'Okay, so here's what we need to do next. Jim, you do this. Sue, you do that. Shirley, you go investigate this thing. And Jim, you go and make sure that we've got this right and check with the lawyers. And let's all reconvene next week, same time. Okay. Thank you very much.' Off we go.

"I was quite impressed with myself. Everybody was very clear, concise, understood what their assignments were, and the meeting even ended on time. Everybody leaves, but as I'm about to walk out the door my boss—my mentor, the CFO—who had lingered behind, pulled me aside, literally grabbed me by the arm, and said, 'Hold on a second, I want to talk to you.' Closed the door and goes, 'You know, Dillon, you are in real trouble.' And I kind of went, 'What?' I'm thinking, *I just held a great meeting. I demonstrated mastery of what I'm doing. What do you mean I'm in real trouble?*

"He said to me, 'That was a great meeting, but your problem is that you still think your job is to be the smartest guy in the room. It's not. Not anymore. If you want to have my job or a job like mine, at this point you can't do it on your own anymore. Or even if you can, you've basically consigned yourself to this job for the rest of your career. At this point, what you've got to do is not prove that you're the smartest guy in the room, but make everybody in the room think that *they're* the smartest guy in the room. You've got to teach them what you know and what you do, not tell them. You've got to demonstrate through actions and through coaching and through how you ask questions that you reveal in a more Socratic way to get them to think of things. To get them to think about how to do this. And to learn from you in a way that when you're not here and you've moved on to your next job, they can carry on.'

"Even when I talk about it to this day, I still get the shivers down my spine. Because I knew on the spot, he was right. It was like a whole new world just opens up before your eyes. And ironically, because I was an economist and forecaster, I've always been good at explaining things in front of audiences. So it was an easy transition to make because I could just go into my, if you will, professorial mode, or the Socratic, explaining to people in terms they understand, but making them feel like they really do understand it and not like dummies. And so it becomes a teaching, a coaching type of environment, as opposed to a command-and-control and direct environment.

"This was one of those seminal moments in one's career where you make the fundamental decision: are you going to be an individual contributor and continue to do individual genius stuff and be the smartest guy in the room, or are you going to leverage your capabilities through others, increasing the impact of what I can bring to the table, but also freeing myself up for what I can do next? And it was on that day my management style changed."

PASSING A TEST

How is Sullivan's bold innovation working out? He points to the downturn of 2009 as a quick and successful test. "We made the decision that this is going to be a new normal. The company is going to be smaller, and we just need to immediately resize the corporate infrastructure. This is what we are going to do. This is what we're not going to do. It was absolute clarity and strategic intent. And because of the organization that Adrian Dillon had built since he came here, they were able to start the execution instantaneously." (When Dillon left for Skype, a successor was ready and able to take his place immediately.)

Nersesian's Electronic Measurement Group also rose to the occasion. "You can't get a better example of how an organization reacts to adversity," says Sullivan. "If you can follow our leadership model, it allows an organization—in his case, of ten thousand people—to react very, very quickly." By contrast, he says, during the tech crash of 2001 people were late in responding. "And when you delay responding, your response isn't very thoughtful." At the same time, senior leaders turned the organization to thinking about the opportunities rather than hammering repeatedly on financial targets and head counts. "The coaching Ron had given me was twofold," says Sullivan. "First, our $45 billion market may have gone down 20 percent, but there's still a big market. So what is the market segmentation, where is the money? Where are people spending money in this downturn moving forward? And so we engaged a group called Parthenon to help us create a dialogue about the market to customers moving forward. Secondly, in the environment we had instituted, we were not going to beat people up on the numbers but really go back and have the discussion about where's the customer, where's the competition, where's our investment, and why?

"As a result of that we had a much more balanced discussion of where to go from here. It allowed people to not have a fear issue. Instead we listened to them and helped them allocate their resources where they thought the greatest opportunities were going forward. I, and Adrian when available, went around to every division and had a dialogue about what they were doing, and how some of the teams would be willing to make more focused bets.

"Because we had moved so quickly, we were able to increase our investment in our bioanalytical and life science opportunity. That business was down 10 percent for the first time since the early 1980s, but we didn't make any cuts there because that's the greatest growth opportunity moving forward. I honestly believe we're going to come out of this downturn as a much stronger company."

CONCLUSIONS

Expertise-based companies can create value and competitive advantage if they are able to develop leaders who have both the technical and general management skills needed to see the business as a whole. Only a small percentage of such companies have the systems and tools to do this, and even fewer have a formal system of reviews and compensation that's needed to move from wishful thinking to having general managers in place.

Especially in emerging markets—India, China, Brazil,

and Indonesia, for example—there is a large population of bright but underutilized people working in silos, particularly information systems. They aspire to be business heads, country heads, or corporate CEOs, and they are frustrated by the absence of social systems like Agilent's. Capitalizing on this raw talent is the foundation for future growth anywhere in the world. As we saw with Dillon and Nersesian, each leader has the responsibility to spot raw talent and get it to the place it deserves, thereby nurturing the capacity of not only the talent spotter but also the organization as a whole.

Though it's also about an expertise-based company, the next chapter takes you to a different place altogether. Novartis has found a novel way to turn specialists into high-potential leaders. Its unique tools help them to discover what they aspire to and what makes them effective, and to draw on hidden inner resources to achieve their goals. Don't sneer at Novartis's unorthodox stress on self-awareness. It has produced a superb group of leaders who outcompete bigger rivals.

Chapter 8

DISCOVERING the LEADER WITHIN

How Novartis Builds Leadership Capability with Self-Knowledge

How much do you really know about your inner core—your beliefs, values, emotional reserves, and feelings? Do you know what triggers your reactions? What makes you anxious and what gives you peace?

How often have you asked yourself a question along these lines?

- How did I miss it? It was so obvious, practically staring me in the face.
- I should have listened to my gut and not done the deal. I knew there would be problems down the road.
- I saw that Chris was faltering. Why didn't I replace him sooner?
- Why can't I give honest feedback? What am I afraid of?
- Why didn't I divest that languishing business unit when I took over? Was I wrong to think that the business unit manager could turn it around? Or did I care too much what my predecessor would think?

Your drive, your psychological likes and dislikes, your motives to achieve goals, and the values by which you achieve those goals are all part of the emotional etchings buried in your inner core. They shape the way you make decisions, exercise judgment, and take action. They affect the people who come into contact with you: subordinates, peers, family. They affect how you see these people. Your inner core determines how clearly you see and perceive, what you select as important, how you think and act, and the quality of your judgments, decisions, and relationships. It affects the way you frame an issue, how you search for information, and from whom. And it very often does these things without Tweeting them to your conscious mind.

Becoming aware of and dealing with your inner core is at the center of leadership effectiveness and development. The more acutely you're aware of it, the better you will be as a leader. You'll be able to judge the fit between the job you now have and where your ambitions are leading you, align your values with your work, and in doing so release your energy and passion and overcome unconscious biases or fears that are tainting your judgment or behavior.

Examples abound of leaders whose emotional overdrive and desire to win for the sake of winning push them beyond the bounds of rationality. A classic case was Sir Fred Goodwin of Royal Bank of Scotland, whose determination to outbid Barclays in a struggle for the Netherlands-based bank ABN AMRO left RBS a ward of the British government. By contrast, Barclays CEO John Varley pulled back from the toxic race, leaving Barclays in a better position among its peers than ever. At the other end of the spectrum are inner confusion and self-doubt, especially during crises when you can't seem to get your arms around the situation. You look enviously at those who can solve problems others see as unsolvable. How do they do it? In part because they draw on their emotional strength and courage to redefine the context, realign the players, and recast the problem in a way that makes it tractable.

Take the example of Andrew Liveris, the CEO of Dow Chemical, when he found himself in a corner during the acquisition of Rohm & Haas. Dow's stock dropped 75 percent in the spring of 2009 from the double blow of the global financial meltdown and the Kuwaiti government's withdrawal from a $17.4 billion joint venture that would have provided $9 billion in cash to carry out the acquisition. Though the deal could destroy Dow's financial health, Liveris was compelled to complete it.

This kind of dilemma tests a person's inner core. The stress affected not only Liveris personally but the entire Dow organization as well. But he had the deep emotional reserves and self-confidence to believe that he could engineer a solution. His tenacity, confidence, and financial creativity made others believe he could pull the company out of the pit. He started by getting ideas from other CEOs who had confronted similar issues. He then convinced Warren Buffett and the family that partially owned Rohm & Haas to make an investment in Dow under a plan that included his pledge to sell assets not vital to the core business. Liveris made his case with confidence and logic, winning the support of his board, investors, creditors, and the rating agencies. Then he executed the plan on time. As of May 2010, Dow's stock price had rebounded almost to pre-stress levels, and he had mapped highly ambitious plans for the next three years.

Is this sort of inner-core strength purely God-given, or can it be developed and nurtured? For an answer we turn to the unusual and successful program for developing leadership talent created by Novartis, the global health care company that produces pharmaceuticals, vaccines, and other health-related products.

HELPING LEADERS UNMASK THEIR INNER CORE

Like every other leader in this book, Novartis chairman and former CEO Dr. Daniel Vasella pays close attention to selecting and developing leadership talent. He lists three leadership qualities that cannot be negotiated away: technical and interpersonal competence, ambition, and integrity. But unlike the others, he includes self-awareness among the development goals for his leaders. An MD by training, with a deep interest in psychology, Vasella believe that a person's abilities and character are driven by his or her inner core, which he defines as a combination of strengths and weaknesses, cognitive and interpersonal styles, and—most important—core values and life purposes. The clearer and deeper a leader's self-awareness, he believes, the more powerful and reliable that inner core becomes. This emphasis on leaders' self-awareness—on making them conscious of their unconscious—is unique in our experience.

Many companies, of course, use psychological assessment when they're looking at people for high-level jobs or considering them for promotion. Most executive search firms use psychologists to assess potential candidates, and specialist consulting firms do these assessments when coaching people. But the assessments are often disconnected from the specifics of the job and its business context, and the people undergoing the assessment often question their usefulness. Further, they are mainly for the benefit of the leaders' bosses and the HR staff.

Novartis's use of psychological assessment is far more sophisticated. Crucially, its distinctive version of talent mastery is designed specifically to help leaders know who they are so they can align their actions, decisions, and behaviors at work with their deepest values and sense of purpose. It gives them insight into their own psychological constructs and unmasks their unconscious thoughts. In the process of creating self-awareness, it builds an intimate connection between up-and-coming leaders and those at senior levels, which is useful for both leadership development and succession planning. Novartis credits this process with helping it move from hiring 80 percent of its top leadership from outside to finding 70 percent of it within.

Greater self-awareness in leaders has improved Novartis's strategy execution by preventing unconscious fears or needs from getting in the way of collaboration and calculated risk-taking. It has also raised productivity in R&D. In the pharmaceutical industry, it can take ten years or more for a product to move from initial concept to earning significant revenues, and the success ratio is dismal. Companies have tried many different approaches to improve their records. Often they reorganize the R&D function. For example, one company has used a venture capital model, breaking its large staff of experts into small independent teams that compete for funds. Novartis focuses instead on improving the quality of decisions in R&D by creating better linkages among scientists in different disciplines.

Vasella recruited a top-notch scientist from academia, Dr. Mark Fishman, to reorient Novartis's R&D machine toward better, more collaborative decision making. Fishman started by identifying scientists with leadership talent in Novartis's research function (called the Novartis Institutes for BioMedical Research). "Scientific expertise is a requirement to lead in R&D at Novartis, to be able to ask the right questions," Fishman says. "Then you need to make the scientists leaders in that environment. Many of those who came from academia had been weaving together teams and working within organizations, even if they didn't know they were doing it. So they had some of the right instincts from the start.

"But they have to understand each individual's possible contribution and be able to put these together in the right context. They have to tolerate the subversive, the person who is a pain in the neck but is making really important contributions. Clarity and honesty are important so that everyone in the room knows that the data are not being bent in any way. And everyone has to be made to feel valued, that they have a contribution they can make."

SELF-AWARENESS AND LEADERSHIP EFFECTIVENESS

Self-awareness can take many forms, any one of which can make a leader more effective. Simply identifying likes and dislikes and personal strengths and weaknesses can open a leader's eyes to the need for specific kinds of support. For example, Vasella recognized early on that he is not much of a process person. A successful CEO, however, has to run several key processes such as budgeting and succession planning. He realized he needed people to complement him in those areas.

While most companies stop at the level of recognizing personal strengths and weaknesses, particularly in competencies such as team building and strategic thinking, Novartis goes to the level of the unconscious, which becomes increasingly important as the scope of a leadership job increases. In bigger jobs, judgment must take more complexity into account and often becomes more intuitive. Most intuitive and instinctive responses are buried in the unconscious and past experiences. The quick, aggressive action that powered an executive up the ranks can become a liability. Neither linear logic nor gut instinct alone will sustain a leader at those higher levels. These factors point to one of the fundamentals of leadership: the greater the scope of a decision and the more variables and uncertainties there are, the more important it is for the leader to be aware of unconscious drives and biases that could affect emotions, reason, and intuition.

People in higher-level leadership positions also need to be aware of how others are affected by what they say—and don't say. In other words, they must think about second- and third-order consequences of their actions and look at an issue from varied angles. Human beings inevitably have blind spots, and developing self-awareness and a sense of wholeness as a person greatly sharpens a leader's ability to understand what others are experiencing and what drives them. A leader who lacks self-awareness or a feeling of inner balance will be handicapped and biased in evaluating, motivating, and inspiring other people as individuals and in teams.

In the culture of Western organizations, business leaders are generally expected to keep their emotions under control or at least not to show them. Too many interpret this as suppressing them to the point of ignoring them. Counsels Vasella, "When you have feelings like impatience and irritation, you have to ask yourself, 'Why am I feeling this? What is going on here to make me impatient or angry?' To use one's own emotional reactions as a diagnostic tool is very important."

Vasella describes how he pays attention to his own feelings in the course of daily business and tries to become more self-aware of the reasons for them: "In a discussion, an encounter, an interview, we all will have feelings and emotions. These emotions can be due to our own history. Or they can be the reflection of what is going on in the person or people we are with. If I become impatient in a meeting, it can have different causes. Perhaps people aren't telling me what's really true to them emotionally, what is really behind what they are saying. They are just playing roles and masking the reality as they see it. Or perhaps someone is very obsessional, going from one detail to the next detail to the next detail, or is simply superficial and talkative. Or perhaps there is something in the issue that troubles me and that I have not yet articulated for myself."

Being aware of your feelings in real time and pinning down what is triggering them will lead to much more incisive questioning and give-and-take with other people. That in turn will influence the behavior of others toward you. The moment you sort out the roots of those feelings, you begin to feel the generation of psychological energy and expansion of personal capacity.

TECHNIQUES FOR GOING DEEPER

As Novartis's CEO for fourteen years, from its inception in the 1996 merger of Ciba-Geigy and Sandoz, Vasella instituted a series of leadership development processes that have focused more and more on helping key executives to not only deepen their knowledge but also to increase their self-awareness. In the early 2000s, Novartis created an annual companywide organizational talent review much like those of other talent masters (GE, HUL, P&G, and Agilent) and formalized a new set of leadership standards. But it also established leadership self-examination and development programs, for both senior and for junior leaders, that are extraordinary in their emphasis on helping a person to discover his or her deeply embedded inner self.

The most intense of these programs is a three-day weekend mentoring session for a select group of high-potential leaders in the early stages of their careers, and it is a remarkably intense exercise. Since its inception in 2002, more than 150 people in Novartis divisions and global functions have attended the program, a handful at a time. A Novartis division or functional head selects six to eight leaders for the mentoring program and takes them off-site for three days with HR staff and expert behavioral psychologists. Juergen Brokatzky-Geiger, Novartis's global head of HR, or the head of HR for the respective division, is also on hand. The groups consist largely of people who work together and are likely to for some time, so the exercises and dialogues help to create a long-term culture of openness, candor, and collaboration.

The lead-up activity includes assessments of each participant in comparison with other leaders in Novartis and with a wider set of leaders from the outside world. Based on feedback they get from the assessments, the participants draft development plans with the help of the mentoring team. Each chooses a leadership challenge—a significant issue that they and their organizations are struggling with—that they will share with their peers and the mentoring team. It can't be something that's easy or that they've already solved, so the choice itself tests managers' capacity and willingness for self-examination.

The leaders take part in a variety of formal and informal activities and encounters, from conversation over dinner to one-on-one meetings and group sessions with role-playing exercises. As the program unfolds, the multiple observations by the division head, HR people, and psychologists combine to produce a very detailed picture of each person's individual and interpersonal behavior in several different contexts. Participants are led to explore both career and personal issues openly with their peers, a challenging feature that can be unsettling at first. As Kim Stratton, now head of Group Country Management & External Affairs, who participated in the program earlier in her career, recalls, "You're talking sometimes about the way you feel or about things that matter to you, so the subject matter is very different from the normal subject matter you're used to discussing in the Monday-to-Friday business environment."

More revealing is when the person discusses that challenge with the group. Let's say, for example, that due to a change in company strategy, Jay, the head of sales in a division, has been avoiding a hard decision. Kate holds a key position in the organization. She has been doing good work but is showing signs that she may no longer be in the right job given the change in strategy. Jay is going through an inner struggle about his personal values. Is firing a person who has been loyal and successful in the past the right thing to do? If he moves ahead with the change, how will others view him—as fair or as ruthless, the type of person willing to sell his grandmother to accomplish his goals? How will his personal brand be perceived from here on?

The dialogue between Jay and others in the program about his hiring dilemma uncovers the root of Jay's inner struggles. Kate has performed well and been given the best ratings for the past five years. She's highly effective with peers and a great cross-functional team player. It's obvious that Jay likes her and appreciates how much she has helped him. Jay's fellow participants query him about what is required to succeed given the changed strategy. Jay tells them that building a stronger network of strategic relationships with customers' higher-level executives is at the top of the list. He thinks Kate might be able to do it, but only with lots of personal coaching over a long period of time—which might slow the execution of the new strategy. The give-and-take of the dialogue forces Jay to think about whether Kate has the natural aptitude for building these relationships. It also brings to light Jay's poor history of bringing in outsiders and his worries that replacing Kate might make the situation worse. In the process Jay starts to reflect on how he is handling the situation and why. "Am I being defensive? Am I avoiding something? Is my concern for fairness preventing me from doing what is right for the business? Am I afraid to hire someone from outside because my record of doing so is poor?"

As people get immersed in the discussions, Brokatzky-Geiger and the division or function head give feedback in real time to help the person with his leadership challenge. Along with the psychologist, they also get insight into the person's inner core, and they compare notes behind the scenes. Brokatzky-Geiger explains: "We see how they carry themselves, how they connect with each other, how they act when tired and frustrated, how they treat others in team situations. Over three long, intense days, we learn the private side of the person. Because the mask is going away in this program. There are certain exercises that challenge people more and more in how they act, and make it impossible for them to keep a mask in place."

Everyone is observed by leader-practitioners, people who know the business context and the real external landscape. Even the psychologists learn the nuances of the business. Nowhere else can a leader get such valuable feedback.

There's time between the group discussions for informal conversation and self-reflection to help participants make their own discoveries. "The opportunity to speak to the other associates about their experiences and what they're getting out of the weekend helps crystallize where you are in your journey," says Stratton. Self-reflection allows the person to come to terms with reality. "The goal is that these people get to know themselves extremely well," Brokatzky-Geiger says, "and then through that to help them bring their private interests and the company's interests together, to match their core values and purpose with those of the company." Often the participants discover consciously for the first time their innermost personal and professional goals and ambitions—who they want to be, what they want to do in life as a whole and why. Finding that and aligning it with their work unleashes tremendous energy.

THE RIGHT CONTEXT

Many organizations hold off-site meetings where people are asked to share personal information publicly, and sometimes the results are not pretty. The difference at Novartis is largely in the context. The participants are not subjected to previously concocted questions or templates. Discussions take place with people who understand the business and the reality of the organizational settings where the participants work. Besides company leaders—the division head and head of HR—participants can draw on peers to provide insight into messy dilemmas they face. The context helps them wrestle with issues such as:

- What is bothering me and eating my inner energy away? How can these problems be articulated very specifically and then framed and reframed, thereby making conscious what is buried in the unconscious?
- Why was I suppressing this issue and not getting a clear solution? Is it because I have no imaginative alternatives or I do not like the consequences of the alternatives? Or that I have a fear of response to the actions that need to be taken because the situation is so uncertain?

- Am I using the old success formula for a new situation and becoming overconfident?
- Which of my core values is getting in the way of shaping the right solution? Do I need to recalibrate expectations? Do I need a sounding board—a trusted person who will help me clear up the confusion and isolate sources of anxiety and stress?

A decade or two ago few people in business would have been willing to reveal these inner thoughts, fearful that they would be used against them. But most cultures today are far more open when it comes to talking about personal details. People share intimate information through social networking, or track it down on sites such as Google. More and more of us are learning that being transparent about personal dilemmas and feelings is preferable to having others come to the wrong conclusions by using information they pick up elsewhere.

RESETTING EXPECTATIONS

The off-site experience helps both Novartis and its most talented and ambitious managers to reexamine views they've long taken for granted and open their eyes to new ones. As they reach a fuller understanding of their drives and motivations, some realize—and acknowledge to their peers and the mentoring team—that they either cannot or will not make certain sacrifices to reach the highest level in the company. Some ambitious people who had been set on becoming the head of a business with P&L responsibilities recalibrate their goals and choose another path to, say, being an executive with a functional rather than bottom-line responsibility.

Others may have second thoughts about accepting a foreign assignment even if turning it down means slowing or even derailing their career expectations. The toll on personal life of uprooting a family may be a deal breaker, especially when success in another environment is not guaranteed. Some people are fearful about living in developing countries. Drawing out this information benefits both Novartis and the young executives. The company can envision the right long-term roles for talented people it wants to retain instead of grooming them for the wrong ones.

Companies that don't acquire deep enough insight into their people's core values and purposes and do not help their talent to acquire insight into themselves can waste precious resources. We have seen this many times, even in talent masters. Despite its exhaustive knowledge of its people, for example, GE has more than once invested heavily in preparing an executive for a big job only to discover much too late that the person wouldn't take it because of personal reasons. As Brokatzky-Geiger put it, "Whenever you get to know yourself or somebody else better, you can revise your judgment and act accordingly."

In the final stage of the three-day off-site program the participants draft one-page "leader plans" for themselves, which they present to their peers and the mentoring team. A leader plan captures all the manager's assessment results and key learnings from the exercises and interactions. Most important, it lists his talents, skills, and values and articulates what he discovered about his inner core. Some of the items may be hopes, not current realities, but these are no less useful, and perhaps even more so: they reveal to the person what he stands for, or aspires to stand for. That's the main theme that pulls all the pieces together. It becomes a mission statement for the individual.

Over the following six months each of the managers has three or more individual coaching sessions on key developmental areas. These concentrate on helping the managers move from awareness and insight about their potential to practice and accountability.

The big breakthrough in self-awareness for most people is

the discovery that they overleverage their professional skills and underleverage their inner values. Their heartfelt values and sense of purpose are reserved for their families or philanthropic activities, and largely disconnected from their leadership in business. Consequently, these bright, high-achieving leaders have often failed to develop their authentic interpersonal skills and their ability to learn from, collaborate with, and influence other people.

Novartis recognizes that these are essential qualities for its business. Teamwork and leaders who can foster it are especially important for continued success in the global pharmaceutical industry. Coordinating efforts in virtually every country of the world becomes more complicated all the time as governments, regulatory agencies, consumer groups, and financial markets respond in different ways to advances in medical science and changes in medical practice. Innovating a pipeline of prescription drugs to replace those going off patent increasingly requires that large teams of specialists in varied scientific and medical fields share information and work well together, not just internally but also with outside people and regulatory agencies.

Stratton had gone through several 360-degree assessments before joining Novartis, and each time they revealed an impatience when she wanted to achieve ambitious goals in a hurry. What hit home for her at the Novartis off-site was the disconnect between how she achieved her goals especially in times of stress, and what she truly valued in her life. "It came out during the weekend that one of my strengths was around empathy, and I knew that I wanted to build on that. But I don't want to be sitting around at age seventy-five thinking, *Okay, great, you were an empathetic person, three cheers.* As I kept reflecting over the six months following the session, my core purpose began to crystallize: I want to realize my full potential as a female business leader and to ensure that my colleagues and my family reach their full potential. So I don't want to lose my speed and drive, but when I take it to the higher level, I can remind myself, *Kim, please take care when you're in this situation.* At the end of the day, if I leave people feeling bruised and unempowered and not fulfilling their potential, actually I suffer as much as if not more than they do because I'm not meeting my own core purpose. I may have won the battle, but I've lost the war. This is not something I arrived at right away or solely as a result of the mentoring weekend, but it's quite profound."

Stratton notes a crucial difference between the typical assessments and the Novartis program: "Quite often when people are giving you 360-degree advice, they focus on the deficiency. What made the difference for me was focusing on how the outcome feeds back into my core purpose. It's more holistic."

SEEING THE NOVARTIS SYSTEM WITH FRESH EYES

Joe Jimenez, who succeeded Vasella as CEO in early 2010, learned the value of self-awareness after he joined the company in 2007 as head of its consumer health division. He'd previously been president and CEO of H. J. Heinz North America and H. J. Heinz Europe. He was used to the demands of top-level business leadership, and he came from an industry, consumer packaged goods, that paid a lot of attention to leadership development.

Jimenez was struck not only by the formality and depth of assessments at Novartis but also by the way they produced a clear diagnosis of each individual's needs in different areas. The payoff, he says, came not so much in his first Novartis assignment but a few months later in his second, when he was promoted to run the company's core pharmaceutical division. After ten years of double-digit growth, the pharma division was facing several patent expires and an increasingly tough environment, and performance in 2007 started to suffer. Jimenez wanted to build the future strategy on the culture that Vasella had created, centered on patient centricity. Jimenez diagnosed the problem as a lack of external focus on the needs of patients, the end consumers of pharma's products, and the changing behaviors of physicians and health insurance providers, the customers whose choices determined pharma's sales results.

The pharma organization didn't want to see this, says Jimenez. "People were saying 2007 was an aberration, and if we just kept on our current path, then we'd be fine. I had to completely change that view and mind-set." He had forged his leadership style in what he calls "a very hard-charging environment," and now he was working in "a Swiss culture that was more reserved." Thanks in part to the depth and rigor of the assessment he had gone through, "I saw myself becoming less patient and more directive," he says. "The assessment helped me to rethink the way I was approaching the situation and to adapt my style to be effective in the Novartis culture. Instead of forcefully driving it through the organization—even though the external environment was rapidly evolving, necessitating change inside Novartis— I recognized that I had to engage it from the bottom up. So I immediately backed off and said, 'Okay, let's benchmark where we stand. Then let's look at how we can address this in a way that makes us more nimble and flexible.' "

This transformed the situation. Instead of battling over a long period of time to effect change, Jimenez gained support for the patient-centric, customer-focused approach. Building on Vasella's strategy, he took the pharma division's top one hundred leaders off-site, where he helped them draw a clear picture of the external environment and the business challenge. Afterward, he asked each of them to think about and send him within fourteen days what they personally were going to do over the next six months to become more patient-centric and customer-focused. This brought Jimenez "an incredibly rich variety of personal commitment letters" that became the basis for "putting the wheels back on the pharma division."

Note the virtuous cycle here. Becoming more self-aware made Jimenez more alert to the pharma division's collective personality, so to speak. This enabled him to build on strengths in his leadership behavior in a way that made the entire organization more self-aware, and thus more alert and responsive to customer needs. As Jimenez sums it up, "The leaders in pharma said the process made them take ownership of the initiative and change their own behavior first. This allowed them to develop as leaders in terms of being more externally focused, so they could in turn help their people become more externally focused. It changed the whole tone of the pharma division."

Jimenez's experiences in his first year at Novartis drove home for him the value of rigorous psychological assessments focused on enhancing leaders' self-awareness. He told us, "Other companies too often define leadership development in a cursory way without that deep up-front assessment of what will really make a person a more effective leader. They don't identify the root cause of the problem, if there is a problem, or the key opportunity that the leader has. The thing that Novartis does better than any other company I've seen is that up-front piece." Insight into people and diagnosing the inner core and values of a person help you become more effective in your work with others. Such insights into people also help in diagnosing the numbers differently and making better decisions and executing them better.

Novartis is now leveraging its assessment processes in two areas of special importance: developing leaders who can adapt their leadership styles to different cultures, and nurturing scientist-leaders who can manage research and development programs to meet key business objectives. Its program of developing self-awareness has the added benefit of building leaders out of scientists and technical experts in ways that other companies can't. As an example, Jimenez points to Trevor Mundel, a very dynamic physician-scientist promoted to be head of global pharma development. Crucially, Jimenez and his senior leadership team saw that Mundel had to make strides in self-awareness in order to handle this enormous responsibility.

"We recognized that Trevor had the leadership skills, as well as the scientific and technical skills, to run the entire development group. He was both charismatic with high aspirations and he was very creative. And we recognized that we needed to work together to change the development process at Novartis to enhance our productivity.

"From a leadership development standpoint, however, after we put him in that job we realized how powerful his vision was and how we had to help him align his group around him quickly to move at the ambitious pace he had set. I would tell him, 'Look, Trevor, you have to slow down and ensure that the 7,500 people in development are coming along with you.'

"Partly by giving him a personal coach, we helped him understand that he had to give the group a digestible amount of change before he moved to the next thing. That helped him grow as a leader."

Mundel now leads a decisive shift in the development strategy. The traditional pharma model has been to work on drugs for common diseases that affect large numbers of people. But as Jimenez observes, this strategy has produced diminishing returns in recent years for all pharmaceutical companies. Despite the reservations of many within Novartis's R&D group, Mundel, along with Dr. Fishman, president of the Novartis Institutes for BioMedical Research, has pushed for a focus on rare diseases that may affect very few people but have genetic mechanisms in common with a constellation of related illnesses. A Novartis drug called Ilaris is one of the first fruits of this approach. Initially developed for Muckle-Wells disease, an inflammatory rheumatological disorder that only a few thousand people in the world have,

Ilaris has the potential to treat a wide range of problems, from arthritis to chronic obstructive pulmonary disease, diabetes, and gout. If successful, this approach could be a new business model for the pharmaceutical industry. And Mundel can move forward with it knowing that he doesn't have to look over his shoulder to see if his 7,500 colleagues are with him.

CONCLUSIONS

- You can liberate your capacity and courage as a leader if you continually plumb the depth of your inner core. Only by doing this can you understand the role it plays in the changing complexities of your job and discover how to deal with the part of the core that compromises your effectiveness—or contains hidden resources that can accelerate it.
- Your competence in continually drilling into your unconscious and discovering your self-awareness helps you to open up others, drive candor in meetings, work with others, match the right people with the right jobs, and take risks on people and expand their effectiveness.
- An often undervalued part of a leader's work is daily interaction with people. Knowing yourself can help you to know them and greatly expand your ability to get things done through others without resorting to manipulation, which betrays the others and can eventually haunt you.

We're going to look next at a group of companies that have only recently set out to become talent masters. There are two things you should note about them: in each case, the CEO was deeply committed to, and totally involved in, the process; and all understood that people come before strategy.

Part III

BECOMING A TALENT MASTER

Many companies don't feel a sense of urgency about their leadership talent until their businesses fall apart or they need to engineer a major strategic shift. These kinds of situations are famous for wholesale and often unfocused changes at the top. Talent masters understand that there's a difference between trying to patch things up and rebuilding the organization's talent for the long term. How skillfully do they select the leaders charged with executing changes that will build the pipeline of future leaders? How will they embed values and behaviors in the organization? What kind of processes will they need for developing those leaders now and for the future? How quickly can they get the ball rolling? In today's rapid-change business environment, they won't have the luxury of building their processes over time as past talent masters have done.

In the three chapters that follow we look at how four companies have tackled this challenge. As it happens, in each case the driver of change was the need for a new strategy. Goodyear's was a plan for transforming a commodity business into one that marketed to consumers; UniCredit set out to create a unique pan-European bank from a collection of country banks; CDR faced a fundamental change in its business environment; and LGE aimed to strengthen its global presence by serving customers better in local markets. In each case their leaders understood that people come before strategy.

We've organized their stories topically. So in chapter 9 we examine how their CEOs decided on the types of leaders they needed—or as Goodyear chairman and CEO Rich Kramer puts it, analyzed the leadership competencies they had, the competencies they needed, and the size of the gap between the two. In chapters 10 and 11 we return to each company for an in-depth view of the practices and processes it adopted as it built the soft and hard components of a talent-mastery system. Chapter 10 deals with the "soft stuff"—values and behavioral norms that undergird talent mastery. Chapter 11 describes the mechanisms and processes each company has developed. We conclude by listing the qualities required of a CEO who aims to make his or her company a talent master.

Chapter 9

GET the RIGHT LEADERS

Whether it's just a few key replacements or a wholesale turnover, starting on the road to talent mastery almost always requires changes in leadership. Talent masters in the making are conscious of the short- and long-term implications of their choice of leaders. They select leaders not only for their business skills but also for their impact on the organization's ability to grow talent.

Here's how Goodyear, UniCredit, Clayton, Dubilier & Rice (CDR), and LG Electronics (LGE) made changes in leadership part of a bigger plan to master talent.

GOODYEAR: RENEWING WITH HELP FROM OUTSIDE

Goodyear Tire & Rubber was in deep trouble when Bob Keegan joined it as COO in 2000. Automobile tires were a commodity business in which big automakers, some of them fighting to stay alive, pitted one supplier against the others for the lowest prices. During the 1990s, Goodyear had to get clear of a staggering debt burden incurred earlier while staving off a furious proxy battle by British greenmailer Sir James Goldsmith. While Goodyear paid down debt, its archrivals, Michelin of France and Bridgestone of Japan, were buying up other tire manufacturers and grabbing global market share. Goodyear responded in 1999 by buying a majority interest in Dunlop tires in Europe and North America, which increased its debt load again. Many questioned Goodyear's ability to remain independent or even survive over the long term.

The job appealed to Keegan, then fifty-three, because Goodyear was up against many of the challenges that had confronted Eastman Kodak, where he'd run the global consumer business. Both had strong global brands, faced hard-charging foreign competitors, had geographically diverse manufacturing and sourcing operations, and tended to pay more attention to research and manufacturing than to marketing. But it didn't take long for him to discover that Goodyear was in even worse shape than he had imagined. As he puts it diplomatically, "The depth of Goodyear's problems had not been fully identified and analyzed by management or the board, although there were directors who knew we needed to make some fundamental changes."

Yet before the decade was over, Keegan—who became CEO in January 2003—had turned Goodyear into a growing global power player with a promising future. From 2002 to 2008, revenues grew 40 percent and operating income rose 116 percent. So different is the company that its leaders and employees came to call it the New Goodyear. How he did it holds an important lesson for anyone running a company with dim prospects: it is never too late to begin developing leadership talent, but you must be willing to confront the limitations of your current leadership. Leadership was in fact the centerpiece of his new strategy, and he executed the change with extraordinary speed.

Keegan started to work on creating a new model for the business even before he became CEO. "The old model was manufacturing-oriented, very insulated, very engineering-focused, very driven by the automakers," he says. "We called our new strategy the market-focused model." It would get Goodyear out of the commodity trap of selling primarily to original equipment manufacturers at low margins by going direct to consumers. The so-called aftermarket offered opportunities for differentiation, and Goodyear had the core resources to create it: a technological prowess that created such successes as the Aquatred and a world-class line of high-performance tires, its globally recognized brand name (who hasn't seen the Goodyear blimp on television?), and a strong worldwide dealer network.

He understood better than many corporate leaders that people come before strategy. His transformational plan would be nothing more than a brave idea without new leaders who could make it work. "We looked at the situation and said, 'We've got to change the whole model of our company,' and I mean the whole model—not just the strategic model, but how we executed and how we actually got things done."

People grow timid in a company beaten down by years of not succeeding. They fear change and aren't willing to take risks. The corporate DNA degrades into incrementalism—doing more of the same old things. The standard fix in these cases is to get rid of deadwood, bring in a few key leaders, hire a consultant on change management, explain the strategy to everybody, and get to work. But Keegan knew that would be like putting a recap tread on a shredded tire carcass. "We realized that fundamentally this culture just wasn't going to work for us if we wanted to evolve into a different kind of company. We'd never get from the old model to the new model without a significantly different philosophy and style of leadership that could change the whole culture."

Keegan had an important partner for his ambitions: Richard J. Kramer, now Goodyear's chairman and CEO who had left PricewaterhouseCoopers to join Goodyear as vice president of corporate finance in 2000, about six months before Keegan arrived. Goodyear had been one of his clients, and he understood well what the company was and what it could be. Kramer shared Keegan's strong views about developing people. Pricewaterhouse, a service business with extremely high standards, demanded that its rising stars groom younger accountants. "I knew a client-service business is a people business, but I also believe that tires are a people business," Kramer says. "Whether it's working with people internally or working with our customers, it's all about people, hearing what they say and watching what they do.

"One of the most important things that Bob brought to the table was a very critical view of the competencies that we had at Goodyear, the competencies we needed, and the size of the gap between the two." Kramer and Keegan, sharing a view of Goodyear that only outsiders could bring to it, worked together to overhaul Goodyear's leadership DNA as they filled the gaps.

Keegan had sharpened his views on leadership development when he was traveling the world fixing troubled businesses for Kodak. "There isn't an easy answer to how someone comes to understand the value of and the methodology for identifying and developing leaders," Keegan says. "For me it evolved empirically. As I had more experiences I saw what worked and what didn't. Over time I saw that successful leaders exhibited some common traits. They had to be team builders, and have high IQs and analytic abilities; they had to fit the chemistry of the organization; and they had to have a lot of courage to innovate and try new things and to do it faster than others might. That's what works." He distills his learning into five principles that he wanted Goodyear's leadership talent to reflect:

- Business is a team sport; it isn't ultimately about individuals.
- The best decisions don't come from the smartest person in the room; they come from a group of smart people gathered in the room.
- Leaders need to know what they don't know.
- Leaders must be courageously innovative.
- Leaders must be passionate about their business but remain unemotional when making key decisions.

It's not easy to build a performance-driven meritocracy in a hurry. There wouldn't be time to create a leadership development infrastructure along the lines of GE or Procter & Gamble and move people through it; only the immediate infusion of a critical mass of leaders would change the company's trajectory. Keegan identified his top internal talent almost as soon as he arrived, and quickly began recruiting outsiders to blend with them. "I told myself that if I can find talent internally I will, but I won't settle for second-best just because someone has been here twenty years when someone from outside with ten years less experience has produced an outstanding record of accomplishment."

Keegan replaced twenty-three of Goodyear's top twenty-four leaders in the first two years, either with outsiders or with people promoted from within; he also brought in hundreds of outsiders to fill positions in every business unit and function in all of Goodyear's geographical locations. The new team was relatively young—many in their thirties and forties, a few older—with outstanding skills in their specialties, including consumer marketing.

Steve McClellan, thirty-seven, who had joined Goodyear straight out of college, was named vice president of Goodyear Commercial Tire Systems in September 2003. Darren Wells, thirty-six, who had been assistant treasurer of Visteon Corp., joined Goodyear in August 2002 as vice president and treasurer. In 2004, Keegan persuaded Tom Connell, fifty-four, to leave his post as vice president and corporate controller of TRW Inc. to take a similar position at Goodyear. Pierre Cohade, forty-three, whom Keegan had known at Kodak before the French-born executive joined Groupe Danone to run its global water and beverage division, was lured to Goodyear in 2004 as president of the company's Asia-Pacific region.

Why would such people want to join a company widely perceived as on the ropes? Keegan's answer was to show them that he had a plan that would offer them a faster track to success than they could expect from their current employers. The best companies draw the best talent in disproportionate amounts. They literally have too many good people to accommodate on a narrowing executive pyramid. Some of those people naturally become impatient—and willing to take a risk, an important characteristic Keegan wanted in his leaders. Goodyear would be taking chances too. Junior people will usually have gaps in their resumes; they won't be as seasoned or as well rounded as more experienced executives. But they will be ambitious and eager to test themselves. Not all will make it in the long run, but enough will that you can make a fundamental change in an organization's culture. "I'm selling the chance to accomplish something, to be a leader sooner than you would be somewhere else," Keegan would tell them. "You're taking a risk and I'm taking a risk. One or both of us could be wrong. You may be the wrong person for the job or we may be the wrong company for you. But if we're both right, then we've done something special for you and for our shareholders."

The outside hiring naturally created anxiety. "The steps I initially took were a bit of a shock to the company because we just hadn't done that before," he says. When a company brings in so many outsiders, particularly in a "company town" such as Goodyear's Akron, Ohio, people become even more fearful of losing their jobs. "But that quieted down rather quickly because of both the talent and capability of the people we brought in."

It helped in assimilating the newcomers that Keegan had a deep belief in teamwork, developed when he played sports in high school and college. "Business is a team sport," he says—and he says it with passion. A superior resume is useless to him if he detects that a potential hire would not be a good fit with the team he is building. Demonstrating teamwork in action, the new leaders won the confidence of the Goodyear hands. The corporate psychology began to change from fear to optimism as people saw new business possibilities and developed self-worth and energy.

Intimacy is harder to achieve with outsiders, but Keegan minimized hiring mistakes by engaging himself and other leaders in intensive interviewing. In the process he established, a candidate meets not just with the person to whom he would report but also with most of the senior leadership team. That provides the multiple inputs that lead to hard and factual judgments. He also sits down for discussions with people who will be reporting to him, which means that no one will be surprised by the new hire or can complain about not having had any say. What's more, the candidate gets a clear picture of what the position entails. "We make sure people from outside know as much as possible about us," said Keegan. "We want them to be sure it's a great fit for them too. We may not have the fastest process, but we do have one that is thorough and analytic."

With new leaders on board, Keegan was ready to move forward on two fronts: changing the business, and changing the way Goodyear builds talent.

UNICREDIT: USING THE TALENT SYSTEM TO EXECUTE A NEW STRATEGY

Alessandro Profumo always had a gut feeling that paying more attention to people would pay off on the bottom line. It was rooted in Profumo's early experience as a young executive in an Italian bank. Years later, when he was in the midst of creating a Europe-wide bank, talent management became a central part of his strategy; it was the means to unite disparate people and cultures in common values and goals. In just a few years—and despite the setbacks of the 2008 financial meltdown—his team built a new performance culture with leadership development as the focal point. The resulting model centered on Profumo's passion for accelerating talent development, aided by a seasoned HR leader who was sensitive to this issue in helping him execute the strategy that has given UniCredit a unique competitive advantage.

Profumo's ambitions were never small. Starting as a bank clerk in 1977, he rose rapidly in the financial industry. At age thirty he left banking to be a consultant, first at McKinsey and then at Bain, Cuneo & Associati. Four years later he joined an insurance company, Riunione Adriatica di Sicurtà, and rose to the position of general manager for the banking and parabanking sectors. He built a reputation in Italian financial circles, and in 1994 the chairman of Credito Italiano, UniCredit's forerunner, needing a younger person to groom as a replacement for himself, invited him to join as deputy general manager. His appointment to chief executive officer came just three years later.

Soft-spoken and modest, Profumo acknowledges that he was unseasoned. "I was thirty-eight then, and didn't appreciate what it meant to be a CEO of a bank," he says dryly. "Despite my experience, my learning was more intuitive than structured. But it became my most exciting experience in terms of professional growth." UniCredit had been formed through the merger of seven banks with Credito Italiano; Profumo managed the integration smoothly and put the bank on a new growth trajectory. His lack of structured experience actually turned out to be an asset, because it allowed him to bring fresh thinking to the business. In particular, he questioned the bank's career plan, which took into account only the top fifty leaders. "At the rate we're growing," he told the leaders, "we need to be looking at three thousand people." This was a radical idea, but despite great skepticism in the ranks, top management backed him and the new plan became a reality.

"We learned through the process," says Profumo. "We were really trying. There were times when we wondered whether we were like the sorcerer's apprentice in the movie *Fantasia*—we had started something and we could not know how it would come out. But I always had a feeling that the direction was right." Though UniCredit had grown to be Italy's largest bank, Profumo was looking for a much bigger arena. In 2005, he unveiled what the *Financial Times* called his "big vision based on a gamble"—a plan to merge with HypoVereinsbank (HVB), a major bank in Germany, Austria, and Central/Eastern Europe. Industry observers shook their heads—the new UniCredit, as it was named, did indeed seem to be a complex and risky gamble. Three years later the financial crisis stressed the bank deeply, leading to more predictions of failure.

But today the vision has clearly paid off: UniCredit has been able to come out of the crisis on its feet. It is one of the few banks to make a positive net income in every quarter—and, more important, with no help from the government. The secret ingredient that confounded the skeptics? It was in large measure Profumo's out-of-the-box thinking on talent management, which both strengthened its competitiveness with stronger leadership and united its disparate cultures.

The reshaping of UniCredit's leadership began with a key hire in July 2005: Rino Piazzolla, a nine-year veteran of GE's HR staff, most recently as the vice president of HR for GE's Infrastructure business. Previously he worked in Italy and the United States for S. C. Johnson and PepsiCo.

Piazzolla came aboard about a month after Profumo had set his strategy in motion. The merger had expanded UniCredit's scope from a few countries to twenty, and doubled the number of its employees to around 170,000. "The challenge was how we were going to bring all these people under the same roof," says Piazzolla. "In Europe, cultural diversity could be a major liability or a major asset. For us it would be the pillar upon which we were going to build this company. Alessandro Profumo had this vision of managing talent in a different way. I didn't know exactly what he meant, but clearly he had in his gut that we needed to do something different." UniCredit had been making some efforts at talent management, sending people to leadership courses and business schools, and hiring consulting firms to work on leadership issues. The efforts didn't amount to much, because they weren't really connected with the business or ingrained into the fabric of the company. To reach his goals, Profumo would need new unifying values, new social systems and organizational structures, and a new talent management system. He had found in Piazzolla the person to help him do it.

PRIVATE EQUITY: NEW TALENT FOR A NEW GAME

It may have been a defining moment in the evolution of private equity. In 2010, with Jack Welch already aboard as an advisory partner, Clayton, Dubilier & Rice (CDR) added four more stellar former CEOs: A. G. Lafley of Procter & Gamble, Ed Liddy of Allstate, Paul Pressler of Gap, and Vindi Banga of Hindustan Unilever. Their name value alone makes CDR the talent powerhouse of the industry, but the company brought them in for much more than their marquee value. It saw their talent as vital to taking its business into a new era.

In the roughly half century since the first pools of investors were organized to fund businesses outside of the stock exchanges, private equity (PE) has become a major force in the world's capital markets. Beginning with a wave of leveraged buyout deals in the 1960s, PE firms organized by clever financiers played an increasingly big role extracting value from underperforming companies. Typically they would buy a troubled public company by borrowing heavily against its assets, squeeze out costs through better controls, cash management, and expertise in taxation and capital structure, and maybe provide strategic advice. After a couple of years they would sell the business, often by taking it public again. Given the plenitude of mismanaged and underleveraged companies, the money rolled in.

Private equity grew explosively in two great spurts, in the mid-1980s and again in the mid-2000s, fueled by cheap credit. The most aggressive firms loaded their acquired companies with debt, counting on getting out quickly enough to pass on any consequences to the next owners. Few of them knew much about running a business; they didn't have to.

Then the world changed. The PE business took a big hit when the economy turned down in 2000, but that was only a warm-up for what happened when capital evaporated in the 2008 financial tsunami. Between 2007 and 2009, the value of private equity deals in the United States fell from a peak of $575 billion to $43 billion, a 65 percent drop, according to the private equity research firm Pitchbook. In today's capital markets and business environment, it can take five or more years to find a buyer for a portfolio company. This means that PE firms have to build lasting value with the help of partners who have the experience in operations and talent management to strengthen the portfolio companies.

CDR turbocharged its new competitive game by recruiting Welch, Lafley, Liddy, Pressler, and Banga, who joined other seasoned former public company leaders. These executives are lending their eye for talent and hands-on approach to coaching other leaders. CDR had already hired Bill Conaty to help its portfolio companies build their own talent mastery. In fact, it and other PE firms are themselves becoming talent magnets, opening new career paths for bright public company leaders and not just retired CEOs or second-tier managers. Prominent among them are Dave Calhoun, a former GE vice chairman in his early fifties, now running AC Nielsen (owned by a consortium of KKR, Carlyle, Blackstone, and Thomas Lee Partners), and Fred Kindle at CDR, former CEO of ABB, also in his early fifties.

One of the first to understand how talent can create value in the numbers is TPG, the fourth-largest private equity firm in the world. From the outset it specialized in improving the operations of its portfolio companies. Its point man on leadership development, partner Jim Williams, joined TPG after a career of unusual breadth: managing partner of the Hay Group, a global consulting firm specializing in human resources development; head of strategy, HR, IT, and marketing for Kaiser Permanente; and subsequently CEO of the Kaiser Health Group, a $4.5 billion spin-off headquartered in Seattle. He loved doing deals and working on operations, but before long his partners began asking him to focus on developing leaders for the portfolio companies. "They said, 'Look, you've got a real nose for talent. The most important decision we're making after the investment decision is who we're going to have run the company, and we're not great at doing this. It would be the highest and best use of your skill to really focus on that element.' "

Williams now splits his time between deals and operations, but it's clear that the partners had it right. He plays the leading role in talent management at TPG and has helped to institutionalize processes for both finding top leaders and developing the right people for the right jobs. He's involved from the very beginning, sitting at the table in every deal decision. "I am expected to have a point of view about management," he says. Sometimes—rarely, he says—the team may be irreparably bad, with no way to fix it fast enough to make the deal work. More often he'll conclude that the bad management team is fixable and he will have ideas about what to do. Then there are the winners: "This is an A-team, and our challenge is going to be to keep them and connect with them and make sure we love them."

LGE: ACQUIRING GLOBAL TALENT

A company deciding to be a serious player in the global marketplace has to take a close look at its existing talent. Often the skills that got it to where it is aren't equal to the challenge of taking it to the wider arena. Yong Nam, CEO of LGE (whose majority owner is the LG Corp. holding company), found an innovative way to bring the right people in without bruising its Korean leadership.

You couldn't imagine two more different companies than Goodyear and LGE: one struggling to escape the legacy of a commodity business, the other a rising player in the insatiable world market for consumer electronics—LGE produces cell phones, flat-screen TVs, air conditioners, and appliances and is challenging the world leaders in all categories. Yet Bob Keegan and Yong Nam had this much in common: each needed a big infusion of outside genes to change cultures driven by manufacturing and R&D to ones in which leaders understood global consumers and markets, and could seamlessly coach, support, and mentor others across borders.

In the decades since its founding in the 1950s, LGE had grown from a small local manufacturer of radios under the Goldstar brand to a major player in the global market for electronics and telecommunications. (It currently is an independent company with LG Corp., the holding company, as its largest shareholder.) The company's hard-driving Korean workforce had given the company an edge in low-cost manufacturing, superior adaptation of technology, and fast product development cycles. But when Nam became CEO in 2007, he believed that the homogeneous Korean talent that had made the company successful had to be globalized.

Nam had an ambitious vision of what LGE could become: not just the best Korean brand, but the best brand in the world. He created a transformation agenda that would build a global consumer brand, create a high-performing, marketing-driven organization, and change the company's DNA to succeed not just in the near term but also ten and twenty years out. The transformation agenda consisted of:

- Realigning the performance management system to focus on profitable growth and ROIC, not just market share
- Restructuring the portfolio to be in the businesses where LGE could and should be number one

- Aligning all product/market strategies against clear customer segments and needs
- Building one global brand
- Investing in design and innovation
- Globalizing the organization and HR systems

Many of these changes weren't revolutionary, but the organization wasn't exhibiting or being assessed for those behaviors. Nam had to get people to behave in a way that was consistent with where LGE was heading. His challenge was to globalize the talent pool and supporting systems fast without demotivating LGE's strong Korean base, and to move from a manufacturing-and-R&D-driven culture to one in which leaders had insights into global consumers and markets. He needed leaders who had the capacity to define a strategy and sell it, engage and empower people to contribute their very best, and build cross-cultural teams.

Earlier in his career he had spent time in the United States, and one of the key lessons from that experience had stuck with him. He had seen a gap between LGE's manufacturing perspective and that of the U.S. consumer. He wanted LGE to understand the consumer in those local markets better than anyone else and to attract the best local talent for functional business leaders in those markets. This, he observed, was no easy task. "Making those individual country subsidiary units the best employer in that country was a critical issue of mine," Nam says. "But locally hired people were not motivated, because the leadership team dispatched from Korea did not integrate them. Turnover was so high that the best in class simply didn't want to join. With that, we would not be able to make LGE a strong brand in that local market and build a strong organization."

Hiring the world's best functional experts, most of whom were non-Korean, would show LGE's commitment to becoming the best on a global scale and help attract top local talent. Bringing them into a tight Korean culture was the challenge.

Just as people come before strategy, the software of talent mastery—values and social systems—needs to precede the structures and processes of talent management. We'll see in the next chapter how our diverse group of companies have traveled different paths to remarkably similar goals.

Chapter 10

SET the RIGHT VALUES and BEHAVIORS

As we've said throughout this book, becoming a talent master means establishing the values and behavioral norms that sustain candor, rigor, and meritocracy. People have to know beyond a doubt that they are expected to search for and develop other leaders' talent, and to do so with the same drive for accuracy that they apply to operations and finance. Making talent development a goal that is measured and rewarded helps, but much of the work is done through role modeling. Leaders establish the code of conduct through their own actions, questions, and openness to differing opinions in the struggle to pin down each leader's unique blend of traits, skills, judgment, relationships, and experience. Formal processes are necessary, but any company intent on becoming a master of talent must attend to the soft side of talent mastery. It's what makes all the difference.

GOODYEAR: A MANIFESTO FOR CHANGE

The old Goodyear mind-set was driven by the need to keep volume up in its high-fixed-cost plants. It took huge orders at razor-thin margins from the big automakers. The new Goodyear would have to improve efficiency and cut costs, but it also needed a new mind-set geared toward generating profitable growth: attracting consumers with new products and strong marketing, and investing in emerging markets. Building the engine to produce new products based on learning what consumers wanted would be a monumental task. Bringing in one leader at a time would be too slow and wouldn't build momentum to make the change. New leaders from the outside had to form a critical mass and would not only make different decisions but make them differently, based on different information. They would have to set new priorities and make new allocations of resources. More important, these new leaders would work with the remaining internal Goodyear people to execute the new model and break the victim mentality.

Bob Keegan created several means to get the new leaders to work as a team. For one thing, he captured in a chart the shift required in each of what he called the seven strategic drivers of the business. Named the market-focused business model, the chart was not only a plan but also a pragmatic values statement that described what the business would be in the future and how it would operate. Leadership, for example, would go from being insulated to a mix of inside and outside talent based on proven performance. Distribution would no longer be an order-taking function but a way to build customers' businesses by meeting customer demands, moving from push to pull. Says Keegan, "The first question out of everyone's mouth was 'How do we rank the drivers?' The answer was there wasn't a ranking; each of the drivers was of equal importance—except for leadership. It would be unequivocally the first among equals."

The market-focused business model became a vehicle for unifying the organization. It even helped Goodyear navigate the recession. Says Joe Ruocco, who became Goodyear's head of HR in 2008, "We had been following the strategic drivers, and when the recession hit, the question in my mind, as a newcomer, was how the strategy would shift in bad times. What was incredible to me was that not only did the strategy not change, but that the first thing we did was say, 'Hey, we need to focus on these seven drivers. They're

MARKET-FOCUSED BUSINESS MODEL

OLD MODEL (MFG)		NEW MODEL (MARKETING)
• Insulated	Leadership	• Blend of talent from inside/outside • Proven performance
• Engineering focused • OE-driven	Product Leadership	• Consumer-relevant innovations • Launch of first replacement market • Outstanding new product engine
• Take orders • Push product based on availability	Leveraged Distribution	• Build our dealers' businesses • "Pull" product orders based on customer demand
• Focus on volume • Fill the factories • Absorb raw materials costs	Build Brand Strength Advantaged Supply Chain	• Intense focus on targeted segments • Targeted OE fitments with high replacement pull-through • Profitable growth focus • Price/mix to offset raw materials • Investment in emerging markets
• New manufacturing facilities • Acquisition of manufacturing assets • Filled high-cost plants	Lower Cash Structure Cash Is King	• Drive efficiency in all parts of the business • Upgrade existing facilities to HVA • Target investment for high-growth markets • Exit nonstrategic businesses • Reduce high-cost footprint/expand low-cost • Low-cost sourcing/procurement • VEBA/USW agreements

Under the old model, Goodyear's mind-set was driven by the need to keep volume up in its high-fixed-cost plants. It took huge orders from the big automakers and pushed the product out to the dealers. The new Goodyear would have to reverse this mind-set by improving efficiency and cutting costs, and by generating profitable growth: attracting consumers with new products and strong marketing, and investing in emerging markets. Building a consumer-based product engine would be a monumental task demanding a critical mass of new leaders from outside who could set different priorities and make different kinds of decisions. Most important, they would have to role-model and teach their people a new mind-set by working with them to execute the new model and showing them how to win—not to be victims.

just as important and just as valuable during bad times as they are in good times.' "

Another far-reaching innovation was a monthly business operating meeting. Here the global leadership team reviews the operating performance of strategic business units and sales and operations planning for the prior month and estimates trends for the coming month and year. These are not point estimates ("next quarter we will increase market share by X percent and sales by Y billion dollars") but detailed scenario plans focused on external conditions that influence the point estimates, such as anticipated competition and changes in interest rates. These reviews teach newly hired people a lot of detail about the business, but they convey more than specific knowledge. They demonstrate the importance of speed as senior leaders use quick market intelligence to make decisions with the operating leaders on the spot. What's more, the social process gets outsiders and insiders to work together with urgency, as senior and operating leaders are jointly engaged in making key decisions. The outsiders know how to be market-oriented, create differentiation, be decisive, and make changes necessary for Goodyear to prosper once again. The insiders, who are intimately familiar with the company's technology, manufacturing, and logistics, know how to take costs out. Working together in this social process develops the leaders' capabilities for adapting to changes in the external environment. The discussion of scenarios between newly arrived outsiders and long-standing insiders also provided an opportunity for a culture of candor to begin to take hold and helped insiders and outsiders build confidence in each other's point of view.

The old Goodyear's hierarchical structure dissuaded people from speaking up to offer a new idea or criticize the way things were being done. But getting to the realities of the business and leaders' talents required new levels of candor and trust. It's taken time to build those habits, but today the senior leaders know that to put your head down and not speak out is tantamount to career suicide.

Getting people to talk openly about personal strengths and shortcomings—not only their own but those of others—is the toughest piece of changing a talent management culture. "A development need is just that, a development need," Conaty says. "It only becomes a fatal flaw if it isn't addressed. But most organizations find it very difficult to have those candid conversations. They can't bring themselves to tell someone, 'You're a beauty queen but you've got a few warts that need to be taken care of.' If I can tell someone that and they can hear it and not take it the wrong way, then we can fix the warts." Change starts at the top, he adds, recalling that when Jack Welch began giving his direct reports candid feedback on their personal development needs, their ability to have similar conversations with their direct reports became much easier. They in turn passed the practice right down the line.

Keegan set the expectation. "What we want are people who are willing to express their opinions, and we're really getting good at doing that because we have the right people in the leadership groups," says Keegan. "They're reaching out to people and asking for ideas and they aren't saying, 'That's a dumb idea'; rather, they're saying, 'Thanks for the input.' And people know now that if you're asking for help, that's absolutely a positive. If you're asking for help, you're looking for an opportunity." Adds Kramer, "We're making a great deal of progress in having candid, performance-based discussions with people, but we need to continuously improve, especially deeper in the organization."

UNICREDIT: VALUES THAT UNITE A CONTINENT

UniCredit's pan-European strategy required unprecedented levels of teamwork across national boundaries. For the strategy to work, people had to transcend cultural differences and adopt new modes of decision making. Alessandro Profumo and Rino Piazzolla knew that setting performance expectations and actually changing people's mind-set are two different things.

Profumo and Piazzolla began by focusing on values. "The key to having a vibrant leadership pipeline is to work on the value system before the performance management system," says Piazzolla. "The first thing I did—it was a week after I joined—was to read all the UniCredit materials they had on the Web, how they were describing the company and its mission. I categorized the information into three blocks: corporate culture, leadership, and know-how in general. Then I went to speak with Alessandro and said, 'Are these the standards you would like to hold people to?' And he was surprised. He said, 'Yes, that's how I want to do it, but how did you find out?' "

More than surprised, Profumo was relieved. He had worried that Piazzolla might come in married to some inflexible "GE way" program for talent management. He knew that would not transplant successfully into UniCredit's culture—and so did Piazzolla. "The people that have failed to implement talent management programs or performance management programs à la GE in their companies failed in my view because they applied mechanically something that was part of the culture of the other company," he says. "What we have tried to do is to take the tools and core processes of GE and apply them as a custom-made suit. In the first six to nine months, people would say, 'Hey, Rino, this is not GE.' And I always pointed out that what I was proposing was based on what I learned about UniCredit's own mission and values."

UniCredit had been working on a values proposition before Profumo and Piazzolla began their transformation. Some one thousand employees contributed ideas in what UniCredit called its Value Laboratories. It was an initiative led by the people in the corporate identity and HR teams where the employees were engaged in a series of discussions and work groups with a goal to define a set of ethical standards they considered important in their day-to-day activities. "The leadership wanted to know what values were important to their employees," says Piazzolla, "but once they had the information, they were saying, 'What do we do with it?' " As he and Profumo reviewed the material, they concluded that it had the potential to be the cultural foundation of the new UniCredit. "It could bring the culture of all these banks together," says Piazzolla. "It would be a unifying element." They met with the management committee—the top fifteen to twenty leaders in the company—to get their input. And after receiving the committee's endorsement, what they launched in September 2005 was a unique and thoughtful document on UniCredit's values and philosophy of business called the Integrity Charter.

One part of the charter's preamble is about profits, and it would surprise most non-Europeans. "We talk about the importance of profit as a precondition of freedom," says Piazzolla. "When I read it the first time I thought this was like explaining why we have to breathe. In the American companies where I worked, the value of profit is something that you don't need to point out. Well, in Europe you have to explain why you're out to make money. Yet as I went through it, I saw that these reflections on the ethical value of being profitable were quite interesting. And in the financial crisis, they turned out to be a great ethical anchor for us. Like everyone else, we were damaged by the crisis itself, but not through any ethical failings of our own."

They implemented the charter with a top-down communication plan that delivered a clear message to the banks: *This is what we stand for, and there will be consequences for not complying.* "Nobody could doubt that it would be taken seriously," says Piazzolla. They also promoted it with an Integrity Charter day, where people put aside their work for two to three hours to talk about the charter and how they should apply it in daily life. Now held every September, the Integrity Charter day has grown increasingly elaborate. For example, says Piazzolla, "in the most recent one, every discussion group had to recognize an individual that epitomized one of these Integrity Charter principles. It was a bottom-up election of people. In the end we had a champion for each business and each function, and we brought them all to meet with the management committee and explained why each one was recognized. There was no money involved; it was just pure recognition. But there were people in tears because they never thought they were going to be recognized for something that wasn't directly connected with business results. It was a really powerful leadership tool for us in the management committee."

UniCredit bolstered the Integrity Charter with an ombudsman system to provide a mechanism for employees to register complaints and issues with an impartial arbitrator. There's an ombud structure in every country where Uni-Credit operates, ranging from two to twenty or so people depending on the size of the company. What distinguishes it from most other systems is that all the ombuds are recent retirees of the company. The idea was to give selected retired people opportunities to stay involved with the company; more important, it would provide highly credible ombuds who knew banking intimately—people who, as Piazzolla puts it, "understood that how you deny a loan is not just a mechanical exercise but a matter of judgment." The leader of the ombuds organization, for instance, is the former head of audit staff. "He knows all the ins and outs and is doing a terrific job," says Piazzolla.

One of Piazzolla's earliest tasks was to shape up his own staff, which needed major surgery. Profumo always paid more attention to it than his peers in banking did, but he didn't have the knowledge and tools to make it an effective business partner. "Their skills were fundamentally the old personnel administration skills," he says. They were totally unprepared to help business leaders think strategically about people, or to help them understand the importance of candid feedback and the concept of development needs. When Piazzolla challenged them, they felt that their authority was threatened. He replaced many of the leaders with outsiders who were able to drive and role-model the new agenda, and armed them with tools and techniques perfected at GE, such as external trend analysis, assessment of potential as leaders, and strategic knowledge gap analysis.

PRIVATE EQUITY: CHANGING THE MIND-SET

The transition to a new era in private equity had to begin with a major shift in values. Joe Rice, a founding partner of CDR, among the oldest private equity firms, explains the issue. "One reason firms have been so slow developing operational capabilities is that almost all of them were started by financial people," he says. "To get good operating people, you have to be willing to share the economics and the decision process, which is hard to do if the partners are all financial people who've been very successful. You think, *Is this guy really going to be valuable?* One of the discussions that goes on around here is, 'What's the relative contribution? Should operating guys really get as much of the firm as the finance guys are getting?' That's been the case in spades in most other firms."

Rice recalls the firm's evolution from its early days. "At the time I started CDR I'd been in the private equity business for twelve years in a firm that was entirely a financial firm. I decided sometime in the early 1970s that we were at a terrible disadvantage doing what we were trying to do if we had a firm solely composed of financial people, because financial people truly don't understand how to run a business. They can run the numbers, and the numbers will always go straight up, but when things get in trouble, they don't have anything they can do but fire the CEO. That's really not a satisfactory thing, because you go through a long period of time where you see the business deteriorate, and it's only when it's really in bad shape that you fire somebody, and then you have to rebuild the whole thing, and because the business is in the tank, it's hard to get someone to come in. For any number of reasons it seemed to make sense that if you're going to be in this business, you really ought to have an operating capability."

TPG more or less had the new values in its genes. From its beginnings in 1992, it specialized in deals that required more attention to management than most. "Our appetite for talent is higher than normal, simply because most of the time when we're involved, there's going to be some level of transformation required," says Jim Williams. "If we're buying a broken business or a division of a business where we know there's going to have to be a lot of rebuilds going, we write that level of change into our deal thesis. We were one of the first guys to have an operations group that really focused on how we run the business." All of TPG's partners have run sizable businesses and have been partners—senior or managing partners in some cases—at prominent consulting firms.

The firm's first deal was buying Continental Airlines in 1993, and few in the private equity game gave it much chance of succeeding. Continental was a seriously troubled business struggling out of its second bankruptcy, and the deal was financially complex. "But the deal thesis was born out of a really deep macro- and microeconomic study of the industry and Continental's competitive position," says Williams, "and we essentially remade the management." They brought in a seasoned airline CEO and a former Bain Capital partner to manage the transformation. Within a few years Continental was on its way to becoming one of the industry's more successful players. When it merged with Northwest Airlines in 2010, its management had been so effective that it wound up in the pilot's seat.

"TPG was basically born at that point, and our whole model since has been around making operating changes and transformations," says Williams. "We were quick to recognize that talent is a key lever, if not the key lever." CDR has also differentiated itself from its peers with its operating expertise. Now it is intensifying its talent management with the help of former GE CEO Jack Welch, an advisory partner since 2001, and Bill Conaty, who has been working with the firm since 2007 to build a human resources infrastructure unique among PE firms.

Now we turn to the hardware: the tools and techniques, processes, and operating mechanisms that our companies use to do the work of developing strong and self-renewing leadership talent.

Chapter 11

GET the RIGHT TALENT MANAGEMENT PROCESSES

G reat leaders and sound values are necessary but not suffi-
cient conditions for keeping talent front and center in the
everyday running of a business. Companies need a consistent,
disciplined rhythm for revisiting talent. Formal processes
provide discipline in identifying leaders with high potential,
pinpointing individuals' talents, giving them opportunities to
grow, and tracking their development. Talent masters in the
making must step back and take a hard look at their existing
processes to be sure they are producing the output desired,
including the intimacy true talent masters achieve. HR can
help reinvent the talent management system, but not without the active participation and support of the CEO.

GOODYEAR: STEPPING UP FROM INFORMAL TO FORMAL

Bob Keegan made only minor changes in Goodyear's human
resources department during the first few years. "Because we
were undertaking such deep change and such intense change,
I consciously decided not to create another major disruption
to add to everything else we had going on," he explains. "The
HR people knew the company, they knew the people, and in
most cases they could assess who was performing and who

wasn't. They had a pretty good set of succession planning tools and were very helpful."

Keegan relied essentially on informal processes that established new behaviors and values. He developed his leadership team by setting a tone of urgency and candor through example and coaching. A hands-on leader by nature, he spent his time not on outside involvements but on core strategy, operations, and customers. He took part in almost every major meeting or intervention, and constantly kept the organization up to speed on whether they were making the expected progress. In his meetings and informal contacts, he repeatedly pressed people to understand and act on the strategic drivers.

By 2008, Keegan was ready to take Goodyear's talent management processes and HR operation to a higher plane, and began searching for the person who could do it. Ruocco's name quickly emerged as a leading candidate. "I was looking for the same general characteristics that I look for in any executive," Keegan said, "but I also wanted someone who had been absolutely immersed in a world-class HR system and company."

As vice president of HR for GE's consumer and industrial business, Ruocco looked like just the right choice. "But Bob Keegan doesn't take anything for granted," says Bill Conaty, whom Keegan called for a rundown on his former colleague. The Goodyear CEO spent well over an hour with Conaty on a Saturday morning phone call, grilling him intensely about Ruocco's ability to play on a team and act as a partner to the senior leadership. After talking about Joe's technical qualifications, which were superb, Keegan wanted to drill down into how well he would fit with the Goodyear team. "He was very intent on making sure that Joe was a team player, someone who would come in and make a difference from day one not just as an HR guy but as a business partner to the rest of the leadership team," says Conaty. "I was pretty impressed that he'd dig that deeply." Conaty predicted that Joe would be a strong team player with a good understanding of operations, who would fit well with the Goodyear senior executives. His assessment confirmed what Keegan had observed in his own meeting with Ruocco. Says Keegan: "It was clear that Joe had all those capabilities as well as the team chemistry that I knew would work here."

The all-important chemistry didn't take long to show itself. "After Joe had been with us for two months he and I met with the board to review succession planning. We go broad and we go deep with the board on succession, and we had an absolutely outstanding session over a couple of hours. So the chemistry was right, the background was right, and Joe has continued to make a big contribution. He not only prepared the board presentation but also weighed in heavily with me on his assessment of Goodyear's key players."

In his first two years, Ruocco added crucial structure and processes to Goodyear's talent development. "What used to be a succession planning process is now a total human resources review focusing on organization, talent management, and leadership development," he says. "It's somewhat similar to the GE Session C process."

Ruocco and his team developed individualized development plans for Goodyear's top one hundred leaders, brought increasing rigor to external search and selection, and introduced new tools for performance management, many of which are automated. For example, managers now have the tools to plot their people on a retention grid that measures how much Goodyear wants to keep a given person and what the risks are of losing that person to another company. High-potential individuals who are at risk of being lost get extra attention to reduce that risk.

"We are driving toward an integrated HR operating system, with the cornerstone being a robust talent management process designed to attract, develop, motivate, and retain a deep bench of top talent," says Ruocco.

"Joe took what they had and intensified the process," says Bill Conaty, ticking off his contributions. "He helped Bob really concentrate on building a more robust internal pipeline. He has fostered a true business partnership among HR, the CEO, the CFO, and the business unit leaders. He has traveled extensively around the globe with both Bob Keegan and Rich Kramer in getting to meet and assess Goodyear's global talent. He intensified their version of Session C—the global organization and talent review—by applying the GE playbook and other world-class best practices. He's really pushing candor in executive assessments to identify critical development needs for executives to work on to improve their game. As Bob pointed out, he's established a good relationship with the board, becoming their steward of doing the right thing about executive compensation, governance, and transparency.

"Joe also significantly upgraded the HR talent. That's something Bob didn't want to do without having a world-class HR leader; picking a few hotshot staffers without changing the top leadership would have been pointless. One very important thing is that Joe and Rich Kramer have forged a terrific working relationship, similar to what Joe had with Bob. That often doesn't happen when a new CEO takes over. I'm thinking of a recent case where one of the newly promoted CEO's first acts was to fire the HR director. HR leaders too often win over the CEO but not the rest of the organization, because they do everything to please the boss and as a result lose credibility with the rest of the organization."

Experiential learning—learning in a different and challenging job—was a mainstay of Keegan's talent development process. As practiced by talent masters, it's used to build people's capacities and capabilities by shifting them into new businesses and disciplines. Given the opportunity to quickly learn the company's strategic and operational aspects through a variety of silos, they greatly expanded their capacities and capabilities. (A leader from finance placed in an operations position in a plant, for example, will broaden his talent base from profit and loss to understanding how people work together and looking at the business from multiple perspectives.) They discover new talents and inner resources, learn to listen more acutely, develop their sense of curiosity, sift and sort information fast, and make quicker judgments. Importantly, they learn how to read people better, to figure out whom they can trust and whom they can't, and what their inner drivers and blind spots are.

Jean-Claude Kihn, for example, was a chemical engineer who worked at Goodyear mostly in technical jobs and caught Keegan's eye as someone with high potential. "He'd lived all over the world," says Keegan, "but he hadn't had a true broad business experience, and he hadn't been in the marketplace the way I wanted to see him in the market." Keegan made him country manager of Goodyear's Peruvian operations in 2003, where he not only gained the business acumen that he'd lacked but also won admiration for his leadership style.

"It's a funny story," says Keegan, "because I wanted him for the chief technical officer role, and the fellows running Latin America didn't want to let him go—they wanted to keep him and give him a bigger country. But that wasn't quite the optimal career path for Jean-Claude, because he's become in just two years an outstanding chief technical officer for the company."

Arthur de Bok joined Goodyear in 2002 as vice president for sales and marketing in Goodyear's European business. With thirteen years at Procter & Gamble, he brought marketing and product management expertise that Goodyear just didn't have. Says Keegan, "He was a very strong leader with a good strategic mind, and a guy that everybody just likes to be around. You could put him in any country. He'd do well. Within a couple of years, he took on the whole consumer business for us in Europe. Within a couple more years, he ran all of Western Europe. Another year, he took on Western Europe and Eastern Europe. So in a very short period of time, he was able to progress because he had good innate talent, built great teams around him, got really out-standing results, and had the courage to take on the very tough decisions that anybody running Europe has to take on almost day to day."

And of course Rich Kramer, now Goodyear's CEO, was a major beneficiary. Keegan had spotted his leadership potential and gave him bigger and broader roles in which to grow. From the time Keegan took over, Kramer moved through six jobs, progressing in a remarkable way from vice president of corporate finance to CEO. In retrospect it was close to an ideal CEO succession plan.

As head of strategy, Kramer got beyond the nuts and bolts of numbers and worked hand in glove with Keegan in determining the future of Goodyear—where the strategic bets would be made and what the company's portfolio of businesses would be. From there he moved to the CFO job, where he was responsible for executing the strategy. It was a unique opportunity denied to many who direct business development and strategy but rarely get the experience of an operational or CFO-level job.

The CFOs with the best chance of making it to CEO have been in the cauldron of operations. Kramer was given responsibility for North American Tire, not only Goodyear's biggest operating division but one with thin margins where Kramer had the challenge of taking out cost. "By definition that job was a big stretch," says Kramer, "and I was very con-scious of the opportunity the company was giving me. But I already knew most of the people, I knew the customers and the finances, and I felt comfortable with the business aspects."

Kramer and Ruocco spend a good deal of time visiting facilities around the world, paying attention not only to operations but also to people. "If a plant manager gives us a tour, we'll grill him about who could take his place, and then we'll grill the region manager about what the plant manager could do next and who would replace him if he was moved," said Kramer during that period. "We're trying to get everyone thinking more about people and evaluating them better, to develop a continual cadence of discussion about people choices. The more you make people talk about who they would put in significant positions and why, the better able they are to see their own logic and whether it's weak or strong. If one person says he thinks a certain person would be best for a bigger job, we'll ask him, 'If that person were outside Goodyear and submitted a resume for that job opening, would he be the one you would hire?' When you do that they start to get it, they understand better what to look for and how to evaluate people."

Foreign assignments were of course a key part of experiential learning at Goodyear. Immersion in foreign cultures would be central to executing the new drivers, including the crucial one of targeting consumer segments in emerging markets. Keegan and Kramer each had international experience, Kramer in France with PWC and Keegan in several countries over a dozen years while at Kodak. They knew that a foreign assignment not only tests a person's business skills, because she is far from headquarters, but also tests her ability to work in and communicate with a different culture. "When I went into England or Spain or New Zealand to run an operation, I always found that people were motivated by different things and saw things in different ways," said Keegan. "They had the same fundamental values, but there was such diversity in the workforce and in the customer base that I had to work hard to understand how to develop talent in those circumstances and how to read the market. You simply learn faster in that kind of environment."

The foreign stints also served another purpose: to begin moving the best people possible into leadership roles abroad. Like many old-line American companies that had gone global after World War II, Goodyear tended to run most of its foreign operations out of Akron. The executives in charge would visit from time to time, but they weren't on the scene with the customers and fully immersed in the culture of the markets they oversaw. That would not suffice for a company with global ambitions. Now senior executives running those operations are intimately familiar with the region, the cultures, and the languages.

One measure of Goodyear's progress in developing leaders is that about 75 percent of its team now is homegrown. During Keegan's first few years as CEO approximately half of the team came from outside. That isn't to say the eventual goal is to promote entirely from within or even to set any targets for insiders versus outsiders. "There's no set number," Keegan says. "We will need to refresh the organization from time to time with people hired from outside. We don't want to become insulated again. But whether the magic number is 75 percent promotion from within or some other number, I don't know. All I know for sure is that it's not 50 percent. Fifty percent would indicate that we're undergoing some sort of major change. I suppose if something dramatic happened in our market, we'd be willing to do that, but it's not in our game plan."

Another measure is Kramer's accession to CEO in February 2010, and then chairman after Keegan retired. Announcing it, James C. Boland, Goodyear's lead director, called it "the logical and anticipated culmination of a well-thought-out succession plan." Adds Conaty, whom Goodyear has engaged to work with the new leadership team, "This is an important inflection point for the company. They've shown that they have a social process that can produce leaders. Now Rich Kramer has got to take it to the next level and be sure it is institutionalized. By that I mean the process has to be unshakable. CEOs can come and go, but the process must keep churning out leaders no matter who is in charge."

It takes time, especially in a company with global scope. "Most of our hiring and recruiting will be global," Kramer says. "How do our people in Thailand or Eastern Europe know who to hire if we want to upgrade the staff? How do we get the right assessments and who does that? We don't have an infrastructure that can do that at this point. That's part of what Joe is building with his global team."

Keegan devoted about a third of his time to talent and leadership development, and Kramer plans to do even more. "We have a lot of good leaders, but they are in the higher positions," Kramer says. "If we had to replace some of those senior positions today, we might have to go outside. The goal is to get them from the bottom up. To create that pool of people we have to take the process we have at the top and cascade it down through the company. Which production managers would be the best plant managers? We have to find them and groom them and move them to the next level."

Keegan's and Kramer's journey over the past ten years shows how effective talent management can change a strategic direction and a culture. "We have a brand that's recognized around the world and a market that is going to be growing at unprecedented rates in coming years," says Kramer. "The number of new drivers in places like China, India, and Russia is increasing at a faster pace than ever before, and we have the brand and the technology to be a formidable player in an industry that is one hundred years old and that will likely be around for another hundred years."

UNICREDIT: SYSTEMS FOR CHANGING A CULTURE

With changes under way, Profumo and Piazzolla moved forward with a process for leadership development. UniCredit's Executive Development Plan essentially serves the purpose of GE's Session C, where top leaders meet to discuss the performance and potential of leaders and connect the decisions about people with the business strategy. Says Piazzolla, "This was a big managerial challenge. None of us has ever experienced the complexity and the scale of what we were going to do. We said, 'Okay, we all have to learn. So the issue is not performance management per se. The issue is executive development—how we make sure we become better executives.' " EDP would create a solid leadership pipeline and succession planning process.

The process normally takes place in a series of five full-day sessions during April and May at the Milan headquarters. But in 2010, they decided to take it out to UniCredit's regional headquarters in Munich, Vienna, and Bologna as well as Milan. Business division and functional leaders, along with their heads of HR, present their organizational and strategic challenges to Profumo and Piazzolla, and then talk extensively about people and the leadership pipeline. All of the top leaders and their people fill out self-assessment forms—what the individual accomplished last year, career aspirations, strengths, and development needs. Each person gets feedback on his or her assessment, and an opportunity to respond. The first sessions were in 2006 and involved around four hundred top executives. In 2010, they will cover more than four thousand, with intimate in-depth sessions on the top five hundred.

The meeting at the top is a culmination of ninety-four sessions held in February and March throughout the group. They are very detailed reviews on both execution and key talent and can take between three and six hours for each session. "What makes me satisfied," says Piazzolla, "is that the business leaders are totally committed to the reviews, and the role of HR is to be the facilitator of those meetings." Business leaders own the content of the discussions. HR owns the process, stimulates candid dialogue, and takes care of the follow-up action plans. In addition, business leaders highlight their best talent. They call this part of the process talent management review (TMR) to show how they are creating a solid pipeline for the future. "And this pipeline building has become a pervasive part of our culture. People talk about it extensively, take it seriously, and every leader feels the obligation to develop other leaders."

UniCredit values are built into the leadership development process. For example, Piazzolla says, the very first session was on the HR function and was between him and Profumo. "It was sort of a lesson on how to do a Session C, and Alessandro knew he could ask me any question. About two-thirds of the way through, we were talking about an individual who was really an achiever, someone that would always get the results the bank wanted, but not a role model for the type of leadership style that Alessandro wanted. Out of the blue he said, 'You know, I don't think this is the type of guy that we want in the company.' And we agreed that people who don't share the values don't belong in our company." He adds, "It was very helpful for us to have that initial review. When Alessandro had his first session with a business, he was just starting to probe and challenge. By the following meeting, people were stunned by how demanding he had become."

The first full executive development process brought in several leadership changes that no one in the organization had expected. "It was pretty shocking to everybody," says Piazzolla, "because while Alessandro always talked about how we needed to have people with high ethical standards and make sure that we all shared the same value system, there were no consequences for those who fell short. Maybe a leader would have been moved to another less central position, but he remained in the company. What we've done in the last three to four years has significantly changed leadership in the company.

"Now everybody understands, particularly at the top of the house, that there is no job guarantee. The performance and value system has consequences and is visible."

A CROWDED UPPER RIGHT CORNER

In the talent review sessions, Piazzolla introduced a nine-block matrix for evaluating leaders, which focuses on performance, values, and potential. "It is identical to the GE nine-block," says Piazzolla, "but the interesting part is that I didn't force it—I didn't say, 'Let's have a nine-block.' We were trying to add a synthesis of how people got measured, I let the discussion go, and we came out with a nine-block. Only at the end did I say, 'Hey, in GE also they have the nine-block.' But in this nine-block, while there are certain core processes that are the same, it is distinctly our own. For instance, we do not have any forced ranking in our nine-block."

It took a lot of teaching to get people to make serious evaluations. As is often the case, leaders had trouble making the tough decisions the nine-block requires. "Everybody was basically putting 90 percent of the people in the upper right corner," says Piazzolla. "Then the discussion was, 'But if our conceptual premise is that we are facing a new challenge and none of us is adequate, how is it possible that everybody's up there?' So the first two years were mostly educational discussion for leaders about how they had to measure. For instance, Alessandro literally moved people from one block to another. He would say, 'Look, Mario doesn't belong there, he belongs here,' and then we had a discussion."

In managing by example and using straight talk, Piazzolla observes, Profumo is reminiscent of Jack Welch. "I never talked about Welch, because we need to do our own thing, but he was behaving in the same way and generating the same level of attention. That kind of role-modeling behavior goes right down to the bottom. Some leaders didn't get it, and guess what: they're not in the company anymore."

UNIMANAGEMENT: A CROTONVILLE IN TORINO

Like GE, UniCredit relies heavily on an educational facility to drive cultural change. UniManagement, UniCredit's own mini-Crotonville, is a state-of-the-art executive development center used extensively for talent development, for cultural

integration, and for meetings with customers. Like Crotonville, it's located off-site—in this case in Torino, an hour
and a half from headquarters in Milan—to make it clearly
a neutral site for multibusiness, multicultural learning. It is
even a separate corporate organization, whose CEO is Anna
Simioni. In UniCredit since the end of 1997 after eleven
years in strategic consulting in Europe and the United States,
Simioni believes that there is a strong link between a person's learning, attitude, and capability to be great in what
he or she is doing. "This is even more true today in banking,
where there cannot be vision without learning. To achieve
our mission, we need great leaders, and I think there's a lot
we can do to enhance our learning skills and attitudes—our
learning capability."

Established just after the merger, UniManagement was
designed to be the unifying center of the group, a central
transmitting station for values and a melting pot where people from different businesses—from investment bankers and
asset managers to retail and commercial people—could learn
from one another. To accomplish this, UniManagement's
underlying philosophy is "learn by doing," which includes
both real-work collaborative problem solving and innovation as well as business simulation and internal case studies.
It has an agenda similar to Crotonville's since it joins people
from different countries and cultures and strongly focuses on
cooperation, innovation, and creating a common leadership
model. In terms of numbers, in 2009 almost 8,500 participants spent around 19,000 learning days at UniManagement.

The physical environment is more like a TV studio than
a classroom setting. The central meeting area—called the
Agora, after the open Greek forum square—is a modernistic
circular airy space, with giant video screens hanging from
exposed girders. Everything is flexible and allows everyone
to experience visually the spirit of the group that is expressed
through a common overall view of the business. Different
types of breakout rooms are designed for specific purposes.

"Energy Rooms," for example, are designed to facilitate idea sharing; every surface can be written upon, even the tables and floors. "Conversation Rooms," with their round tables and kitchens, create a relaxed atmosphere to promote easy and open interactions.

One unique feature is that UniManagement uses artists to graphically portray the key messages the presenters are conveying. An artist will stand behind the presenter and capture the themes in drawings and words on a twelve-foot-long storyboard. Color copies are made after each presentation and distributed to all participants. The artists are business-savvy, and they know just what to focus on. They also serve as a reality check: if a presentation is not coherent, its flaws will be obvious for all to see.

"Basically there are no teachers but instead facilitators and some subject matter experts," says Piazzolla. "We wanted the people to have a self-learning environment, and we provide facilitation tools for them to make it more productive. And that's been incredibly effective, because it takes people completely out of their normal reality and it brings them into a different gravity. So they have to relearn and be rewired completely. And it has been extremely helpful in driving our cultural change."

Senior leaders, including Profumo and Piazzolla, spend serious time at UniManagement. Every quarter the top one hundred executives come for a day and a half to talk interactively about business and strategic issues. Once a year the top four hundred come in for two days. In 2009, the theme was "Banking Reloaded," and in February 2010, under the umbrella of "We Leaders of UniCredit," the conversation centered on accountability for the group's new mission and what it implies for the four hundred leaders. At the end of the meeting the four hundred were asked to send personal letters to the CEO stating their 2010 contribution to the new mission as well as the key challenges they will face and what they will achieve.

"Now we have also started bringing customers in to help us redefine banking," says Piazzolla. "Our purpose was to listen clearly for their key expectations and how to fulfill them. Based on this input together with all the customer satisfaction data and reputation survey, UniCredit is redesigning its commitments to its customers. So it has become the place where things get developed. We are using this place to be the incubator of the new culture of the company.

"People are learning. They have smiles on their faces. They're upbeat, they want to work. It's really a great melting pot. And the cross-culturization is unbelievable. For example, Simioni spoke about one meeting she attended during the financial liquidity crisis. The Germans and Italians were wringing their hands and looking for help from their governments. The Eastern Europeans said, 'You guys must be nuts. We've seen how that works! If you think this is tough, you should have been in our shoes twenty years ago—you would have seen a tough life. This is not so bad. Let's fix it and keep the government out of it.'

"And it's another force driving candor into the culture. We've seen it happen. Candor is relative and evolutionary. It's not instinctive in banking culture or Italian business, but people are starting to see its importance. The critical drivers are UniCredit values and the sincerity and openness of the CEO. Alessandro is really walking the talk. He has good instincts and key hires to help him drive the change, and he studies the world's best practices. He pushes for openness, honesty, and consequences for results both in performance and in values."

UniManagement is a workshop in candor. When people went at first, they were reluctant to say what was on their minds. But then they experienced the atmosphere of thirst for new learning, openness, and trust. Now they go there and cut loose. We're convinced UniCredit wouldn't be able to pull off its monumental change without UniManagement as the central transmitting station for values and culture.

PUSHING THE PROCESS DOWN

Talent management at UniCredit is still a work in progress. After all, you don't get to be a GE-grade master of talent overnight—particularly in banking, which in Piazzolla's words "has always in my view been fairly bureaucratic and introverted. They didn't need to do the things that other companies had to do in order to generate excitement in the company. One thing that surprised me when I came was that everything was around salary. Motivation and success were totally correlated to money."

UniCredit has achieved intimacy with talent among its top five hundred leaders, with a good feel for their strengths, development needs, and promotion potential. For the rest, it continues to push the process down. In our first executive development session, Piazzolla recalls, "it was one big wow that the majority of the leadership positions didn't have a solid pipeline of successors. We asked for a page with a list of talents. We got lots of lists, and then when we asked, 'So do you really know these people?' often the answer was, 'No, it was given to me by HR.' That was one extreme. The other was a guy who was candid enough to leave the page blank and say, 'I realize I don't know the talents in my organization, so what I decided to do is to make this commitment: the next year you will see a page with people that I personally know.' "

Four years later, UniCredit has pinpointed replacements for each of the top five hundred leaders, 90 percent of them internal candidates. Profumo admits candidly that he has no one to succeed him today, but "we have identified many colleagues in their late thirties and early forties that can be the next CEO in five to ten years."

Many leaders still struggle with the concept of development needs. It's not a mind-set that comes easily to people conditioned over years to think that they're doing the best job possible and that any criticism—no matter how constructively intended—is a personal attack. Most leaders were disoriented and depressed at first. "This tool was new for them, it was rocket science," says Piazzolla. "Education is important; you have to explain the logic."

At GE, it took a generation before it was fully accepted, but UniCredit may get there sooner. Says Piazzolla: "Once leaders fully understand the implications of the feedback culture, they support it. Today we have many people asking for feedback that will help them grow. We foster this, and can see that this idea of managing and developing talent is taking hold and even becoming a bit of an obsession. The managers are learning that it is not something extraneous to their culture. It is their tool to develop people, and they own it." The UniCredit board of directors, he adds, supports the new talent development process. "They had to rewire themselves to see that critical feedback doesn't mean a bad job, but they understand that we are working seriously in building the future leadership.

"So these are the things that we are trying to build. They are not different from what GE has done for many decades. For most banks it's new."

CDR: LEARNING FROM GE

CDR was ahead of most of its peers in recognizing that a private equity firm needed operating people in positions of high-leverage decision making. By the time its current CEO, Don Gogel, joined the firm in 1989, CDR was relatively hands-on in picking deals and overseeing its portfolio companies. The financial and operating partners sat together to vet possible acquisitions, and the operating guys would work with each company's leaders to strengthen operations. "We would look at properties that had operational gaps and fix them," says Gogel.

CDR also was beginning to learn about leadership issues.

For example, in 1989 it bought IBM's printer business, which was spun off under the name of Lexmark. The $1.6 billion deal was one of the biggest ever by a PE firm at the time. Lexmark had no leadership to speak of—IBM had only a few P&L centers where leaders could develop management skills, and Lexmark was not one of them. "We had to build a company," says Gogel. "We needed different kinds of processes, people, culture. For example, there was no incentive compensation; IBM required dual sourcing, which was not relevant to faster product life cycles. Broader talent management was the key." CDR brought in many outsiders, among them a new CFO, head of sales, and people with retail experience, since IBM had not sold through retail channels. Gogel and operating partner Chuck Ames, a former head of B. F. Goodrich, personally wooed a badly needed product development manager from IBM. Paul Curlander had been the project engineer for IBM's first laser printer, and had since risen to become a vice president. He didn't want to leave. Says Gogel, "To him, nothing was better than being a vice president at IBM. And here were these flaky guys from New York telling him they wanted him to join their company and run this development function, and telling him that he'll love it." Curlander took a lot of persuading, but the effort paid off: today he is Lexmark's CEO.

Still, talent management remained secondary until the turn of the century. "Our original instinct was to exercise our governance with the talent that was there," says CEO Gogel. "As deals grew bigger we might look at a few other executives, like the CFO. But there was no robust assessment of talent." Instead, the firm recruited business leaders vigorously. It developed a close relationship with Spencer Stuart, one of the leading executive search firms, but the main driver was Gogel himself. He kept close tabs on company CEOs around the world, talking with them and learning from them, always with an eye toward the possibility of a future operating partnership or advisory role. In fact, his inventory of candidates was a form of succession planning. "This was our strength during the 1990s," says Gogel, adding that he still interviews a CEO every chance he gets. CDR developed its own leaders through an informal apprenticeship system, where principals and younger partners work for senior partners, observing them in deal negotiations, reviews, and evaluations to develop their skills and absorb the organization's culture.

How you coach and support a management team is an evolving work of art, Gogel adds. "The job is to make them successful. If we don't, one of us has to come in and run the business. Historically, in one of three cases, our guys have had to move to Oklahoma or Dallas and sit as CEO until a business was under control. We've done better in the past eight or nine years because we've gotten better at talent assessment."

What really focused CDR on talent was the economic slowdown between 2000 and 2002, which pushed three of its companies into bankruptcy. "Suddenly the game was at a different level," says Gogel. Companies were having to deal with the complexities of competition from abroad, managing global supply chains, and dealing with fast-changing markets. Operating partners were having to step in and run the ones that had gotten into trouble.

That's when Gogel began bringing in more seasoned, high-powered executives as operating partners. Among them were George Tamke and Roberto Quarta, who joined in 2000, and Jim Berges and Charlie Banks, who joined in 2006. Tamke and Berges were former vice chairmen of Emerson Electric—a company celebrated for its operational excellence. Quarta, who was CEO and later chairman of BBA Group PLC, a U.K.-based aviation services company, now heads CDR's London Office; Banks was CEO of England's Wolsley Group, the world's largest distributor of plumbing and heating products. Also operating partners are Fred Kindle, former CEO of Switzerland-based ABB, and Edward

Liddy, the former CEO and chairman of Allstate (who did a stint at AIG at the government's request during the financial meltdown). Each oversees one or more portfolio companies as chairman of the executive committee.

Gogel would assess the operating partners regularly in candid one-on-one meetings. Some bristled a bit at first—as top executives of major companies, they weren't used to being questioned so closely. "But we do it for everybody," says Gogel. "It's part of the apprenticeship system." Today he also asks them to do a formal self-evaluation each year.

CDR took a big step forward in 2001 when it brought in Jack Welch."We didn't do it because he was a celebrity," says Gogel. "What attracted us was the GE thought process and system that Welch developed. Those work better than anyplace in the world, and we thought maybe we could replicate some of that. We got him here by saying, 'Do what you want.' And the two things he liked were doing deals and running the operations reviews."

Welch quickly became a major force in CDR's leadership development. For many years the firm had run operations reviews where both the financial and operating partners sat down with business leaders twice a year for in-depth discussions. Originally focused mainly on performance, the reviews had increasingly been taking people into account. Welch catapulted them to another level, rigorously linking people to business results and bringing the famed take-no-prisoners style of coaching we described earlier to a business that had never seen anything like it. Says Gogel, "There was resistance at first. These guys thought they were pretty good, and they are. But we had developed a culture where people were reluctant to criticize one another. That went away after the first meeting. Jack said, 'You guys are too nice. Throw a few punches. Challenge. That's your business.' And then he showed them how.'" Welch effectively became the chief coach at CDR, teaching senior leaders to drill down to the core issues and reveal cause and effect. In turn, those leaders cascaded the style down to the businesses. "Now you wouldn't know who the tough question has come from," says Gogel. "The style has become Jack."

Six years after Welch joined, Gogel engaged Bill Conaty to help CDR strengthen its talent management processes. Gogel's charge to Conaty was "I want CDR to be known as the private equity company with the best HR practices and people." After searching for leadership issues and needs in each portfolio business, Conaty developed a far more rigorous talent review process than anything the firm had before. For example, each portfolio review is preceded by an in-depth talent review that includes each CEO and his direct reports, and covers their accomplishments, misses, leadership capabilities, development needs, and future potential, as well as their personal development and succession plans. The reviews are followed up with informal appraisals throughout the year, so that talent management becomes an institutionalized and repetitive process.

UPGRADING HR PRACTICES IN CDR'S PORTFOLIO

Conaty also brought new life to the portfolio companies' HR functions. There are many good HR people in those companies, he says, "but they were in their own cocoons, isolated from the rest of the world. Most didn't know each other. I saw a real opportunity if we could pull them all together, get them acquainted, expand their personal networks of resources, and share best practices."

He organized a CDR Human Resources Council that brings HR leaders together formally twice a year, but much more often informally. Hosted by the various businesses on a rotating basis, the meetings start with a dinner for social networking. The following day is spent discussing best practices. "We frame it so that the formal discussions feel more informal," he says. "We start by talking a little about each business—where it's going, what are the challenges for the business and for HR, key talent gaps, retention issues, labor issues, compensation, health care. We also talk about how engaged employees are, and we ask everyone if they have any best practices to share. I repeat the charge I got from Gogel. After the meeting they go away fired up and empowered, realizing they're not just by themselves on an island and that they can learn a lot from each other." Conaty also encourages them to expand their personal networks by attending the semiannual meetings of the Human Resource Policy Organization, a high-powered professional group with some three hundred corporate members. He tells them: "With your help, I want to distinguish CDR in the private equity world as having the best HR leadership talent and practices."

Conaty's work with the HR council has also added new depth and robustness to CDR's top talent reviews by revamping the so-called heat charts, which rank leaders' performance on various criteria by color codes. The charts cover the CEOs and their direct reports, and were originally focused mainly on financial results, with green, yellow, and red colors to indicate "passing," "caution," and "troubled." The HR team expanded the criteria to include leadership potential, retention concerns, and whether the leader has a succession plan in place. They also added a page showing each executive's key strength, key development need, and a key action to address. At the end, the leader reports on what he or she has accomplished since the last annual review.

"It has caused the portfolio CEOs and HR leaders to be more thoughtful about this process, especially issues around potential, retention, and succession," says Conaty. "Say you got green lights on performance and potential, a yellow around retention, and a red for succession. That should set off an alarm bell, and you'll get questioned on it right there. How can we make that yellow a green? If you've got a key executive whose retention can't be ensured—he wants to be a CEO somewhere—then you better have a near-term retention hook and a succession plan in your pocket. And the more we do this, the more it will really sink in."

There's plenty of room for improvement, Conaty is quick to point out—for example, it still can take months to identify CEO succession candidates. But today the firm is emerging as a talent master to watch in the private equity business. After all, don't you wish you could get *your* operational advice from the likes of Jack Welch, A. G. Lafley, Vindi Banga, and other talent masters?

PROCESS AT TPG

TPG's talent management processes are relatively simple, partly because the firm puts a lot of effort into recruiting the right talent and partly because it has an extraordinary talent master in the person of Jim Williams. Besides working with a number of search firms, says Williams, "we spend a big chunk of time developing our networks, and we work them pretty hard." The firm has hot lists of people they know they want to work with, and for the past seven or eight years has been hosting conferences for CEOs, CFOs, and HR leaders; speakers include luminaries such as Ford's Alan Mullaley and former Walmart CEO Lee Scott. TPG attendees are expected to network vigorously. "They're part of an informal social process, you might call it," says Williams. "When they learn they can talk to each other, they then build those networks after the conference. You give them enough time and room to do that, and it's almost boundaryless. It's been, frankly, a real secret sauce."

Williams has been recruiting highly experienced HR

people from operating companies, such as Anish Batlaw from Novartis, to help the portfolio companies keep talent development and assessment front and center. With responsibility for TPG's portfolio companies in China and Southeast Asia, Batlaw worked closely with the CEO of an automotive distributor in China to ramp up the team by recruiting world-class experts in supply-chain management, information systems, and leaders who could execute in the context of fast growth. In two years, the distributor's revenues grew by three times and its profits by five times, a great return for both TPG and the Chinese entrepreneur.

While the talent management processes aren't elaborate, they are thoroughgoing. Most PE firms bring their portfolio company heads in once a year to give presentations on how their companies are doing. At TPG, Williams and a core group of the partners undertake in-depth operating reviews every week of four to six of the firm's roughly sixty portfolio companies, dedicating part of the time to assessing talent. In addition, Williams holds major semiannual talent reviews of all the portfolio companies, with follow-up reviews in the following quarters.

"In the early days this was seen a little bit as a paper process, but it's actually quite alive because it helps facilitate some tough conversations," says Williams. "I'll take our sixty companies and say, 'Here's what we have, and here's where it's going well, and here's where it's not going well.' Some of the deal guys feel like it's a little bit of a report card, but we're reviewing the talent and the priorities."

LGE: AN INNOVATIVE TALENT TRANSPLANT

As we saw earlier, CEO Yong Nam could not achieve his vision of making LGE the global consumer electronics leader without a large infusion of outside genes. But seeking world-class talent meant bringing non-Koreans into a homogeneous Korean culture.

In a creative and innovative stroke, he found a way to bring a cadre of non-Korean functional experts into the company without igniting a culture clash. He brought them in at a high level, reporting directly to him. He did not, however, give them any immediate line responsibilities. Their mission was to form a corporate center of excellence to provide world-class functional best practices to the line managers and provide training to LGE people throughout the world. Nam hired a chief marketing officer from Pfizer, a chief procurement officer from IBM, a chief supply chain officer from Hewlett-Packard, a chief strategy officer from McKinsey, and a chief human resources officer from Ford—all non-Koreans.

This arrangement allowed the non-Korean executives to quickly add value in their area of expertise while giving them enough time to learn about and understand LGE and Korean culture and establish personal credibility. Nam reasoned that if his new recruits were immediately immersed in the responsibilities of a business leadership job, it would be hard for them to gain support from a mostly Korean management team. This way they could help Nam broaden the LGE culture while he helped them bolster their credibility and build their networks. If things went well, some of these executives could go on to eventually run businesses.

Nam's approach reduced the risk that the non-Koreans would fail in their new jobs because of cultural differences. Nam explains: "It was relatively easy for the organization to accept that I wanted to be supported by functional experts from around the world, so the risk of these people failing was pretty low. In theory and reality, we were incenting people in the organization to develop their own skills and capabilities by learning from these experts rather than having them feel controlled by people who had hierarchical control over them."

Nam had to deal with the issue of differences in compensation practices between Korea and places such as the United States as he was upgrading and globalizing LGE's leadership. He needed to compensate his new direct reports in line with market practices, knowing it could cause a stir with Korean executives. The Koreans knew such differences existed, and it was hard to accept within their own company, especially because in some cases the new people took longer to gain traction within the organization. Nam withstood the noise, and after a while the newcomers had added significant value to the company and this became less of an issue.

The business functions strengthened, and by 2010, one of the leaders brought in as a direct report to the CEO was ready to become a line leader for his home country. The officer, James Shad, had impressed the management team with his deep expertise in go-to-market process and management. He also had shown a high level of business acumen and a personal style that embodied the cross-cultural leadership characteristics that Nam saw as the role model for global LGE operations. Remarkably, Nam was willing to make this bold move in one of LGE's most important markets—the United States. Nam also showed that introducing new talent to LGE at senior levels was not just for foreigners. A Korean national educated at Harvard and developed in the McKinsey organization was brought into LGE as the business audit team executive vice president during 2007. He also was moved to an operating role as chief operating officer of LGE's expansive European region in 2010. This showed Nam's resolve to bring in people based on how their talents matched those needed to drive the change, not just to bring national diversity to the senior management ranks.

The diverse set of highly talented functional leaders had another effect: it demonstrated that LGE welcomed talent from anywhere in the world and would support it with expertise. LGE became a magnet for top domestic leadership talent in many countries. With encouragement and support from Nam, key regional presidents established chief operating officer positions in select countries in Europe, Africa, and North America. This boosted business results in each market and accelerated the localization strategy.

Nam supported the new talent with best-in-class HR practices guided by global, not Korean, standards. Korean command-and-control style leadership had worked well when LGE was largely driven by cost, but it was getting in the way of helping people grow and fostering creativity and innovation. Talented people sometimes left to pursue their ambitions elsewhere. Moreover, for LGE to continue to grow and succeed as a global business, people had to be able to work well together. Like almost all global companies, LGE had moved to a matrix structure as it became global, and collaboration across geographies, functions, and projects was crucial to speed, agility, and winning against the competition. Yet the behaviors necessary for a matrix organization to work were not being explicitly recognized and rewarded.

Nam outlined four new leadership criteria. He used them in selecting and assessing leaders, and by talking about them often he made it clear that every leader was expected to do the same with his or her direct reports:

1. Capacity. How much bandwidth do people have to absorb knowledge and grow? Do they possess both macro and micro insights on the business? Nam gauged this by asking challenging questions and observing those who could see the business from both perspectives. That was an indication that they could take on a broader range of responsibility.

2. Passion and aspiration. Are they driven to succeed on their own or do they have to be driven from above? Are they passionate about the business and their careers? Selecting leaders who continually raised the bar on their own performance meant that Nam would not have to do the pushing. That freed time to discuss strategy and vision. Raising performance goals would take care of itself.

3. Motivation. Are they personally motivated, and can they excite and energize others? Leaders had to be able to help people realize their potential, to engage people from the beginning, empowering, observing, and coaching them when they were in trouble rather than directing them.

4. Team player. Are they capable of coaching and supporting others versus being hierarchical and demanding? Even as CEO, Nam had to collaborate with partners and vendors and find resolution to the inherent conflicts of interest. He recognized the limitations of imposing your point of view on others and shooting down other options. He looked for leaders who could come up with third options that created win-win solutions among teams, businesses, functions, and partners.

Early in his tenure as CEO, Nam felt the HR function needed a hard look. The Korean HR leader was a solid individual but didn't have the background to globalize the function. Nam knew that LGE needed to revamp its HR processes and systems to support global growth. The changes required ranged from the compensation system to the leadership framework and talent development practices. He recruited Reg Bull, a Brit who had spent most of his career at Unilever. He also sought the advice of Jean Kang, who had been GE's country executive in Korea and had recently retired. Kang steered Nam to Bill Conaty to help accelerate the HR agenda; Conaty accepted his offer, and soon after conducted a session for the entire senior team on leadership, culture, developing a pipeline of leaders, and succession planning.

When Bull had to resign because of health problems in his family, Nam asked Conaty to help select his replacement. The search led to Peter Stickler, an American with a lengthy career at Ford Motor Company. Notably, he had been a senior HR leader when the business was navigating from being an international company to a global one and when the HR function was shifting focus from transactions to transformational process leadership. Both Conaty and Nam agreed that Stickler had the right technical capabilities, experience, global perspective, and interpersonal skills to take LGE's HR function to a higher level.

Nam tapped his HR experts to help him design a set of formal and informal people reviews that would help these criteria take root in the organization. The formal organizational development and people development sessions occur annually in July and August. In those reviews, Nam spends three to four hours reviewing each of his direct reports who leads a business unit or functional area. He also reviews the direct reports of every subsidiary CEO, business unit CEO, regional headquarters president, and company president, covering the top 250 leaders in high-leverage positions. All told, the reviews represent three to four weeks spent on people reviews and people decisions.

Nam reinforces the behavior he wants LGE to demonstrate in dialogue sessions he conducts with groups of employees as he travels from location to location. He role-models the more open Western-style form of communication by giving them a thorough update on the business and its future prospects. He then solicits comments and questions and makes a point of showing genuine interest in what people have to say. The style is pretty much countercultural to the top-down Korean mode, and at first employees were far too deferential to Nam's position as CEO to ask candid questions in these discussions. They felt they were being graded by Nam. Sensitive to the issue, Nam asked them to write their questions anonymously and submit them in advance. Gradually they became comfortable with candor, and today's employee groups are even animated in stating what's really on their minds, a major feat in a company that had been so command-and-control.

The company now has six non-Korean leaders running

operations in other countries—the United States, Canada, France, the Netherlands, Sweden, and South Africa. And Nam hasn't neglected the home office in Seoul. The chief information officer and chief HR officer are American. The chief marketing officer, chief technology officer, chief strategy officer, and the process excellence and global supply chain leader are all non-Koreans. In three short years, Nam has set his Korean company firmly on the road to becoming the global leader that he envisioned.

CONCLUSIONS: CHANGE STARTS AT THE TOP

No company ever got to be a talent master without the wholehearted commitment and participation of an enlightened CEO: one who understands that building talent is the most important priority and will be their legacy. The enlightened CEOs we've met throughout this book had nine characteristics in common. These qualities add up to a template for anybody setting out on the road to talent mastery:

- They understand that talent is the key to the future. Strategies come and go, market share and profits wax and wane, but an organization that can build a self-renewing team of first-rate leaders is prepared to handle anything that tomorrow brings.
- They make talent management as rigorous as financial management.
- They personally lead the social processes that support and reinforce talent development and make themselves role models for the entire organization. They make it clear that building organizational capability is part of every leader's job.
- They devote a good deal of their time to knowing, discussing, and calibrating their leaders. They take every opportunity, planned or spontaneous, to meet

their high-potential leaders on their own turf, to observe them, and to give them feedback.

- They focus on the content of succession planning, not just the process. They think about and discuss the demands of the job and the specific qualities of those who might be prepared to do it. They plan carefully for their own succession.
- They recognize the importance of entry to the leadership pipeline and devote time and attention to it.
- They establish a performance culture by making company values explicit and enforcing them, and establishing performance goals and measurements with clear rewards and consequences.
- They set the tone for candid dialogues and insist on candor in evaluations.
- They continuously raise the bar on learning and performance.

Part IV

THE TALENT
MASTERY TOOL KIT

The goal of *The Talent Masters* is to light a path for all companies to build a better, more secure future for employees, shareholders, customers, and partners by developing robust talent pipelines and same-day succession plans. We hope it inspires you, but first and foremost we want it to be actionable. This section is designed to help you translate the ideas and practices described in the earlier pages into actions you can take Monday morning.

One of the principles of talent masters is an enlightened CEO. This is not meant to suggest that leaders have to wait for a spiritual awakening or epiphany but rather to say that CEOs should realize the tremendous responsibility they bear for the future of the company. It is their actions, decisions, and behavior that signal to others that talent matters, that it can be identified, understood, and managed like the resource it truly is. The right words are important, but words are not enough. Time and regular attention send stronger signals. Linking rewards to developing talent is stronger still. Don't divorce results from the leaders who produce them, and don't talk about leaders in abstract terms. Bring realism, rigor, specificity, and candor to discussions as you link people and numbers.

With or without guidance from the CEO, leaders at any level can sharpen their skill in developing talent. Practice your power of observation and test the accuracy of your judgments in pinpointing other people's talents. Here are the elements of the tool kit. Use them to significantly improve your ability to develop talent. Make them a part of your daily routine.

- Principles of Talent Masters
- Does Your Company Have the Culture of a Talent Master?
- The How-tos of Mastering Talent
- A Mechanism for Differentiating Talent
- FAQs and Answers
- Guidelines for Your Next Talent Review
- Crotonville on Any Budget
- Six Ways HR Leaders Can Become More Effective Business Partners
- How to Ensure Smooth Successions
- What Feedback Should Look Like
- Leadership Pitfalls
- Lessons Learned on Talent and Leadership Development

PRINCIPLES OF TALENT MASTERS

For quick reference, here is a brief recap of the principles we enumerated in chapter 1.

1. An enlightened leadership team, starting with a CEO who really "gets it" and sees talent development as a competitive advantage.

2. A performance-driven meritocracy, a willingness to differentiate talent based on results *as well as* the values and behaviors behind those results.

3. Explicit definition and articulation of values, citing strong company beliefs and expected behaviors.

4. Candor and trust, leading to better insights into people's talents and potential, focusing on development needs to accelerate personal growth.

5. Talent assessment/development systems that have as much rigor and repeatability as systems used for finance and operations.

6. Human resource leaders as business partners and trustees of the talent development system with functional expertise equal to the CFO's.

7. Investment in continuous learning and improvement to build and continuously update the leadership brand in sync with the changing world.

DOES YOUR COMPANY HAVE THE CULTURE OF A TALENT MASTER?

The mechanics of talent development—when to conduct reviews, who should be in the room, what criteria to consider, and so on—are relatively easy to replicate. A good HR department can design processes based on best practices observed elsewhere. Harder to copy and key to developing leaders are the cultural or social aspects of talent development. Here senior management must drive the effort to instill the values and behaviors that make leadership development an integral part of running the business.

The following checklist will tell you whether your organization has the culture of a talent master.

True or False?

1. Senior leaders are heavily involved in recruiting and developing leadership talent at all organizational levels.

2. A candidate's behavior and values are considered before hiring.

3. Leaders at every level are vigilant about spotting new talent in the ranks, not just among the people reporting directly to them. They see it as a major part of their job.

4. Leaders are thoughtful and rigorous in pinpointing people's specific talents and where those talents would flourish.

5. Leaders don't hesitate to give hard-hitting, timely feedback on individuals' development needs to improve their performance.

6. Poor performers are confronted and given the opportunity to improve or face the consequences of removal.

7. Operational, budget, and strategic business reviews are used in addition to specific talent reviews to get insights into a leader's natural talents, and sometimes lead to major decisions about which leaders should be in which jobs.

8. Leaders spend time with leaders at lower organizational levels to see them in action doing their jobs. They are hands-on developers of talent.

9. Leaders with the highest potential are spotted early and moved quickly into jobs that will expand their capacity and capability.

10. Judgments on leaders are based on hard evidence and cross-checking of observations by multiple people.

11. Leadership development is attacked as intensively as delivering financial results.

12. Developing other leaders is expected and rewarded.

THE HOW-TOS OF MASTERING TALENT

Selecting Leaders

1. Get senior leaders involved in selecting leadership talent.

The quality of the seed has a huge effect on the fruit years later, so don't hand off recruiting to whoever is convenient. Have your seniormost leaders involved in the recruiting process from the campus level to the top of the organization. They will have the instincts and judgment to spot business savvy and raw leadership talent. Knowing how important it is to recruit the best talent and how much the company will be investing in their management trainees, senior leaders at Hindustan Unilever make the time to interview entry-level candidates for the company's high-potential pipeline. While it might be impractical for CEOs of larger companies to participate at the ground level, they should be knowledgeable and comfortable that the right role models within their companies are serving as their "face" in scouting talent.

2. Hire for leadership, not just functional or academic expertise.

Don't look only for technical expertise and hope that some of your experts will turn out to be leaders. Look for people who have demonstrated leadership in some area of their life. Even when a high level of technical or scientific proficiency is required, look for those experts who have the desire and potential to lead others and help them grow, as Novartis and Agilent do.

3. Learn about the person's values and behavior before hiring.

Think about the values and behaviors leaders will have to demonstrate to succeed at your company, and screen for it. Well-designed interviews can test for things such as teamwork, interpersonal behavior, intellectual honesty, and temperament before you make an offer. Hindustan Unilever creates opportunities to observe people in a group setting as part of their screening process, and GE, P&G, and others test for cultural fit based on the candidate's competitiveness—academically, athletically, and socially.

4. Be humble enough to bring in outsiders when you have to, but take steps to ensure their cultural assimilation.

It's sometimes necessary to recruit leaders at higher organizational levels, to change the culture (as at Goodyear), for critical expertise (as in GE's Ultrasound business), or to raise the bar or globalize (as at LGE). Do observational research along with your usual reference checking to be sure about the fit. Then back the newcomers with visible signs of support from the top. LGE's new functional leaders had time to adapt to LGE's closed Korean culture—and vice versa—because they started as advisors to the CEO rather than as line leaders. Jack Welch reinforced his commitment to Omar Ishrak, brought in a couple of organizational levels below Welch to run Ultrasound, by letting everyone know he was "his guy." When Ishrak attended his initial corporate business review and was awaiting his turn to present the Ultrasound story, Welch impatiently asked, "When is my friend Omar going to present?" He was assured that Omar would be presenting shortly; others got the message that he was invested in Omar's success and open to the changes he was proposing.

5. Be honest about who has the greatest leadership potential.

Make your best judgment about who has the potential to rise to the highest levels of the organization and do all you can to accelerate their growth. Watch carefully to see if those initial judgments were correct, and don't get locked into predetermined stars whose shine may be dimming. Keep an eye out for others you might have missed or whose leadership talent emerges later. Crystallize what enabled them to deliver excellent results, and consider whether it will be relevant to their success in the future. Bear in mind that while high-potential leaders deliver results, results alone don't indicate high potential. Embracing values and maturing leadership style are usually the differentiator between former and future stars.

Developing Leaders

1. Make talent development your obsession.

Spend at least a quarter of your time trying to understand people's talents and helping them grow, and try to improve your judgment about people. Welch, Immelt, Lafley, and Keegan stated that they spend between 30 and 40 percent of their time on people decisions. Dig in several levels below your direct reports. Look at the person from multiple perspectives, and take time to think about where the person would flourish. Filter out personal biases by gathering evidence and facts. Bill Conaty and Jack Welch, and later Jeff Immelt, talked about people all the time, always with an eye toward figuring out what makes them tick and how to unleash their talents. That's how you will expand your own capacity. When you spend time and energy to help leaders reach their potential, retention takes care of itself. GE has historically retained over 95 percent of the top six hundred senior executives they didn't want to lose. This metric is tracked closely and reviewed with the board of directors twice a year.

2. Drill to the specifics of each leader's talent, just as you would drill to the root cause of financial performance.

Every individual has his or her own unique blend of traits and talents. Each has areas where judgment needs to be improved, whether it's anticipating shifts in the external environment, building teams, or segmenting a market. Be rigorous in identifying the one or two things that will accelerate or unblock the person's growth. Keep linking business issues to the leader's actions, decisions, and behavior until those talents and areas for development are clear and specific. P&G recognized Deb Henretta's ability to understand the consumer and build relationships and gave her a big job in Asia, where those natural talents were able to expand. Ron Nersesian at Agilent saw in Niels Faché an entrepreneur's action orientation and a technologist's attention to detail. Nersesian coached him to keep in mind the strategic context when negotiating global partnerships and helped him become a general manager and later group executive.

3. Give frequent, honest feedback.

When it comes to knowledge workers and leaders, development often occurs as the result of some kind of trigger, whether it's a stern lecture, a teaching experience, or a trusted person hitting you with a verbal two-by-four. Leaders use every interaction to understand people better and watch for those coachable moments when they can provide feedback as a possible trigger. Adrian Dillon's career took a whole new turn when his boss showed him the downside of being the smartest guy in the room. Feedback is best when it is targeted, constructive, and candid. The senior leaders at Hindustan Unilever travel far and wide to visit young leaders in the field. They log their feedback in a "Management Trainee Contact Book," which helps to accelerate the young leaders' development. Jack Welch, Jeff Immelt, and other leaders at GE follow up formal reviews with informal coaching sessions to reinforce the learning and accelerate leadership growth.

4. Make talent development an explicit part of every leader's job and hold him or her accountable for it.

Leaders show the importance of developing other leaders

largely by example. At GE and P&G, business reviews inevitably include questions about people, so leaders have to know their people well: who is doing well, who needs more runway, who needs exposure to a different part of the business or a different culture. Developing talent becomes part of the DNA. Agilent keeps leadership development top of mind by making it an explicit performance objective and tying compensation to it. The CEO reviews organizational capability and performance twice a year.

5. Provide intellectual opportunities for additional growth.

True leaders continuously build their skills and relationships, hone their personal traits, and improve their judgment. Experience is a great teacher, but leaders also need intellectual stimulation to really excel. The educational piece helps leaders deal with nuances they might not be aware of if they have their head down doing their job. If you don't have a Crotonville, use local universities and in-house experts to conduct teaching sessions for intellectual stimulation and cross-fertilization, live or online. Novartis used outside experts to make leaders self-aware of their psychological blockages. UniCredit has effectively used its UniManagement training center to expand its leaders' perspective in keeping with the company's pan-European strategy. Be specific about the learning you observe and what that says about a leader's future growth trajectory. Continuous learning, at the speed of change, is a critical success trait for contemporary leaders facing new global challenges every day. The worst thing for a leader is obsolescence.

Making Leadership Assignments

1. Give leaders jobs with lots of room for growth.

When you get to know a person's talent really well and imagine what it could be, you'll know what kind of assignment is a good fit. High-potential leaders need jobs that challenge them. Be clear about what you expect them to gain, whether it's testing to see if a new skill can be acquired or etching more deeply their judgment about people or business. Actually experiencing a different culture is top of the list for leaders in companies that are expanding globally. Tumultuous events occur frequently in other parts of the world. Having traveled the world throughout her career, P&G's Deb Henretta wasn't sure she needed to move to Asia, but living there and dealing with one crisis event after another helped her develop a sense of calm. Some of the best GE leaders developed that same sense of calm from their stints in other parts of the world. That ability to stay calm and maintain perspective is a distinct leadership quality that expands dramatically when operating outside your comfort zone. P&G's Melanie Healey's vast experiences both growing up and working in dangerous parts of the world gave her both the self-confidence and peripheral vision to succeed despite difficult surroundings.

2. Take a corporate view when giving assignments.

Leaders who become CEOs in their forties or fifties will have worked for many bosses along the way. A single boss cannot be allowed to hold back a talented young leader. Leadership talent must be cultivated and protected as a corporate resource. When giving someone a new job assignment, consider whether the person's new boss will be nurturing or suppressive. Leaders at GE sometimes have to wait for the right assignment, but senior leaders keep an open dialogue with the person so he or she knows what the company has in mind. Immelt thought he was in line to run GE's Appliances business, but Welch and Conaty waited for a better fit while reassuring Immelt he was on their near-term radar screen for a big move up. Shortly thereafter, John Trani left the medical business to become CEO of Stanley Works and Immelt was rewarded for his patience with the top job at Medical

Systems. The key point here is that Immelt trusted the system and Welch to deliver on the promise, and it paid off.

3. Think creatively about where a person will excel.

It takes keen judgment to know which next assignment is best for an individual leader. Incremental moves are appropriate for some leaders but too slow for those with the highest potential. Horizontal moves can be great accelerators of growth. Average performers in one job can sometimes be high performers in another. It's a matter of finding the right fit. Agilent's Niels Faché was losing his spark in a job that required more maintenance than forging new ground, so his boss moved him to a completely different track, exploring mergers and acquisitions. Elsewhere at Agilent, Adrian Dillon saw that a person's natural inclination toward long-term planning was perfect for strategy but not for jobs that required fast action. The core values and ambitions of some leaders at Novartis suggested that the current jobs were not right for these leaders, and a different career direction would work better for those individuals and the company.

4. Keep a database of employees' skills and experiences.

It goes without saying that companies need a system to keep track of cash and financial data. Companies need similar tools to systematize their knowledge about up-and-coming leaders. A database can collect incredible amounts of information on employees throughout the world—what languages they speak, what countries they'd prefer to work in, their mobility, their performance, their track record. It is not a substitute for judgment any more than the mere collection of numbers is, but it frees up time and mental energy for insights into developing people's talents. As Dick Antoine says of P&G's database, "When a job opens up, we don't miss anybody." Creating such a system was one of Bill Conaty's first undertakings as head of HR at GE. Now whatever GE needs to know about a leader, bingo—they can get unlimited data about the person almost instantly. These computerized global employee databases ensure that all candidates are on equal footing for consideration for bigger opportunities. They also pressure employees to keep their resumes current in order to be considered for promotion.

Assessing Leaders

1. Do formal reviews informally.

Business leaders take pride in knowing how the business is doing based on the numbers. Some have them memorized and check them daily between the quarterly budget and operating reviews. You need to have the same feel for your leadership talent by reviewing it formally at least twice a year and preferably more often. Keep asking questions until you know who is doing well, who is having trouble, who needs a new assignment soon, and where the capability gaps are. Build your skill in reviewing people and getting to their core talent by practicing it repeatedly. And insist on candor and realism. When UniCredit CEO Alessandro Profumo started giving candid feedback regarding development needs, people found it hard to accept at first, but the company pulled together as people came to see that performance would be visible and recognized. The most beneficial feedback is informal and timely. If you take every opportunity to give employees informal feedback on their performance, you eliminate that one very uncomfortable discussion when the employee says, "This is the first time I've ever heard about that issue. I believe you're picking on me."

2. Use business reviews as people reviews and vice versa.

Take the time to connect business results with the people behind them. Who is doing what to cause the results?

Remember that business outcomes, including financial results, are lagging indicators produced by people. Follow hunches to get to the people issues sooner. GE uses every budget and operating review as a chance to learn more about people, not just what they're doing but how they think. Decisions to promote or reward a leader are as likely to be made in an operating review as in a Session C or similar talent review. Agilent makes leadership a routine topic in business reviews. Extend the review if you have to allow time to explicitly discuss people. No business operational or strategic review is complete without examining the people implications involved in executing the strategy.

3. Don't judge performance by numbers alone.

Drill below the surface to learn how the numbers were achieved or what stood in the way of achieving them. Did the person miss because the boss insisted he retain a weak team member or because the price of a critical resource suddenly spiked? Drill just as deeply when the leader makes the numbers. This is where you'll test a leader's values: did she sacrifice the brand for the sake of more sales? It is also where you'll spot great talents. Lindell Pharmaceutical discovered a gem in Sue by noticing *how* she had achieved her extraordinary sales numbers: by helping Lindell's pharmacy customers improve their prescription fulfillment and financial results. It was brilliant and sustainable. Senior managers started talking about how to give her more runway.

4. Consider what the leader leaves behind.

You learn even more about a leader by looking at the business after he or she leaves the job. Is the group better off because of his leadership or does the next person have to clean up a heap of problems? Interview people to find out. A senior leader or someone from HR can do this, provided the person is highly trusted. Use it as a development tool to give the person feedback, not to play "gotcha." P&G invented this practice as a way to develop leaders and ensure it was promoting only the best. They look over a five-to-seven-year period at the enduring value a leader did or didn't create. High-potential leaders leave the organization stronger in relation to the external environment than what they inherited.

5. Sort misfits from failures.

Success and failure are often conditional, so be careful how you use those labels. When a leader falls short in one job, rethink your assessment of the person's talent and search for a better fit. That's how GE ended up with a great leader in charge of its corporate R&D. Mark Little was the right leader for GE's gas turbines business under normal circumstances, but because of dramatic changes in the external environment and massive technical failures that he did not create, GE had to bring in a more seasoned technical leader fast. Little's career was sidetracked temporarily. He had many strengths that were too good to lose, and fortunately, he persevered and had a great career at GE. When a leader falls short repeatedly, admit that your judgment about his potential may be wrong. Find the right job, or as a last resort dismiss the person, but treat him with dignity and encouragement so that he will find his place elsewhere.

Recognizing and Retaining Leaders

1. Tell people how they fit in.

Don't assume your stars know that you know who they are. Remind people that their contributions are recognized and how you see their potential. People deserve to know how you see their future. That will give leaders with the highest potential more reason to stay. Money is just one of many ways to tell people they are valued, and in today's environment, there's not much of it to spread around. Words and public recognition are powerful supplements. Telling someone they're doing a great job doesn't cost a penny. Virtually all the masters of talent give frequent, positive reinforcement, and they make it personal.

2. Spread financial rewards throughout the year.

Salary reviews are great opportunities to sit down with leaders eyeball to eyeball and reinforce their motivation and commitment. Increase the opportunities for those candid personal interactions by having separate discussions around bonuses and other forms of compensation. GE spreads the financial rewards given to its top six hundred or so leaders by giving salary increases at various intervals based on the person's assignment starting date, bonuses in February, and stock options in September. Leaders at GE also step outside the schedule when they see the need to reward extraordinary work or to retain someone. GE doesn't hesitate to grant off-cycle raises or restricted stock units in the midst of Session C. That puts spice in the game as word spreads through the informal network that exists in every organization. A side benefit of discussions at frequent intervals: no one gets an unpleasant year-end surprise.

3. Allow for judgment when compensating leaders.

Make compensation rigorous but not overly formulaic. Beware that efforts to make compensation objective often have the opposite effect. Formulas are no substitute for good judgment and knowing your people well. GE uses judgment to factor in the "difficulty of the dive"—in other words, how effectively the person performed versus the industry competition. That's why leaders of the low-margin, slower-growth industrial division could get greater percentage boosts than those who run flashier, high-growth businesses. Just be sure your thinking is rigorous and fair and provides additional upside for achieving stretch goals.

4. Differentiate.

All people may have been created equal, but they don't perform equally well. Allow those differences to surface and give greater rewards to the leaders who make bigger contributions. Did the person make an individual contribution or make the team more effective? Did she take the viewpoint of the corporation as a whole despite the fact that it affected her area adversely? Differentiation forces candor, as in "Tell me again why I'm getting this and Sharon is getting that. What am I doing wrong?" Don't back off from a merit-based performance management system, even if people gripe. Your hope is that it will force candid discussion on performance. Make your judgments and stand behind them.

Driving Differentiation

This is a mechanism to help you drive differentiation around rewards and recognition. The percentages are something to aim for. They should not be used so mechanistically or formulaically as to cause inequity. Feel free to customize it for your own business.

		← Potential		
		High Potential	Moderate Potential	Topped Out
Performance & Values ↑	Top Talent ~30%			
	Highly Valued ~60%			
	Less Effective ~10%			

FAQs and Answers

Q: My company isn't big on developing leaders. Can I develop myself?

You must. While talent masters continuously seek ways to develop their leaders, they expect those leaders to take responsibility for their own growth. In fact, a drive to continuously learn and improve oneself is an indicator of leadership potential. Ask for input from bosses or peers and look for ways to build on your talents, at work or even outside of work. Volunteer for projects to gain experience and expand your perspective. Look for a mentor to help you build capabilities you need to move ahead. Don't rely only on performance evaluations for what to work on; at many companies, they are backward-looking and not developmental. Solicit help or do your own assessment and decide whether to work on skills, personality, relationships, or judgment. Read books, take classes, ask questions. Work to excel in your current job, then ask for more challenges. Make it clear that everybody must grow and everyone should bear accountability for personal growth. CEOs aren't exempt; in this highly volatile and fast-changing external landscape, it is imperative for them to grow too.

Q: We're a small company. How can we give younger leaders learning experiences without putting the company at risk?

You can easily expose leaders to other functions, other parts of the business, higher levels of decision making, and even externalities just by getting them in the room with other people. For example, a manufacturing person will benefit tremendously from direct contact with customers. Creating advisory boards or arranging for leaders to participate in industry associations outside the company can expand their view. But leaders do need practice running a P&L. Consider creating a small one, and if the leader is successful, expand its scope. It's also a good idea to use high-potential people in a consultative role, seeking their inputs on things that are not part of their day job. And have them lead cross-functional teams on projects that can take the small company to the next level.

Some small private-equity companies, such as Baltimore-based Sterling Partners, recruit young graduates and have them sit in on reviews of portfolio companies in addition to carrying out their usual entry-level tasks. The young leaders learn by observing the partners in action, asking questions, linking numbers with operations, and comparing people among the portfolios. This exposure accelerates their development.

Q: What's the trick to finding HR people who have a grounding in business operations?

Break the hiring mold by looking for people who are already in a business leadership job and have good instincts about people. Dick Antoine, former head of HR for P&G, was running the supply chain before he was running HR. Bill Conaty spent five years of his career in operations before making the shift to HR. For people who have spent their careers in HR, consider rotating them to assignments elsewhere in the company. Working with finance people, for instance, will broaden the HR person and build credibility. Meanwhile, the numbers people will become more aware of people issues, and the match-up becomes mutually beneficial. At GE, Conaty made sure people in human resource leadership training spent one full assignment outside the HR function, preferably on the corporate financial audit staff to gain business partnership experience.

Q: What can a midlevel HR person do differently?

People issues are the downfall of many leaders. To be a successful partner to business leaders, you have to work on improving your judgment in dealing with these issues. They will run the gamut. Just when you think you've seen every situation possible, something else comes along. The more you test your judgment, the better it will be. The good news for HR people not in the top job is that they can offer a perspective or possible solution to a problem and test it with someone more experienced. That is, once you have an action in mind, you can huddle with more experienced HR people. Go up a notch in the organization and ask, "What would you do?" or "What do you think of this plan of action?" By listening to those whose judgment you trust, your own judgment will improve, and you'll feel more confident as a problem solver. That's great training to be a future partner to the CEO.

Q: How can I make a sound judgment on a person's personality and values?

The best way to inform yourself about another person is through close observation. Watch how the person handles herself in a group or dealing with a tough issue. If you can't observe directly, ask questions and get 360-degree input from others closer to the person. In reference checking, for instance, ask for examples of how the person might typically handle a particular situation, such as a peer or a boss contradicting her viewpoint. Is she open to others' views or stubborn and defensive about her opinions? Actions speak louder than words; look closely at what he's actually accomplished versus what he plans to do. HUL's three-day mentoring session is a chance to observe leaders' actions and behavior. Its length and intensity make it impossible for people to mask who they really are and what is most important to them.

GUIDELINES FOR YOUR NEXT TALENT REVIEW

Whom to include:

- The seniormost leader, ideally the CEO, who will lead the discussion
- The head of corporate HR
- The leader of the particular business, unit, department, or function you are reviewing
- The HR person who works with that leader, if any

How to schedule it:

- Hold it at the leader's site, not headquarters.
- Schedule it before your annual strategy and budget reviews.
- Schedule a follow-up session no more than three months later, perhaps by phone.
- Plan to spend a few hours to start. Don't rush; allow extra time when the process is new.

What to bring:

Up-to-date and background files with summary evaluations, detailed assessments, and photos of each group leader being reviewed and each of the leaders reporting up to him or her from one and two levels below. An employee database will make access to this information much simpler.

How to set the tone:

The best way to get candor is to ask questions and challenge people's statements. They will soon realize that you are seeking honesty and directness.

What to talk about:

Don't jump into the specifics of any individual until you've been updated on the business. Unless this is your first such session, remind yourself ahead of time what issues to follow up on. Ask what the current challenges are, what external or internal issues people are worried about, and what might arise in the next twelve to eighteen months. A good opening question is "Do we have the right leadership team in place to execute the business strategy?"

Look for linkages between those business issues and people. Is the business changing in ways that demand different capabilities? Are competitors making moves that affect talent—shedding employees or making a hiring push? Does this business unit contemplate a change in organization structure? Why or why not? How well prepared is the team to play the game two years out? What gaps exist? What actions will be taken?

Make explicit who could replace the leader now and in the coming years.

As you discuss each individual, probe for specific facts and evidence and ask the group to consider what pattern is emerging. What talent is this person demonstrating? Where might this person really shine, and what would she need to do to get there? Don't limit your focus to high performers. An average performer in one job could be a higher performer in a different job.

Use an agenda, but deviate from it for the sake of fruitful discussion.

A Typical Agenda

1. Business Leadership
   - Business priorities
   - Current organizational chart with names, faces, positions, and time in job
   - Matrix of ratings on performance and values for high-level leaders
   - Succession plan for direct reports
   - Any anticipated restructuring or leadership changes

2. Pipeline
   - Broad list of leaders one and two levels below CEO direct reports
   - Overall ratings for these leaders
   - Diverse best bets for promotion
   - Nominations to attend executive education courses or other developmental actions
   - Review of entry-level recruiting for corporate training programs

3. Growth and Culture
   - Describe the way you are driving the business goals and priorities in your organization
   - Review plans to accelerate business and talent growth in key areas, such as emerging markets
   - Discuss results from discussions about top company priorities
   - Discuss feedback from employee opinion surveys or social audits

CROTONVILLE ON ANY BUDGET

Continuous learning is a given for masters of talent. They emphasize experiential learning, and enhance its value by giving their leaders intellectual stimulation and training on specific topics through in-house or external educational programs. The educational piece helps leaders understand nuances they might not be aware of when they have their heads down doing their jobs. It helps leaders learn tools and concepts that may be too new to have been tested, and exposes them to thought leadership, which often stimulates new ideas and leads to innovation, particularly around management.

Not every company is big enough or prosperous enough to support a training facility like GE's John F. Welch Learning Center (otherwise known as Crotonville) in Ossining, New York, or UniCredit's UniManagement facility in Torino, but they don't have to be. Here are other options and things to keep in mind.

Turn leaders into teachers.

While it's important to have some outside teachers who bring an external perspective, you already have a great educational resource on your payroll: your existing leadership talent. Establish programs in which senior leaders teach other leaders. At P&G, the CEO, vice chairs, and business presidents teach in education programs for general managers and other top talent. At GE, too, senior leaders conduct teaching sessions, along with outsiders. At Intel, former CEO Andy Grove made it a rule that all officers, including himself, must teach at least one week a year. When leaders teach, topics are guaranteed to be relevant, and discussions will broaden people's understanding of the business. Yes, it takes time, but the time is well spent to build the organization's leadership bench. In the process you will also be developing the top leaders who conduct those classes, because teaching tends to sharpen a person's thinking. Leaders will benefit more if they do fewer PowerPoint presentations and deliver less company PR to the attendees and conduct more interactive teaching in which people can challenge the teacher's thinking. Leaders can hold classes online via webcasts.

Localize learning.

Large, dispersed companies could set up internal programs at their various sites to give promising leaders frequent exposure to top executives in the company. A customized leadership assimilation or development program might include the top twenty to thirty leaders at a location, who would gather for two to three hours a week over a six-month period with a different member of the company's senior management each time. During that period, the younger leaders would be exposed to various functional or business perspectives, and those senior leaders would get to know the up-and-coming ones. Some time might be spent getting up to speed on hot-button issues or specialized topics. Occasionally an outside expert could be brought in. Costs would be low, yet people who want to learn would get a lot of mental stimulation. Such a program is a great development tool and also a great retention device for people who feel they're running out of opportunities to grow. One CEO instituted a practice in which some fifteen to twenty upper-level high-potential people meet with him quarterly from 4:00 to 10:00 p.m. with no preparation or set agenda. The CEO throws out for discussion a very important current topic having to do with the external environment, and sometimes it is only indirectly relevant to the company. People do their own original thinking and at the same time bond with each other. The practice encourages them to keep up to date on important current topics.

Use technology to facilitate learning from peers.

One of the real advantages of Crotonville is the social exchange. People learn as much from their classmates as they do from their instructors as they get exposed to different business issues and practices. Their view of the business and the external world expands. It doesn't cost a lot to gather a cross section of people to participate in an exercise or engage in a discussion on an important topic. These exchanges can occur in the company cafeteria or across oceans virtually, perhaps with occasional face-to-face group meetings. Once social relationships get established, communication across distances is easier, and learning is ongoing.

Work with local universities.

Many schools will customize development programs to be taught on campus or at the company site. The key is to get your high-level leaders involved as a tag team with professors, so the learning is relevant to the business. Many CEOs are teaming up with a university professor to co-teach in the university and even to do research and write papers. Andy Grove joined with a professor at Stanford, and together they wrote a groundbreaking paper on cross-industry disruption.

Differentiate and educate.

If you are willing to differentiate among your leaders, chances are you will have a very small percentage of people who truly have the potential to rise to the highest level. Tuition for executive education programs at business schools or leadership training centers might be affordable for those select few. The issue is selecting who should attend. Not every great GE person goes to Crotonville. You've got to be willing to make those calls for your best people, and not use the educational training class as the consolation prize for coming in second on a missed promotion.

SIX WAYS HR LEADERS CAN BECOME MORE EFFECTIVE BUSINESS PARTNERS

1. Understand your business and industry dynamics.

Know the financials and key operating levers that affect your business. In order to get respect from the CEO and senior business team, you need to understand the business issues and challenges that are confronting them on a day-to-day basis. When you can effectively focus your attention on HR issues that impact their business issues, you will find a much more receptive audience.

2. Build your HR vision and strategies around the business model.

Too many HR leaders get enamored with new initiatives that do not have a direct impact on the business bottom line. They may be fun, but if they're not affecting business performance, they're nonproductive exercises. For example, we worked with one company that had a fourteen-page performance appraisal for all professional employees. This appraisal process may have won an award in an HR contest for comprehensiveness, but it turned off every leader as well as every individual being appraised. It was absolute overkill, and a time drain for the people expected to use it. We shortened the form to two pages, replacing HR jargon with business language and making it more practical and valuable.

3. Become problem solvers versus problem identifiers.

Too many HR professionals see their role as discovering problems and making a hand-off to the operations leader for the fix. The real way for HR to add value is to remove issues from the CEO's plate instead of adding to the existing pile. Bill Conaty personally made a practice of keeping his CEO informed of delicate issues that he was working on that might ultimately come to his attention. Those issues might include anything from retention or promotion to compensation or allegations of wrongdoing. He made it clear that he was going to do everything in his power to solve the issue without the CEO's intervention. By contrast, one CEO remarked in his appraisal of his HR leader, "I really like my HR leader as a person. She has a good personality and is fun to be around. But every time we have a meeting, I bring my list of issues to the meeting, and the HR leader brings her list, and when the meeting concludes, I end up with both lists." This is the ultimate indictment of HR professionals who are great at identifying problems and not so great at fixing them. Become the person who is welcome at the CEO's door versus the one where the CEO looks up from the desk thinking, *Here comes the grim reaper with another dump truck full of unsolved problems.*

4. Take your work seriously, but don't take yourself too seriously.

Since the HR function could be viewed as the ultimate arbiter of fairness, balancing business needs with employee advocacy in the organization, your personal style contributes greatly to the receptivity of your decisions. If the HR leader projects arrogance or a power-broker style, your credibility sinks like a rock. Despite the nature of your problem, keep it light and maintain a good sense of humor to keep the CEO loose. Lord knows CEOs have enough other staff members who will keep them uptight, so you need to lighten the load. Even in the darkest times, you have to realize that you're only human, and by staying cool you've got a much higher chance of solving the problem. A lot of operational leaders are highly passionate and emotional. That poses a great opportunity for an HR leader to provide a sense of balance and calm in the storm.

5. Have the personal independence, self-confidence, and courage to push back or challenge the system when necessary.

Don't salute every command. Understand that CEOs aren't infallible in their thinking just because they draw the biggest paycheck. But pick your spots. One of the main reasons Bill Conaty got the top job as senior vice president of HR for GE in 1993 is that Jack Welch valued the fact that he pushed back on the system during one of the highest-profile integrity/compliance issues that the company had faced in a long time. GE had to exit and discipline a large number of executives, and Conaty felt that the company needed to differentiate the discipline based on the individual's involvement in the issue and prior contributions. It would have been easier to treat everyone involved in the same manner, but that didn't feel right to Conaty, and he said so. Conaty wasn't sure how his point of view would be received, but he stuck to his guns and spoke his mind. That was one of several times when he put his job on the line. In some companies, he might have been history, and he was prepared for that possibility. But that didn't happen in GE, where candor, courage, and convictions are highly valued. In the end, those who deserved to be fired were fired, while others with lesser involvement were disciplined appropriately. The entire corporate team was comfortable with the final outcome. Another lesson for HR leaders is that when you stay true to your personal values and convictions, those moments can make or break your career. In Conaty's case, it propelled his career forward.

6. Never forget why you're at the table.

HR leaders have an obligation to balance their strong business partnership role with their employee advocacy role. But effective HR leaders can't be perceived as being in the CEO's pocket or they'll lose credibility and objectivity throughout the organization. If you're viewed as a direct extension of the CEO, people will filter the message. It's a very delicate balance, where occasionally an HR leader slips too heavily into the business-partner role and neglects employee advocacy. CEOs don't need another financial or operational expert, since there are many staffers already present to provide that advice. But they do need at least one leader thinking about the people implications of their decisions. One of the nicest tributes Bill Conaty ever experienced came from Brian Rowe, the former CEO of GE's Aviation business. This was in 1993, as Conaty was leaving Aviation to take the top corporate HR job. He had worked with Rowe for three years, from 1990 to 1993, and at Conaty's going-away party Rowe's parting comments were: "This is the first HR guy I've ever known that really cared about human beings." So the last piece of advice for HR leaders: never forget the "human" in human resources.

HOW TO ENSURE SMOOTH SUCCESSIONS

Companies that want to ensure smooth successions must first of all know their business and their leaders well. That intimacy will allow them to anticipate when a leader will soon be ready to move out of a job and who is getting ready to step into it. Succession to the CEO spot and other high-leverage jobs, however, requires exceptional vigilance and the close involvement of the board of directors, which owns the CEO succession decision and should weigh in heavily on other key positions.

CEO Succession

Throughout this book we have emphasized the importance of knowing leaders intimately for the sake of leveraging a person's talent and helping that person develop. The same holds true for the CEO job. The board of directors, which selects the CEO, must know the candidates well. That is a strong argument for choosing an insider, and masters of talent almost always do. P&G and Goodyear are great recent examples of a well-orchestrated internal CEO succession plan.

Because of the strength and diversity of their leadership bench, talent masters have more than one viable contender for the top job. The board and the outgoing CEO know each of the contenders well and therefore have a clear fix on what particular talents they will bring to the job.

The most important piece of advice regarding succession is therefore to build talent throughout your organization following the principles outlined in this book. Look for CEO potential among your newest recruits and accelerate their growth by giving them jobs that are big leaps, not incremental moves. As leaders succeed and move into high-leverage jobs, create opportunities for the board to get to know them through things like board presentations, dinners, and site visits. A unique practice at Tyco Electronics is to devote two hours of every Management Development and Compensation Committee meeting to a business unit, whose leaders present and discuss their unit's future organization structure, leadership capability requirements, and key players in the top two layers. The committee learns a lot about the people in each business unit, including those who could be future CEOs. Some members of the business units also attend the board meeting and are invited to cocktails and dinner with the board, where one or two directors sit with the leaders to get to know them. This practice is repeated every year.

At talent master companies, HR gives the board annual reports on the composition of the company's overall leadership, but they also acquaint the board with individual leaders several levels below the CEO. That way board members build their knowledge and intimacy with those leaders over time. A side benefit is that directors often have great insights into people and can make useful suggestions about how to further develop a person's talent. This intimacy allows the board to act quickly if the company loses its CEO unexpectedly.

Companies where leadership development is somewhat ad hoc can follow these steps to improve the process of selecting their next chief executive:

Two to Three Years Ahead of Time

- Carve out time for the board, the CEO, and the head of HR to identify and discuss all potential CEO candidates. Do not settle on one or two prematurely, and don't look only at the CEO's direct reports. Make this an urgent item on the board's agenda. Have HR assemble a tight package of information on each individual.
- Discuss the challenges the business will face in the near future and the longer term for the purpose of clarifying what skills and qualities the future CEO will

need. High integrity, strong character, and good communication skills should be givens but are not enough for the job at hand.

- Let the emerging business needs narrow the field of candidates. Be careful not to let past psychological contracts, loyalties, or past performance dominate. The CEO, head of HR, and board should remind each other to look forward.

- Continue to create opportunities for the board to get to know the candidates in a variety of settings. Make job changes or create new jobs to test a candidate's capabilities. This is a time when functionally organized companies will want to test leaders with specialized expertise in a P&L job, even if it means creating such a position.

- If the list of potential candidates whose talents match the needs of the job is thin, bring in outsiders while there is still time to test them in jobs below the level of CEO.

When the CEO's Retirement Is Imminent

- Have the board spend half a day nailing down the company's situation and defining the absolutely essential skills and traits for its next leader. These are the non-negotiable criteria for the job. The Management Development and Compensation Committee can take the lead, but the full board must be engaged in this discussion.

- Compare each of the final candidates to the non-negotiable criteria. In most cases one candidate will emerge as a better fit than the others. Be sure to identify the potential weaknesses of this candidate and brainstorm ways to compensate for them (recall how GE sought the support of the VP of operations when it appointed Jim Campbell to run the Appliances business).

When the Inside Slate of Candidates Falls Short

- The world changes fast, which means even talent masters might fail to produce a CEO who is prepared to take the company where it needs to go next. Smaller companies or those that don't have P&L opportunities for their leaders might simply have no choice but to seek a leader from outside. This is when boards turn to headhunters to fill the slot. Still, the board must control the selection process and not delegate it to the recruiting firms.
- Take the time to clarify the essential or non-negotiable criteria, and explain them to the recruiters. Ask them to state in their profiles of various candidates how the individual meets those criteria. Narrow the field using that filter.
- Have the board interview the final two or three candidates by having two or three directors meet with one of the candidates. Then the directors can pool their observations and impressions. Remember the value of multiple inputs, and drive for specific evidence to overcome personal biases and superficial first impressions.
- Make reference checking as rigorous as other forms of due diligence. Ask pointed questions to better understand the person's behavior and values as well as his or her skills. Dig below the track record to learn how that performance was accomplished.
- Allow ample time for the full board to discuss all the candidates, identifying their particular talents and their fit with the business.

Specificity and Nuance Make the Difference

When it is time to choose the next CEO, the succession process should force the board to challenge preconceived opinions and assumptions and reach a collective understanding of the job and the candidates. Succession, like other aspects of talent management, is fundamentally a social process. The focus must be on the rigor of the dialogue and sharing of multiple perspectives, from which sharper, more accurate insights into the job, its context, and the candidates will emerge.

Define the job in specific terms.

Every CEO job poses a unique set of challenges. The board has to know what they are for the coming years—a tall order in a world that is in constant flux, but a prerequisite for finding the CEO who is most likely to succeed. It's easy to say that no one can predict the future, but the board must think through various scenarios that could unfold, then step back and ask, What will it take to succeed under those conditions? The answer will come through group discussion, and that discussion should continue until the answer is reduced to three to five specific criteria.

Every CEO will have certain desirable traits. Early in the search for a successor to Jack Welch, he, Bill Conaty, and Chuck Okasky created a profile of "The Ideal CEO" (see page 294). They knew the next CEO would not meet all the criteria; no human being could. The description established a high standard but did not in itself define the future CEO. Similarly, many companies list qualities that should be considered "givens," things like integrity and the ability to communicate and motivate people.

The board must go beyond those exercises to define the unique set of non-negotiable criteria. These will likely be a mix of skills, experience, capabilities, and personal traits. Take the example of a health insurance company in 2010. The board might ask, What will it take to succeed as CEO in the dynamic, politically charged health care environment, and how does the board feel about the company's current direction? Growth may be an imperative for competitive reasons and for shareholders, but the health care landscape is changing and societal concerns are gaining voice. A chief executive would need to drive both innovation and productivity, be able to participate in policy making, have a consumer orientation, and lead organizational change. It might not be easy to find someone with those capabilities, but without them, the company will suffer. A large manufacturing company whose domestic demand is dwindling may need to build markets in other geographic regions. In that case, experience leading market expansion, ability to work with foreign governments, and a willingness to take risks may be non-negotiable criteria for the next CEO. A company that has missed several financial targets over the past few years may need to reestablish its credibility with Wall Street. The ability to deal with investors and analysts might be a non-negotiable criterion.

The point is that when the set of criteria for a new CEO looks like that of any other company, the board has not done its job. It takes time, but the board has to keep talking until it has separated the givens and the wish list from the handful of criteria that are absolute must-haves.

Get to the nuances of the person.

It's common for directors to think they know the CEO candidates better than they do. They won't make this mistake if they do their due diligence on people, and especially if every board member is deeply involved. Those who are on the search committee can design and lead the processes for selecting a new CEO, but every director should know the candidates and participate in making the final decision. We stand by our advice for boards to get to know internal candidates over many years, but even when the company has several internal candidates for CEO succession and directors feel they know them well, the board must approach the CEO decision with a clean slate and an open mind. When directors step back and reflect as a group, amazing things happen: preconceived opinions disappear, insights deepen, and matches and mismatches with the non-negotiable criteria become crystal clear. Almost always the directors come to a unanimous conclusion.

The Ideal CEO

Five years before Jack Welch's retirement, GE leaders drew up a list of criteria for what they called the ideal CEO. You probably won't find Mr. or Ms. Perfect (let us know if you do), but it's a useful checklist of qualities to look for.

Integrity/ Values	Unquestioned integrity; capacity to shape company values and culture. Brings values to life in all personal interactions.
Experience (Broad, Deep, Global)	Broad, global business experience; successful management of multiple businesses through the cycle, necessary mastery of business essentials; e.g., financial acumen; markets/ customers; technology; boundaryless operation of key business processes. Proven ability to create/increase shareholder value.
Vision	A visionary . . . capacity to imagine and create new paradigms and future opportunities . . . to drive through and beyond conventional wisdom . . . ability to reinvent . . . move to the second act, the third act, etc.
Leadership	Outstanding leadership skills (all dimensions); attracts, excites, energizes, and motivates the best to continuously stretch for and achieve extraordinary levels of accomplishment. Has the savvy to effectively sequence the CEO action agenda. Understands the need to establish a track record for results before advancing the "social" programs. Has to put "hard" actions ahead of "soft" initiatives (e.g., as restructuring came before Work-Out).

Edge	Insatiable appetite for increasing knowledge/ perspective. Acute listening skills. Sorts facts efficiently; applied intuition for speed/ impact; sound judgment; strong convictions; courageous advocacy, but willing to revisit and reconsider. Effective decision maker. Selects and leverages personal involvement for highest return.
Stature	Statesmanship, charisma, presence, charm; adapts personality/style effectively to different situations; held in high esteem by multiple constituencies.
Fairness	Deep commitment to "fairness." The balance, objectivity, and wisdom needed to make important human and business judgments.
Energy/ Balance/ Courage	Sound physical health and emotional equilibrium. Strong endurance. Beyond resilient . . . thrives on pressure. Comfortable operating under a microscope. "Stomach" to play for high stakes. Understands all elements and all constituencies involved in crisis management. Has the intellectual honesty and bold candor required to establish credibility and bring difficult issues to timely/ effective closure.

Succession to Other High-Leverage Leadership Jobs

Talent masters apply the same rigor and intensity to succession decisions for all their high-leverage leadership jobs. Planning years in advance without locking on to any one person ensures that strong leaders step into those jobs prepared to build on the foundation of their predecessors.

Ironically, many companies do a particularly poor job of succession planning in the HR function. It is troubling to see many major companies going outside to fill the top HR slots because they lacked the foresight to groom insiders. Surely the insiders find it demoralizing to know that they can climb only so high in the organization and that the top job is out of their reach. At companies such as GE and P&G this is not the case, but the list narrows dramatically beyond them.

At GE, Bill Conaty always knew it was his obligation to develop three or four HR leaders ready to step up at the right time. It's no wonder that so many GE HR alums were recruited to the top HR slots in other companies. Because of the development they experience at GE, there's a big world of opportunity available to them externally. It's part of the value proposition that makes joining the GE HR team so attractive in the first place. Dennis Donovan went to Raytheon, Home Depot, and Cerberus; Bob Colman to Delta; Brian McNamee to Amgen; Joe Ruocco to Goodyear; Laszlo Bock to Google; Eileen Whelley to The Hartford; Rino Piazzolla to UniCredit; Mark Mathieu to Stanley Works; and Bob Llamas to AC Nielsen, just to name a few. In fact, GE has an active HR alum group of hundreds who cut their teeth at GE and remain loyal and proud of their GE heritage.

Jeff Immelt and Bill Conaty spent years reviewing and discussing Conaty's personal succession plan. Immelt treated it in a similar fashion to a CEO succession. The intensity stepped up in Conaty's final two years on the job as he and Immelt developed a list of factors they felt were critical to the future specifications of the role and constantly monitored the strengths and gaps of each candidate. They kept the GE board involved and comfortable throughout the process.

They recognized that the role of HR in a talent master company demands different skills and capabilities than the usual HR job, and the succession process has to reflect that reality. They established forward-looking demands of the job and from that deduced the criteria. That search led to the appointment of John Lynch, the best fit among a group of highly capable HR professionals.

GE started by pinning down the future trends and issues the next senior vice president of HR would face. GE would continue to be a competitive and exciting enterprise, and HR would continue to be a credible, visible, value-adding business partner. HR would have to continue to attract, develop, and retain the best diverse and global talent and build a leadership pipeline, anticipating business needs and making GE a source of the best jobs in the world. HR initiatives and outcomes had to be closely linked to the business. And the function itself had to develop world-class talent with both functional skills and business expertise, while continuing to advocate for employees.

Specific challenges were to help drive GE's growth initiative, accelerate globalization, attract and retain great diverse talent despite increased competition for it, deal with compensation and reward systems in a slow-growth economy, deal with the rising legacy costs of health care and pensions, and be a source of coaching and calibration, especially for the highest-level leaders.

That thorough and specific understanding of the job led to an equally specific set of characteristics the new HR leader would need:

- Trust and confidence of the senior leadership team
- Fit with the CEO and CFO
- Ability to be the external face of GE
- Excellent assessor of talent
- Global operator
- Clear thinker and change leader, with strategic capability
- Huge capacity for complex problem solving
- Operationally savvy
- Decisive, with the courage to make tough calls
- Ability to retain senior HR team

WHAT FEEDBACK SHOULD LOOK LIKE

We've said that feedback and coaching are hallmarks of talent masters and that feedback should be candid and specific. Here we use one of Jack Welch's signature coaching devices—the handwritten letter he sent leaders after every review—to show what we mean. Current GE CEO Jeff Immelt continues the practice.

Below are excerpts of letters Welch wrote to Bill Conaty following some of his reviews.

> Dear Bill,
>
> Congratulations on a sensational start. Your incentive bonus reflects how we all feel about you—and this is just the beginning. Your "real-person" skills are just what the company needs.
>
> Bill, the challenge as I see it is simply "upgrading the talent"—not just your own; you have a good start on that—but that on the field. We have too many "war horses" that aren't good enough at the second level. Worse than that, they kill our values with their old-school thinking.
>
> Next year, your biggest and most important Session Cs could be your field Cs on HR. I'd love to see you push to upgrade this crowd—even if they do have "files on their team."
>
> Bill, you are a great member of the team and I'm sure glad you came here.
>
> Best,
> Jack

Clarity and specificity: Welch makes it unmistakably clear what he expects Conaty to focus on in the coming year and why.
Tone: Direct but friendly. The letter gets right to the point. It is written in everyday language.

Underlying message:"You are valued. You have to make some changes that might be uncomfortable; I'm behind you on them."

Dear Bill,

Congratulations on your year and your IC—you are the best I've ever seen at what you do. Thanks for all your help.

Bill, your challenge remains the same—better people in more jobs. Nice moves in Industrial. We need fresh talent like this across the company at the second level. Everyone in your corner of the world on Relations has to be the best—keep weeding.

The issue is, where are the next Bill Conatys? How do we get them up to visible positions earlier? You are working at 150 percent—please demand the same from all around you!

Again, congratulations and thanks for a sensational year.

Best,
Jack

Clarity and specificity: Make more of the kind of changes you made in Industrial.
Tone: Same direct, uncluttered language.
Underlying message:"Talent matters. Succession in HR is important and urgent. You are valued."

LEADERSHIP PITFALLS

Having participated in numerous talent reviews and observed countless leaders over many decades, we have seen many things that keep otherwise talented leaders from rising further. The following are the most common; talent masters and individual leaders should watch for them.

- Misfiring on performance or values, overcommitting and underdelivering
- Being too internally oriented
- Resisting change, not embracing new ideas
- Being a problem identifier instead of a problem solver
- Winning over the CEO but not your business peer group
- Always being worried about your next career move instead of focusing on the present
- "Running for office"—which is totally transparent to everyone else
- Being self-important and rigid, with no sense of humor
- Lacking the courage to push back on the system
- Not developing your own succession plan
- Not growing, being complacent
- Not keeping up with the speed and character of external change

LESSONS LEARNED ON TALENT AND LEADERSHIP DEVELOPMENT

Here is a summary of what we have learned about leadership and its development over the years:

- Company and personal values must be compatible.
- Attracting, developing, and retaining world-class talent is a never-ending task.
- Candor and trust in the system are musts.
- Think of shortcomings first as development needs rather than fatal flaws.
- Differentiation breeds meritocracy, but sameness breeds mediocrity.
- A performance culture has consequences—good or bad.
- Great leaders develop great succession plans.
- Dealing with adversity is developmental and illuminating.
- Large organizations require simple, focused, consistent communications.
- Continuous learning is critical for success.
- Great leaders balance passion with compassion.

CLOSING COMMENT: IMPROVE YOUR GAME

Most of what we believe and recommend to the readers of this book is based on our decades of experiences with major corporations as consultants and practitioners. Our advice to leaders who want to become talent masters is simple. But it's simple in the same way the advice from a golf pro is simple: take a nice, smooth, rhythmic swing at the ball and follow through. Now you know what you need to do, but it will take you a lot of determined effort to develop the swing that the masters of golf perform with ease.

Talent mastery requires the same rigor and consistency to build your skills—in this case, identifying, developing, and retaining the talent you need for a competitive edge. It requires dedicated processes and resources. Above all, it requires total commitment. As a leader of the business, your wholehearted involvement is what will drive the practice and culture of talent mastery in your organization. Without it, you and your people will be stuck in the rough. Not long ago we were talking to a friend who'd recently been made CEO of a company. Talent mastery is his goal, and in only a few months he'd gotten off to a great start. But, he told us, he'd also quickly come to see that if he left, it would be all over—the rest of his team just wouldn't have the staying power. "We're not talking about an initiative," he said. "It has to become institutionalized, and a part of the culture—that set of written and unwritten rules that determines what people do when nobody's looking."

Our underlying premise of putting people before the numbers is fundamental to becoming a talent master since operational and financial results begin with having the right people in the right jobs to create and execute the business strategy. And talent masters recognize that only intimacy among leaders will engender the candor, mutual trust, and confidence that is essential to building organizational capability. Without disciplined practice, that swing will always be off balance and unreliable.

Acknowledgments

We have had the privilege of working with and learning from many of the world's most accomplished business leaders throughout our careers. Many of them have broken new ground in developing leaders and thus have extended the longevity of their organizations. All of them are exemplary practitioners who demonstrate in their daily work a passion and commitment to helping others reach their leadership potential. Their efforts truly create value for their companies and for society as a whole.

We wish to acknowledge the tremendous support we received from the following individuals who were so generous with their time and insights. At Agilent Technologies: Bill Sullivan, Ron Nersesian, Niels Faché, Adrian Dillon, Jean Halloran, Teresa Roche, Christine Landon, and Amy Flores. At Clayton, Dubilier & Rice: Joe Rice, Don Gogel, and Tom Franco. At GE: Jeff Immelt, Mark Little, Omar Ishrak, Jim Campbell, and Gary Sheffer. At Goodyear: Bob Keegan, Rich Kramer, and Joe Ruocco. At Hindustan Unilever: Vindi Banga and Nitin Paranjpe. At LG Electronics: CEO Yong Nam and Pete Stickler. At Novartis: Dr. Dan Vasella, Joe Jimenez, Kim Stratton, Dr. Mark Fishman, Thorsten Sievert, Juergen Brokatzky-Geiger, Kevin Cashman, Kathy Bloomgarden, and Elizabeth Flynn. At P&G: A. G. Lafley, Bob McDonald, Dick Antoine, Moheet Nagrath, Deb Henretta, Melanie Healey, and Laura Mattimore. At TPG: Jim Williams. At UniCredit: Alessandro Profumo, Rino Piazzolla, Anish Batlaw, and Anna Simioni.

In describing the leadership development systems at GE,

and in particular, the values and social processes that make them so effective, we were reminded of the tremendous contributions Jack Welch has made in this area. He understood intuitively the importance of building on people's strengths and truly revolutionized the concept of leadership development around the world.

Our editor, John Mahaney, was a hands-on partner throughout the writing process. We are grateful to have had the benefit of his intelligence, sage editorial advice, and unfailing vision and support along the journey. No editor is more dedicated to his profession.

Geri Willigan was the glue that kept us all together and moving forward. She helped shape the book through participation in the design, research, writing, and editing, and kept us all focused on the big picture through the twists and turns. Enormous thanks to her; we crossed the finish line.

We also want to thank Charlie Burck, whose drive for deeper understanding helped us draw out the lessons from our own and others' experiences. He mastered the subject, then used his penchant for detail and accuracy, along with his artful writing skills, to bring the stories to life on the page.

Hilary Hinzmann and Doug Sease provided great editorial support at critical junctures, drafting some sections with the ease of the seasoned professionals they are. They were a pleasure to work with.

Last but not least, we owe thanks to Cynthia Burr and Carol Davis of Charan Associates, who managed the project's complex logistics with utmost care and competence.

Index

About the Authors

After a forty-year career with General Electric, BILL CONATY retired in 2007. The company he left behind owes much of its global success to the top-notch human resources organization that he developed and led for over fourteen years. As senior vice president for human resources at GE from 1993 to 2007, he has long been recognized as a world leader in his field. One of the most visible achievements was successfully managing the CEO succession and transition process from Jack Welch to Jeff Immelt, the current chairman and CEO of GE.

Bill Conaty spent his entire career at General Electric. A native of Binghamton, New York, he earned his bachelor's degree from Bryant University in Rhode Island. After graduating from a three-year management program at GE and a stint in the military, he held management positions in a number of GE operations including aerospace, rail, and aircraft engines. In 1990, he was elected a company officer and became vice president for human resources at GE Aircraft Engines. Just three years later, he was selected by Jack Welch to the senior vice presidency of corporate human resources with responsibility for over 320,000 employees worldwide. He served Welch for eight years and Jeff Immelt for six years.

GE is not only one of the largest and most diversified industrial companies in the world, it is one of the most highly respected as well. GE was named by *Fortune* magazine as the "World's Most Respected Company" for seven of the last ten years on Bill's watch. Additionally, *Fortune* ranked GE #1 in developing world-class leaders. In 2004, Bill Conaty was named Human Resources Executive of the Year. The cover story in *Human Resource Executive* magazine hailed his handling of "one of the most important CEO succession challenges of the century."

In great measure due to the management development and training programs Bill engineered, *Business Week* declared that GE had "the most talent-rich management bench in the world." A recent profile in the same magazine praised him for taking "a department that's often treated as a support function" and turning it "into a high-level business partner." Bill's old boss, Jack Welch, calls him "spectacular," explaining that he has earned "enormous trust at every level. The union guys respect him as much as the senior managers." In fact, Bill handed over the top job to a long-time GE HR colleague while staying on to conclude his final successful round of national labor negotiations with GE's unions.

Bill serves as a Trustee of the Board of Bryant University and currently serves on the Advisory Board of Cornell University's Center for Advanced HR Studies, where his legacy will continue with the recent endowment of the William J. Conaty Chair in Human Resources. In November 1996, he was inducted as a Fellow to the National Academy of Human Resources, elected chairman in February 2001, and named Distinguished Fellow, the highest honor, in November 2007. Bill is also a member of the HR Policy Association, where he served as chairman from 2001 to 2007, and is a member of the Personnel Roundtable.

Following his retirement, Bill formed his own consulting company, Conaty Consulting LLC. His client base includes Clayton, Dubilier & Rice, P&G, Dell, Boeing, Maersk, LG Electronics, Goodyear, UniCredit, and several other Fortune 100 companies. He is also active on the speaking circuit, represented by Leading Authorities (www.lauthorities.com) as world leader in HR.

RAM CHARAN is a highly sought after business advisor and speaker famous among senior executives for his uncanny ability to solve their toughest business problems. For more than thirty-five years, Dr. Charan has worked behind the scenes with top executives at some of the world's most successful companies, including GE, Verizon, Novartis, DuPont, Thomson, Honeywell, KLM, and MeadWestvaco. He has shared his insights with many others through teaching and writing.

Dr. Charan's introduction to business came early while working in the family shoe shop in the small Indian town where he was raised. He earned an engineering degree in India and soon after took a job in Australia and then in Hawaii. When his talent for business was discovered, Dr. Charan was encouraged to pursue it. He earned MBA and doctorate degrees from Harvard Business School, where he graduated with high distinction and was a Baker Scholar. After receiving his doctorate degree in corporate governance, he served on the Harvard Business School faculty.

Dr. Charan is well known for providing advice that is down-to-earth and relevant and that takes into account the real-world complexities of business. He views every interaction with business leaders as an opportunity to stretch their thinking and his own. Using his business acumen, insights into people, and common sense, he translates his observations and insights into recommendations leaders can apply on Monday morning. He has expertise in leadership and succession, growth and innovation, execution, and social systems. Identified by *Fortune* as the leading expert in corporate governance and by *The Economist* as a veteran of CEO succession, Dr. Charan provides practical ways for boards to improve their functioning. Directors, CEOs, and senior-most human resource executives often seek his advice on talent planning and key hires, including CEO selection.

Many people have come to know Dr. Charan through in-house executive education programs. His energetic, interactive teaching style has won him several awards. He won the Bell Ringer Award at GE's famous learning center in Crotonville, New York, and best teacher awards at Northwestern and Wharton's Insurance Institute. He was among *Business-Week*'s top ten resources for in-house executive development programs.

Over the past decade, Dr. Charan has captured his business insights in numerous books and articles. In the past five years, Dr. Charan's books have sold more than 2 million copies. These include the bestseller *Execution: The Discipline of Getting Things Done,* coauthored with Larry Bossidy; *The Game-Changer,* coauthored with A. G. Lafley, and *Leadership in the Era of Economic Uncertainty.* Dr. Charan has written several cover stories for *Fortune* magazine and lead articles for *Harvard Business Review.* His articles have also appeared in *Financial Times, Wall Street Journal,* and *Director's Monthly.*

Dr. Charan was elected a Distinguished Fellow of the National Academy of Human Resources. He is on the boards of Tyco Electronics, Austin Industries, and Emaar MGF India. He is based in Dallas, Texas.